PRISONER

Of

20 Years in the Hole at *Hustler* Magazine

by Allan MacDonell

Names have been changed among non-public personalities in this book to relieve innocent parties of embarrassment. All conversations and events are presented to the author's best recollection, often aided by the hindsight of colleagues.

A Feral House Book
ISBN: 1-932595-13-9

Feral House
PO Box 39910
Los Angeles, CA 90039

10 9 8 7 6 5 4 3 2 1

www.feralhouse.com
info@feralhouse.com

Cover by Daniel Clowes
Design by Hedi El Kholti

To William Michael McPadden for his insistence and aid,
to John Rechy for whatever clarity of expression is here,
to the wife, and to A.P. for taking a chance.

TABLE OF CONTENTS

What Kind of Creep Runs *Hustler*?

IT TAKES A special person to work at *Hustler* magazine for 20 years and not crack up. From the dawn of the Reagan Administration well into Bush II, I was bombarded daily by sharply focused images of naked women and bare-assed men locked in the most primal and private activity human beings engage in other than defecation, and I'd been shown that too. I viewed these images, literally 1,000 every day, through powerful magnifying lenses ground in Germany. I evaluated each photograph for its prurient appeal, and selected the most effective among them to be presented to a drooling audience, a large portion of which would have paid a month of their salaries to spend a week on my job.

As a writer, I cranked out service pieces on how to dump a girlfriend before she dumps you, on romancing welfare mothers, on capturing for a moment the erotic affections of rich women, crazy women, gorgeous women, angry women, new age women, promiscuous women, aging women, and women with severe eating disorders. I clarified at least one mystery of the universe in a feature titled "Creeps: Why Women Love Us."

I'd been airlifted to a remote Nevada highway and embedded at a house of prostitution there. I'd infiltrated a convention of soldier-of-fortune mercenaries, and penetrated San Quentin Prison's death row to interview a man convicted of murdering two consecutive wives. I'd tagged along to the south of France with a planeload of porn starlets who plied their trade to private fans at up to $5,000 per scene. I'd spent three hours in a cell with a tape recorder and one of California's most notorious serial killers. I'd hopped a redeye to Atlanta, Georgia, where I delivered a staggering cashier's check to the second ex-wife of family-values congressman Bob Barr.

I entered the strange and titillating environment of Larry Flynt Publications as a married 27-year-old clinging to the shreds of a Roman Catholic education. Tentative at first, jumpy around all the sexual triggers, I quickly adopted a jaded sensualism which was put to the test once my wife had split. Acclimating well, I assumed a supervisory position within the hotbed of anarchy and depravity at LFP. I hired and indoctrinated others to the *Hustler* way. I directed talented underlings in the creation of aberrant literature and curiously lewd photographic scenarios. I trained attractive young women to compose debauched sexual memoirs, and then I made suggestions for improving their grammar. *Hustler* was not the vilest magazine on the market, but we tried.

Private sex videos never intended for public consumption crossed my desk, souvenirs that purported to show Ted Turner in a manic kinky mood with Jane Fonda, young Pam Anderson satisfying the singer from Poison, Chuck Berry despoiling a string of anonymous partners, some of whom treated Chuck (if indeed that was Chuck) to a bite of poo, Anna Nicole Smith playing the nude, inebriated seductress in a hotel bathtub, Mick Jagger captured by a crafty, spread-eagle stripper barely one-third his age, and Courtney Love cavorting with Scott Weiland of the Stone Temple Pilots. I came away with the opinion that all of these tapes were probably authentic, but I had learned to mistrust reality at large.

In 1998, I was plunged into the chamber pot of national politics. Suddenly, at the height of the frenzy surrounding the impeachment of President Bill Clinton, my actions were creating headlines in the *Washington Post* and being cited in *New York Times* and *Wall Street Journal* Op-Ed columns. There I was on prime-time TV, arguing public morality with big-haired news-channel blowhards. Functioning as equal parts reporter and vandal, I hounded down adulterous Congressional hypocrites wherever Larry Flynt's lure of a million-dollar reward could flush them out. Before the smoke and mirrors had cleared, the Speaker-elect had resigned from the United States House of Representatives in the face of my insinuation that *Hustler* had uncovered proof of his extramarital follies.

After having saved Bill Clinton's pasty ass, if not his legacy, I continued to guide staffs of writers and artists in producing the sarcasm, muckraking, celebrity bashing and go-for-the-throat eroticism of America's most iconoclastic stroke book, as well as being overlord on a half-dozen ancillary publications—*Taboo, Barely Legal, Chic, Asian Fever, Busty Beauties, Honey Buns.* At 46, a seasoned veteran of hardcore anti-journalism, I reigned over a fiefdom of quick-witted geeks with graduate degrees and no concept of a career path. Then I made one crucial blunder in my relationship with Larry Flynt, a faux pas so colossal that I must have committed it deliberately. Soon after, I was fired.

From my first day as an axed employee, casual acquaintances, relatives and former co-workers told me I should write the book on *Hustler.* To everyone who didn't have to write it, the book was a no-brainer, but I had to wonder: What is the specific idea? Do I intend to produce an exposé of Larry Flynt? How do you pitch a tell-all of a man who is on record as having had sex with a chicken?

Oprah tosses up her hands: "The man admits to raping a fowl. Are you telling me there is more?"

In fact, there is plenty more, but this book racket is turning out to be more work than I am accustomed to. Trying to make things easy on myself, I reached out to several former *Hustler* co-workers. Many of these are decent, conflicted men and women. A few are porno scumbags. I asked everybody the same questions: What had working in the peculiar biosphere of LFP been like for you? What memories typified or evoked the experience?

Most everyone agreed that their *Hustler* tenure had been weird and less than entirely pleasant. All the former employees I contacted shared one common thing that separated them from me: they'd come to Larry Flynt Publications, and then they continued on their way, having outgrown the *Hustler* environment. Maybe it wasn't a question of growth for all of them. Perhaps a few had simply burnt out on the beaver shots, the institutionalized paranoia and the unrelenting satire. The point is, these burnouts had moved on. My growth, if that's what I chose to call it, had all been confined within the structure of LFP.

I'd come in as an assistant nobody and risen to the top, like scum on a cup of hot chocolate. If this progression had occurred at

Condé Nast, I'd be pushing my publicist for a five-page profile in *Forbes*. When we met during the filming of *The People vs. Larry Flynt*, actor Woody Harrelson, who portrayed Larry in the movie, said, "You're the guy who's got the best job in the world." If so, why did I start my car every morning, then sit behind the wheel for 10 minutes debating whether or not to open the garage door?

A tougher question might be: how did I thrive so long in a bizarro world of bodyguards, cracker-rich hillbillies and high-gloss cumshots? Now here is an interesting question of character: what the fuck was wrong with me?

CHAPTER 1

███████████

Fired!

MOST PEOPLE DON'T have the luxury of reliving their own suicide, but anytime I want, I can power up my VCR and witness myself standing in front of 500 gamblers and a few co-workers, all of whom have gathered to laugh at me as I commit career *hara-kiri.*

Look at that stooped, thin man stepping up to the microphone. He stands within the crowded confines of a hotel ballroom. Waiters clear away dessert plates from a grid of banquet tables, and the guests face forward, skeptically waiting to be amused. A sign affixed to the front of the podium reads, "LARRY FLYNT'S X-RATED ROAST." *Hustler* magazine publisher Larry Flynt sits to the right on the rostrum, silk-suited and egg-shaped, inert but imposing in a gleaming gold wheelchair. Crippled by a would-be killer with a deer rifle 25 years earlier, America's cuddliest pariah looks like Humpty Dumpty put back together again, but older, fatter and dyspeptic. Flynt's glazed emerald eyes stare the camera down. His lips hold a pout of gassy forbearance. The thin man standing to Flynt's left peers out through thick, black-framed glasses, scanning the audience of half a thousand as though it were packed with assassins. The condemned man coughs nervously, not quite prepared to speak. That man was me.

I leaned sideways and squatted level with the jowly, dispassionate face of my boss.

"Hey, Larry," I said, "did you lose a bet? Why are you submitting to this roast?"

He ignored my questions, as usual. His smile might have been enigmatic, or maybe it was just a sneer. "I hope you like your job," he drawled.

Ambivalence plagued me on that point, but now was not the time to discuss it. "You know what I do for a living. I write 'Asshole of the Month.' Why pick me for a roaster?"

"You get paid to fuck with people, and I pay you to fuck with people, but I don't pay you to fuck with me."

His mouth clammed shut, his way of saying that no further discussion would be brooked. I stood up half-straight and faced the cameras, the crowd and my future.

"My name is Allan MacDonell, and I have come here tonight to help honor a man who is bigger than life. Wait a minute; I fucked up already. To honor a man whose head is bigger than life."

Polite laughter. The audience was thick with milling gamblers and their mercenary girlfriends, still grumbling about the price of drinks at the no-host bar. Sitting at the head of this surly mob, oblivious to the complaints about his cheapness, Flynt puffed up like a venomous, red-faced toad. When I was a kid, before we'd ever met, Larry Flynt had been one of my favorite famous Americans. Discounting the bit about being stuck forever in a wheelchair, it was fun to romanticize Larry's reputation as an iconoclast and a rebel, to envy his profligate wealth and his excesses with the ladies. Then I'd gone to work for the real guy, and now this: trapped in a Holiday Inn side room packed full of extras from *Married to the Mob*.

Tomorrow morning, play would commence on a million-dollar grand slam of poker, sponsored by the Hustler Casino, a hillbilly-fabulous card club owned by Flynt and located in a crummy Los Angeles suburb. The seven-figure jackpot had drawn hundreds of high-stakes cardsharps from all over the country. As a treat to the contestants, the casino's management was hosting a pre-tournament dinner. This roast of Larry Flynt followed dessert. Former President Bill Clinton's half-brother Roger and former professional comedian Gabe Kaplan had been recruited to poke fun at the wheelchair-bound sleaze merchant. A decent roast requires more than one past-prime yukster and a sibling liability, but Larry Flynt had been reluctant to shell out for extras. He padded the lineup with unpaid employees, including me. Who am I? Up until that night, I was Larry's trusted editorial director.

I had a dilemma. Larry Flynt is a funny guy. He can take a joke, up to a point. He is also profoundly sensitive and once offended tends to stay that way. He resents anyone overstepping their familiarity with him, but he also punishes timidity. If I cobbled together a string of anecdotes that went soft on him, he would label me a chickenshit, and that evaluation would go into the continually revised mental file he keeps on everyone who works for him.

A few old-timers were lurking around the office, deep-fried charity cases who'd been leeching off Larry since the 1970s when he ran *Hustler* out of a seedy storefront in Columbus, Ohio, and could still walk. The bolder of these weasels were after my top-dog job, and had been ever since I'd clawed my way to it years earlier. Undermining sneaks were constantly sending Larry secret memos pointing out my imagined failings, memos that Larry would forward to me. Any passages that he deemed pertinent were double-underlined. Our sales had been skidding. The entire "men's sophisticate" niche of the magazine market was spinning into the toilet. I could not afford to be notched down in Larry's timidity category.

On the other hand, if I pressed too close to home with well-aimed jokes that twisted the dessert fork in any of Larry's delicate areas, he might decide he hated me. I'd seen him suddenly hate better, smarter men than me, men more indispensable to the well-being of his empire, and he'd cast them out as if they had given him the clap. My commentary would have to talk a fine line, and there was no way of knowing where that line might be drawn. It's not as if I could ask Flynt for ground rules. The man has a sadistic streak. Nothing would make Larry Flynt happier than to watch his editorial director—a snot-nosed middle-aged would-be big shot who thought he was smarter than everyone else—stutter and falter and slowly die in front of an auditorium packed with poker-faced friends.

I have a tendency to rush when I speak, slurring words in a rapid-fire, marble-mouth mumble. I cautioned myself to read my prepared script slowly, one word for every three beats of my heart.

"A major Hollywood movie and countless TV shows have tried to get at the real Larry Flynt, the man behind the image. The movie and TV shows are fine, as far as they go, but if you really want to take a man's measure, you should talk to someone who works for him."

Even now, many months afterward, I have trouble watching the videotape. On the screen, I see a lone, thin man sag slightly within a light trained upon the lectern. The glare off his wet forehead flashes in the camera lens. He looks toward his right. Larry Flynt sits within arm's reach, glowering with impatience.

"I've been on Larry Flynt's payroll for 20 years. And I have the four-figure net worth to prove it."

Light snickering gave me confidence that my enunciation was passable. I shot the cuffs on my Prada suit.

"So I might not qualify for a loan to buy a condo in La Puente, but I am qualified to give a fair and unbiased account of Larry Flynt."

A miracle happened. Laughter came, real laughter, loud and sustained. I was able to pause and gather my wits, waiting for the outburst to subside. My wife, Theresa, covered her mouth and quietly laughed, sitting one table away from where Liz Flynt, Larry's wife, held court. Liz Flynt waved to me. I looked away so as not to be blinded by the flash of diamonds on her fingers and wrist.

"Larry called me into his office this afternoon. Between the door of his office and his desk is about 70 yards of green carpet, the exact color of money. As I walked across this no man's land, Larry glared out at me with pure malevolence, which is how he shows affection to an employee. His evil face made me think of the man in the moon squatting on the toilet, straining to force out a dry turd."

This punch line received less enthusiasm than I had hoped for. The top of Larry's head moved at the periphery of my vision. He stifled a yawn.

"I was afraid that he'd been sitting on one of his testicles all day. Either that, or Doug the bodyguard had misplaced Larry's pocket pussy."

Again, I was allowed to wait while the laughter died down. It didn't take long. My mind concentrated on the task at hand, shutting out all observational data regarding Liz Flynt and refusing to consider the potential reactions of Larry to my immediate right.

"'Allan,' Larry said, 'you say whatever you want about me tonight. It's a free country.'"

For some reason, the crowd found that funny. Puzzled, but pleased, I went on.

"Then he had Doug take me up to the roof of the Flynt Building and show me the view from what he calls the Launching Pad."

I had them. Poker might be their business, but they were suckers for my sly, mordant wit. I stuck with the material I had spent three weekends working on. My jokes shocked me. How could I be so vile, crass and humorless? I'd unconsciously tapped into a raging undercurrent of resentment toward my employer. He'd stiffed me on my annual raise—again—after saddling me with unpaid special projects, then he had the gall to shove me into this false position.

"I hope it is safe for me to say that Larry Flynt is a complex man, and working for him is full of contradictions. Larry Flynt runs the only company in the world where he makes you pay to park in his building, but he promises all employees a free defense attorney with every sexual harassment suit."

That one sank with only slight ripples of amusement, which didn't stop me from mining the vein.

"Most of you here, I'm told, know Larry from the gaming world. He claims he is a world-class poker player. Nobody who works for him can understand how that's possible. We can't imagine him giving anyone a credible raise."

The casino crowd fell for the gaming reference, loud and hearty. This performing was like being an unwilling passenger on a runaway roller coaster: a sensible person might reason he should disembark before the first big dip, but knows there is no profit in jumping off.

"A few years ago, I was at Circuit City with my wife, and we were spending my Christmas bonus. The wife and I couldn't decide if we should buy a toaster or put a Walkman on layaway. I saw a bank of television sets, and I wondered if I would ever be able to afford one. Suddenly, Larry's man-in-the-moon face appeared on a whole row of TVs. He was on *Entertainment Tonight*, live from Las Vegas. He'd just lost a million dollars in one sitting at blackjack. My wife was shaken by this news. She said, 'Allan, what if that man loses *Hustler* magazine in a poker game, and you're forced to go work for some cheap bastard?'"

There is no accounting for what people think is funny. My wife had predicted this jab would fall flat, but hilarity tore through the crowd. I put a hand to my sliding glasses and pushed them back up my greasy nose. I looked up toward the ceiling as if for help. Bigger laugh. Larry Flynt glowers like an alpha toad who has ingested a lesser amphibian, one that is too wiry to swallow. The skinny toad is dead, but still kicking.

"Larry assured me he would never wager something so precious as his beloved *Hustler* magazine. He apologized that my retirement account was another matter altogether.

"And so when I look out at this crowd, I don't see friends and associates of my boss. I see a roomful of fuckers who are hoping to win my 401K money."

I earned an ovation. Had I stopped at this high point, everything that had come before might have been forgiven, but the ride was not over.

"There is a common belief that having Larry Flynt in charge of a porno magazine is like leaving a priest in charge of an orphanage."

A couple of groans. I was confident that I would win them over.

"Part of my job at *Hustler* magazine is to review photo sets with Larry. We take our special magnifying lenses, and we inspect pictures of naked young women."

I mimed this activity, preparing to impersonate the distinctive Flynt drawl.

"'I love a hairy pussy' is something I've heard Larry say far more often than 'lunch is on me.'"

Serious gamblers, in my experience, can't get enough jokes that demean a miserly multimillionaire. Against all odds, I was still ahead. I put a hand on Larry's shoulder, and he turned to me. His green, yellow-rimmed eyes sized me up. His icy stare was the look he'd give across a poker table, calling a bluff.

"The secret truth about Larry Flynt is that he is the most pussy-whipped man I have ever met. He talks a big game, but his wife Liz only lets him wear the pants because it takes two grown men to lift Larry off his ass so she can strip those pants off of him."

I began to understand the emotions of the dive-bombing kamikaze pilot. The end is near. It will be swift and spectacular.

"I'm just reporting the facts.

"Liz Flynt met Larry when she went to work for him as a private nurse. She weaned him off of painkillers, turned his health around and whipped him into shape. Then she persuaded him to marry her. I always wondered how she did that.

"I discovered Liz's secret one night recently when my wife and I went out to dinner with the Flynts ... Dutch treat."

I'd been losing my audience, but again the penny-pinching reference brought them to my side.

"Larry has a wandering eye. Every time any woman from any table in the restaurant stands up to go anywhere, Larry's head pivots, and his eyes track her tits. I could see that this was pissing off Liz, and I tried to warn Larry, but he never listens to me. Finally, nurse Liz reaches into her purse and pulls out this giant enema bag, right there in Wendy's.

"So that's Liz's secret. The corrective enema."

I prepared to soften the sarcasm by bringing the joke around so that I too am a butt of it.

"The sad part about this story is that my wife made me stop on the way home and buy one of those bags."

If you consult the tape and listen closely, you will hear that this stab at self-deprecation wins the affection of the crowd. They appreciate that I am not mean-spirited. I see the humor in myself as well as in those around me. Love inhabits that applause and laughter. Video does not lie. But no love inhabits the face of Larry Flynt. He recognizes my feeble stab at self-abnegation for the meaningless, manipulative gesture it is. As far as he is concerned, I am finished.

"So I could talk all night about Larry's philanthropy and generosity. Because I'm a huge bullshitter.

"But it is time to discuss Larry's professional achievements. When the history is written, what will be seen as Larry Flynt's defining contribution to American culture?

"Will he be remembered for the battles for free speech and a free press?"

"Yes!" responded an enthusiastic butt-kisser in the audience, as if I'd been fishing for that answer.

"Or might Larry's lasting fame be as the pornographer who cared enough to save President Clinton's ass?"

Again, rumbles of affirmation formed, but I snuffed them.

"Perhaps our grandchildren will recall our guest of honor as the man who offered Jenna Bush $10 million to pose nude in *Hustler* magazine. Plus a quart of Colt .45 if she spreads her butt cheeks."

The crowd was thrown off. Had they really thought I was paying serious tribute? There seems to be no end to the limits of human miscommunication. My subtext, for instance, had been lost even on myself. The underlying message was coming clear: I was tendering one of the most passively aggressive resignations in history.

"My vote is that we remember Larry as the guy who invented the Scratch 'n' Sniff centerfold, an innovation that was created in his own image. The Scratch 'n' Sniff centerfold is the perfect representation of Larry's legacy. When you scrape its surface, it's sort of flaky, and it smells vaguely fishy."

I was on a slide, falling flat. Now for the soft ending.

"Larry, thanks for all the excitement over the years. I'm grateful for all the opportunities you've given me. Even this one. I really do love you."

The "love you" came out spontaneously. There's no mention of love in the 24-point type of my roast script. I took my seat, after the feeblest attempt to shake Flynt's hand, and the red in my face deepened as I endured an embarrassment of applause. Finally, Roger Clinton was called to the podium, and the attention shifted to his slow-pitched softballs. I estimated how many weeks would pass before I was *Hustler* history. That "really do love you" bit had sealed it.

The word *love* doesn't occur naturally in my everyday conversation. The wife complains that she never hears it. To this day, I feel a twinge of shame for having made the public avowal to my old boss. Telling someone you love them in front of a crowd is seldom the right thing to do. Take for example the LFP Christmas party of 1998: Doug the bodyguard rolled gold-plated Larry to the center of the cleared dance floor, and the publisher addressed his guests and his minions through a handheld microphone. Bob Livingston, the freshly elected Speaker of the United States House of Representatives, had announced his resignation that very day, claiming that he had been "Flynted."

Larry's voice quavered, and his hands trembled as he recounted LFP's victories of the past year. He cited the company's unprecedented profit margins. The moment was perfect for announcing year-end bonuses, something that had been missing from our annual festivities since Larry's emergence from a narcotic stupor several years earlier. We employees held our collective breath. Larry faltered; something had stuck in his throat. He girded himself, and then forced out the four words that had gagged him: "I love you all."

Saying "I love you" cost him almost as much as if he had offered to give us money. I had felt his pain and admired him for enduring it. Still, not one of us employees wouldn't have rather had a check. In the story of Larry and me, *love* is clearly an overstatement, best left unsaid.

A Concise History of Newsstand Skin

NO MAGAZINE RACK is complete without its sleazy ghetto of high-priced rags placed just beyond the reach but tantalizingly within eyesight of a post-pubescent male. *Barely Legal*, *Black Asses*, *Shaved Orient Tails*, *Sluts and Slobs*, *Juggs*. Lurid in color and content, designed with all the subtlety of a cheap fishing lure, these glossy advertisements for corruption seem to multiply and mutate from month to month like industrious cancer cells. Magazine pros refer to this virulent niche, with no intended irony, as "men's sophisticates."

Men's sophistication was pioneered by Neanderthal visionaries who etched depictions of naked ape copulation onto their cave walls. The golden age of sophisticates began in 1953, when Hugh Marston Hefner, a $65-a-week copywriter for *Esquire*, conceived of a photo-driven publication for men, to be called *Stag Party*. Hefner wisely changed the name and secured nude glamour photos of starlet Marilyn Monroe before rolling out *Playboy* and revolutionizing newsstand sex. *Playboy* dominated the market until a truck driver-turned-photographer named Bob Guccione imported a title from England called *Penthouse*.

Guccione went where no mainstream magazine had dared to go before—below the waist. *Penthouse* models adopted a splay-legged European decadence that was in direct contrast to the rosy Midwestern cheeks turned to the camera by *Playboy*'s centerfold bunnies. *Penthouse*'s encroachment forced Hef's cameramen to lower their sights, revealing wisps of rabbit fuzz.

Playboy and *Penthouse* conducted a gentlemen's competition, a sophisticated sparring that prepared neither Hef nor

Guccione for the rude onslaught of a grade-school dropout from Appalachian Kentucky. Former dirt farmer Larry Flynt, fueled by amphetamines, erotic fervor and financial lust, had willed himself up from subsistence poverty to become owner of eight Ohio go-go bars. Flynt's dives, where the gals were encouraged to mingle with paying customers, were euphemistically called Hustler Clubs. The hardscrabble entrepreneur distributed a throwaway newsletter to his patrons, a smudged, photocopied intimation of the good life as conceived by polyester-clad sensualists. Within the stark pages of this B-bar broadsheet, Flynt's indomitable ego divined the kernel of magazine greatness. In July 1974, the resultant *Hustler* dropped like six pounds of manure in a four-pound bag. The fallout was immediate, far-reaching and impossible to ignore. A provocative blend of raunch and class resentment, *Hustler* rocketed to one of the biggest sales spurts in magazine history. Flynt's million-dollar innovation was the gynecologic close-up. Sophisticates had never been so crass, not even in the early Neanderthal days. The pink genie sprang out of the bottle, and airbrushed subtlety forever hid its blushing face.

Hustler's road to notoriety hit some bumps and, eventually, one long rut. First came obscenity charges, a 1977 conviction, a sentence of 20 years in prison. Out on appeal, Larry launched a First Amendment crusade, his national profile rose, and chances for a reversal of the verdict looked positive. Huge waves of cash were rolling his way.

At the peak of *Hustler*'s stratospheric ascent, its publisher sustained a religious conversion (which he later dismissed as a manic-depressive episode) under the influence of then-President Jimmy Carter's sister, Ruth Carter Stapleton, and devoted himself with public fanfare to the greater glory of Jesus Christ. This abrupt zealotry failed to stimulate revenues. Flynt's Christian virtues alienated far more sinners from *Hustler* than they attracted Bible students to it.

The smutmonger's spiritual growth stopped dead on March 6, 1978. While walking to the local courthouse on the dusty streets of Lawrenceville, Georgia, defending against yet another obscenity charge, Larry was dropped by three bullets from a hunting rifle. The attempted murder left the porn king paralyzed from the waist down. Providence had deprived Flynt's reproductive organ of the very blind, impetuous thrust that he had so blithely capitalized upon in others. Pain, depression and narcotics would claim his attention for the next five years. Flynt's wife, Althea, attempted to fill in as *Hustler*'s publisher, but her efforts stagnated in a pool of office politics and an editorial vision that ranged from self-congratulation to self-contradiction.

In 1983, Flynt underwent the first of repeated micro laser surgeries to sever the nerves that were causing the sharpest of his physical agonies. Like a rich, manic, perverted Rip Van Winkle, he emerged from the years of his painkiller snooze and took stock. The world had passed Larry Flynt by. He had a lot of catching up to do if he were to reestablish his rightful place in infamy.

That's where I would come in.

CHAPTER 2

Portrait of the Author as a Young Sophisticate

MALE SOPHISTICATION LIT UP my world in the Technicolor year of 1964. To all outward appearances, I was a gangly eight-year-old living with two younger brothers, an older sister, a mom and a dad. My father had transplanted the family from a drizzly seaside community outside of Vancouver, Canada, to a freeway-fed suburb in scorched Southern California. Our new neighborhood was smog-choked and prefab. I was unaware of the locale's limitations. My entire being was preoccupied by a sudden hyper-awareness of grown women. Life was a constant high alert for sliding bra straps and glimpses of private skin revealed by tipsy moms at poolside barbecues.

Looking back, I cannot be sure whether this profound urge to breach the undergarments of teacher, babysitter and grocery checker preceded or followed the discovery of my father's cache of salacious pulp magazines. Hidden beneath socks and unused scarves, buried under the house gun, a fat manila envelope disgorged three fascinating artifacts.

To the casual observer, these publications might have been nothing more than disposable entertainment. To me, they represented a Rosetta Stone, the key to all the eternal mysteries. Their exteriors captivated me. It may have been an hour before I managed to look inside. Each cover bore a lifelike, painted illustration centered upon one or more big-busted women whose blouses were a single, stressed button away from popping wide open. The nastiest cover showed a blonde tied to a chair. A uniformed Nazi blacksmith prepared to brand her trembling swells with a red-hot swastika. The second magazine featured a pair of brunettes in elaborate underwear plundering the suit pockets of a simpering man who reclined upon a sofa. The third artifact was a lurid detective magazine, and the focal female appeared to be dead. Interest in that one soon waned.

I returned to the depths of this sock drawer at every opportunity. The magazines were printed on gray newsprint, but they excited every vibrant shade of the sensual rainbow in my imagination. The murky editorial wells presented photo coverage of nudist vacations, topless beauty pageants and innovative women's swimsuits that left one breast exposed. The captions to these photos, despite my deepest, concentrated efforts to decipher them, seemed to be written in a patois completely alien to the language I was being taught. The hours passed like 15-minute blocks while I puzzled over loaded puns and double meanings.

My father's magazines abruptly disappeared, but my curiosity would not be denied. Most afternoons, I would discuss the entrancing puzzlement of inter-gender relations with an older woman from down the block, a prodigiously worldly 14-year-old whose name was Sandra. She wore straight, no-waist dresses that fell short of her knees. White vinyl boots rose halfway up her calves. She was forbidden to have boyfriends over to her house when she was alone. Her divorced dad promised to send her to Catholic school if she ever defied his order.

Sandra and I would fill shot glasses with hard spirits from her dad's home bar and sip debonairly while she played Beatles albums and tutored me in the boy-woman equation. Occasionally she would excuse herself to go to the bathroom, looking back at me over her shoulder with a pert challenge. I would rush the bar and steel myself with a slug straight from the jug. Aside from a stockpile of open liquor bottles, Sandra's father owned ample stacks of *Playboy* magazine. These journals were used as visual aids in my indoctrination. Even at age eight, I recognized the *Playboy* quality as far superior to the smudgy black and white junk my cheapskate dad kept stashed away. The *Playboy*s opened to a possibility of ease and pleasure that became more real with every sip from my glass. Sandra would turn the pages. We leaned our heads over the centerfolds, our hair commingling.

Sandra confided in me. Pausing in her page-turning duties, she told me who she had a crush on and who had a crush on her. I didn't know these high-school baseball players and surfers, but Sandra would model what she planned to wear to their swim parties, and I envied them. Flushed and excited one day, Sandra gushed that she had a date to play strip poker with two Italian cousins who lived in a tract up in the hills. She explained the rudiments of strip poker, then she sent me tottering home. My bicycle wobbled as I envisioned Sandra's no-waist dress being lifted over her head. I crashed into a curb and sprawled on someone's burned-out front lawn, gazing into the hazy sky as the clouds formed into panties and brassieres.

The next afternoon, I rang Sandra's doorbell promptly at 3:30. I'd been anticipating our rendezvous all through my school day, but Sandra refused to allow me beyond the porch. Her father's liquor bottles and *Playboys* gleamed behind her within the mood-lit, sunken living room. Sandra suggested we take a walk, and she steered me back toward my house. She sneered off into the distance, refusing to meet my eyes. I tired of playing coy.

"Tell me about the strip poker. Did you win?"

Murder flashed through her eyes. She towered over me, more than a head taller, and outweighed me by at least 20 pounds. She threw me to the ground of my own backyard and straddled me. Her knees and the white vinyl of her over-the-calf go-go boots pinned my arms to the turf. As my sister and brothers watched impassively, Sandra filled my mouth with grass and leaves, berating and mocking me. Terrified and berserk, I squirmed free and struck blindly at her. She started crying, but continued to abuse me to disguise that fact. My family members declined to take sides. We had a dog back then, and even the mutt knew to distance himself from me. I picked up a coffee can full of dirt and threatened to throw it on Sandra. She took the opportunity to call me a filthy name and withdraw with dignity.

This was only the first time that a wronged woman would force me to do penance for the sins of some other assholes. Just like in the future, her warning signals did nothing to slow my pursuit of male sophistication. A few years later, I was one among a squad of 10-year-old males who uncovered a carton of mildewed *Playboys* while crawling under a vacant house. We were in training for some whimsical James Bond adventure. I'd been saving two purloined cans of Pabst for a special occasion, and my preteen colleagues and I drank contemplatively as we reviewed the material. At day's end, we each took one *Playboy* to keep and returned the remainder to where we had found them, in case their rightful owner should be enraged at their theft. It was inconceivable that someone would leave this treasure trove behind deliberately.

I've listened for decades as people claimed to buy *Playboy* for the articles, but the magazine I took home was my faithful companion for nearly two years, until my mother found it and threw it out, and I never once noticed any words on the pages. What I remember are photos of a supine Jayne Mansfield's upright breasts.

I gravitated to friends whose parents were well-supplied boozers and whose older brothers were willing to share access to their stashed nudie mags. I became able to distinguish between *Stag* and *Swank*, and would do so for hours at a time, especially if a buddy or I had managed to filch some sacramental wine to complement the activity. Despite high grades in English and composition, I remained unable to actually read any of this literature. The words refused to make sense. Physical agitation placed my brain in a place beyond verbal comprehension. Still, the pictures were very informative.

In freshman year of high school, I befriended a kleptomaniac named Bob. He had an attractive brunette stepmother, hardly 20 years our senior, and a pair of older blonde sisters who had inured his parents to adolescent bad behavior. Once we had our learner's permits, Bob and I drove his $200 Chevrolet to outlying suburbs on after-school shopping expeditions. A guilty-looking drip, I would draw all the storekeeper's attention, and Bob would freely kipe everything we wanted: Southern Comfort, Boone's Farm and *Penthouse* magazine.

Penthouse was the first sophisticated magazine that I actually read, a testament to the gripping perversity of its editorial content. The photos were far more distracting than *Playboy*'s or *Swank*'s. Bob would snore passed out on his waterbed. I would be bug-eyed on the beanbag, reading outlandish sex letters in the light from a lava lamp, gulping Ripple and picturing Bob's mom and his sisters, one or more of whom were often only a room or two away. Using the bathroom at Bob's was torture. Frilly underthings were always soaking in the sink and hanging to dry on top of the towels. Touching these things was unavoidable. I tried to differentiate which sister fit into which bra, easily visualizing the silky scraps being tugged and twisted into place. I managed not to sniff the items. I asked Bob how he could stand the constant exposure. He seemed quite unfazed and hit the bong hard.

All this heightened sexual energy naturally led to masturbation, which could have been satisfying, except that the propaganda of my peers held that masturbation was a homosexual activity. I'd been receiving this misguided information since prior to junior high. The images of buoyant, rounded flesh and white vinyl go-go boots that flashed through my mind while I spent increasingly long stretches soaping my privates in the shower were unfailingly female, but my homoerotic suspicions persisted. I was, after all, a male with my hand on a male's pleasure organ. I didn't feel comfortable enough to talk about this confused sexual orientation with anybody, not even with Bob. Especially not with Bob. What if my homosexual fears were grounded, and Bob confirmed them? I could not risk alienating him. Drugs were readily available (this was 1970s high school, for God's sake), but where would I find alcohol if Bob abandoned me? As a shunned homosexual, I would be left to steal my own. Luckily, Bob continued to swipe each new issue of *Penthouse* along with our other essential supplies. *Penthouse* caused me no confusion, and in fact helped clear away my remaining onanistic inhibitions. Interjecting photos of spread-eagled, naked women between my eyes and what my hand was doing eased my mind about incipient deviance.

I graduated from high school in the most desultory manner imaginable and enrolled at the local junior college. The early 1970s was a rough time to be running around stoned every day. All the excesses of the '60s were in play, with none of the idealism. The rose-colored revolutionary optimism was gone. Ex-hippies who had once been pioneers in the counterculture economy had become flat-out future convicts. The first time I saw *Hustler* was while waiting for a hash delivery in the living room of a Vietnam vet. Mason had been scary before he went overseas. They'd kicked him out of high school while I was still in junior high. He'd totaled a few cars he had not owned, been suspected of some burglaries and was given the option to enlist as a Marine. Responsible adults cited Mason as an example of how low a bad kid might fall. There I was, slumped on his swayback couch. Mason kept his scrapbook of in-country snapshots lying under a *Hustler* on a footlocker that doubled as a coffee table, so in my mind, *Hustler* and atrocity were linked from the beginning.

"You look jumpy," Mason said. "Here's some coke. It'll settle you down."

I'd never had coke. This was late in 1974. Coke hadn't trickled down to my level. Mason used a huge, throat-slicing knife to chop the powder on the glass of a framed picture of him in his dress uniform. All I knew about coke was that it was exorbitantly expensive. I snarfed up two fat lines, then wondered why Mason would treat me to a free sample of the drug. My brain clanked into a reptilian gear, and my wonder gave way to the realization that the crystallized snot dripping down my throat was angel dust and not cocaine. Klepto Bob and I had endured some bad angel-dust trips during Christmas season at the end of high school, so I knew I was in for a long night, especially if I was unable to break free from Mason. Six years older than me, he'd spent one of those years in Southeast Asia perfecting a psycho stare. He was skinny, but not the type of thin that gave you confidence in being able to take him. I hadn't really filled out any since I was eight, when Sandra had shoved leaves and lawn into my mouth. Mason almost never wore a shirt and was proud of his scars. He claimed to have been bayoneted and to have eaten the liver of the man who did it while that man sat with his eyes open and watched. It was unclear whether that man had been an enemy combatant or someone from our own side. Mason slapped my leg with the side of the knife.

"Check this shit out." He pushed his 'Nam scrapbook at me. Last time he'd forced me to look at it, I'd nearly fainted. The effects of the angel dust were creeping up my spine, numbing me one vertebra at a time. I looked for some way to avoid the scrapbook and reached out toward the *Hustler* magazine as if it might save me.

"I think I'll look at some girls," I said. I opened the *Hustler*, hoping to hold Mason's yearbook of death and gore at bay. The gambit worked for about three minutes, and then I turned the *Hustler* to what must have been conceived as a public health alert. There in suppurating color were the ultimate effects of syphilis, gonorrhea and venereal warts in their worst-case, end-stage scenarios. Genitals dripping pus, mutilated and eaten away, presented big as life.

"Jesus Christ, Mason."

He laughed.

"I'm going to puke."

"Not in my house, motherfucker. Not again!" I barfed sponta-neously a month earlier while reclining on this very sofa, a forceful arc that had embedded itself in Mason's memory. He clenched the knife in his teeth, picked me up by my jean jacket, hustled me across the living room and threw me down his front steps, a far preferable fate than if he had taken a notion to hold me hostage.

I dry-heaved in the hedge that separated Mason's patch of weedy dirt from the lush lawn next door. Nothing came up. The awaited drug delivery lost its importance. My old karate teacher might be holding. He lived about two miles away. I didn't have a car, so I had a long walk ahead of me in the crisp winter cold. My breath came out like the fog of death, an image that I assured myself was only a wraith of the angel dust. Thank God for *Hustler*. If that magazine hadn't turned my stomach, I might still be back on Mason's sofa, unable to move, with him acting crazy and deadly.

Nobody liked the way my life was going, not my parents, not even me. I suspected there might be more to life than smoking bombers and guzzling tallboys. I transferred from the local J.C. to a real col-lege in San Francisco. The San Francisco university awarded a masters degree in creative writing, if you stuck around long enough. I transferred up there in 1975 before the film-school boom. Most of us directionless bundles of acne and unfounded attitude were still studying ceramics and poetry. A friend from the East L.A. barrio would visit twice a month, driving up kilos of weed. I could beat the prices of anybody in the dormitories.

At college, I put much thought into the appearance of being cool. I felt that having a jerkoff magazine in my room was not entirely sophisticated, although I always consulted any such material were it displayed in the residences of my customers. One smoky afternoon I'd lost the ability to raise myself from the sofa of a pair of pre-law druggies. They had each bought a lid and smoked me out, and I'd become too self-conscious to stand up. I was diverting myself with a *Playboy* book of lingerie photography, of all things, when a white guy who stood close to 6' 8" manifested within the room. He wore a T-shirt that indicated he played basketball for the school. A doctor's son, he had dropped in to peddle spare pharmaceuticals. I asked if he wanted to trade weed for speed, and he declined. What more did I have to say to a guy like that? My attention returned to the airbrushed lovelies in lingerie. The gauzy magazine attracted the disdain of the basketball player. He took a smoldering joint out of my hand and said, "We're into *Hustler*. Are you up for that?"

This jock and his roommate had papered their dorm room with foldouts from *Hustler*. Evidently, the mission of the *Hustler* photographers was to include all three of a woman's primary orifices in each individual shot, moisturized and gaping. Unfathomable today, coeds would come around from the women's floors, in pairs and alone, dropping in to buy black beauties. They'd stay for an hour or two, chatting and sophisticated within this tomb of wall-to-wall gape. In a few years, these coeds would be replaced by serious young women majoring in feminist theory.

Toward the end of my two semesters at college, punk rock was being invented in New York City and London, England. My intuition told me that Los Angeles would be the epicenter of a highly lucrative West Coast punk-rock explosion. Against my parents' strenuous objections, I dropped out of school, took up residence on a friend's sofa and pursued career ambitions in various lowlife Hollywood dives and seedy after-parties. The pay was not great, nonexistent in fact, and the hours were brutal.

Four punk-rock girls who called themselves the Plungers lived in a single-room apartment off of Santa Monica Boulevard, across the street from the Starwood. The Starwood was a rock 'n' roll club owned by Eddie Nash, a storied gangster who would be implicated in the bloody four-on-the-floor murders on Wonderland Avenue in Laurel Canyon. The Plunger Pit overlooked an alley frequented by cruising homosexuals, a pre-AIDS hotbed of man-on-man action.

The Plungers' furniture was all broken and low to the ground. Their place was teeming with dopers and drunks, mostly kids just entering their terrible twenties, jostling shoulder to shoulder. We'd all come from seeing the Dead Boys at the Starwood. I had noticed a flashy brunette moving with attitude through the crowd at the club— pretty, dark, short, with black spiky hair; not at all hard-looking but with an edge. She seemed to be on her own, although she had a nod-ding acquaintance with a few of the usual punks. The band had quit early. I'd wormed my way backstage and given lead singer Stiv Bators synthetic painkillers called Talwin. He washed down the pills imme-diately, and they had produced for Stiv an irresistible urge to vomit just as he hit the stage for the second show.

Talwin ingestion was making me wheezy myself, so I cleared off a place on the Plungers' coffee table and sat down. The brunette I had scoped in the Starwood took a spot next to me on the coffee table. Two lame guys stood talking to her, failing to hold her interest. A beer dangled from her hand, and she tapped her foot in a manner that struck me as forward and suggestive. She made me nervous. My best solution was to take another Talwin. Four of the toxic orange pills remained in my pocket.

To openly pull out drugs at the Plunger Pit was to invite a mooch infestation, so I rose from the coffee table and squeezed through the press of delinquents toward the bathroom. The knob and latch had been ripped out of the bathroom door. I pushed in without knocking. Two of the Plunger Girls had stripped to bras and panties and were presenting their rear cheeks to a rail-thin, black-haired degenerate in a black leather jacket and bone-tight black leather jeans. He wielded a supple thong of leather that hit with a snap. The girls yelped.

I fished out my pills and swallowed two at the clogged sink. In no hurry to rejoin the crowd, I sat on the edge of the tub. Appearing casual, I riffled through a stack of magazines beside the toilet. The Plunger Girls' laundry bobbed in the tub, filled to the brim. A *Hustler* magazine tumbled from the pile of periodicals, and I lifted it to my lap. Emblazoned across the cover were the words WAR: THE REAL OBSCENITY.

The black-haired skeeve's whip snapped on girl flesh, and I looked up. How had I missed identifying this guy? The sadist was Stiv Bators. We grinned in mutual recognition.

The Plungers' bathroom door opened inward, and I yelled, "Get out!" The intruder retreated, and the door closed. One of the Plungers was much rounder, larger and far less welted than her friend. I kicked Stiv to capture his attention.

"Whip that one," I said, pointing. "Right there."

Stiv raised the lash to comply, and I leaned backward to stay clear of its arc. Balance pranked me, and I toppled into the cold, fluid embrace of the bathtub behind me. I sank like dumb weight through engulfing waters and lodged beneath the Plunger Pit's soaking laundry. I looked up at the world through sitting bath water. The two partially naked Plunger Girls and Stiv Bators fished me from the tub.

"I'm okay," I sputtered, pointing to the breasts of the smaller girl. "Now whip this one here."

The girl cooed encouragingly, and Stiv slapped her chest with his lash. The bathroom door pushed inward. Again, I yelled, "Get out."

A girl walked straight in. She was the spiky brunette, the girl whose assertive foot-tapping had driven me to take sanctuary in this perilous bathroom. In two glances, she assessed the situation. Composed, slightly contemptuous, she moved past the panty-and-bra girls and whip-waving Stiv Bators, hiked her red mini and took a seat on the toilet. She tricked me into making eye contact and winked. Playing coy, sopping in stale water, I turned to the wet *Hustler* on my lap and fanned its pages. The magazine opened to photos of a hollow-eyed American soldier sprawled in tropical dirt and caked in blood. The back half of his head was blown away. I recoiled and shut the magazine.

Slap. Stiv continued his corporal enjoyment of the Plunger Girls. The brunette on the toilet regarded me blankly. I forced myself back to the editorial well of the *Hustler* and was confronted by severed limbs, charred flesh, heads with no bodies. These gruesome visuals, I was given to understand later, were not a gratuitous ploy for shock value, but were intended as serious commentary upon a society that criminalizes depictions of physical love while glorifying acts of brutality. The gore and the Talwin roiled my stomach. People puked at Plunger Pit parties all the time, but they were ridiculed mercilessly, and I didn't want to be included among them. The enticing brunette had positioned herself between me and the door, or I might never have spoken to her. "I have to go outside," I said.

Perhaps she interpreted a seductive subtext to what I had said. She followed me out through the party throng and into the West Hollywood night. We leaned against a block wall and watched gay romance in the alley. Her name was Juliet. Her father was French, and her mother was German. Her parents had been born in Europe and had come to the United States to escape the ethnic conflicts that arose every time their respective families met. Juliet had recently dropped out of art school and was selling shoes at a West L.A. chain store. My nausea passed, and the simultaneous notion struck that Juliet and I should make out. So, in effect, some may say that I am indebted to *Hustler* for hooking me up with my first wife, but eventually, *Hustler* became one of the excuses Juliet would use to leave me.

I needed a reason to be hanging around all these punk rock parties. Rather than learn to play guitar, I started writing for *Slash* magazine. The publishers and editors were a pair of couples, older than the rest of us, pushing 30 if not already there. Like me, they sensed an imminent wealth explosion in servicing the punk rock population. Under pen names Basho Macko, Mumbo Jumbo, Nervo Pervo, Heebo Jeebo and Alex Mackaral, I supplied concert reviews, record reviews, interviews, a snide gossip column. I hoped the founders would one day remunerate me for my contributions. Ten or 15 dollars would have been appreciated.

Juliet and I moved into a prewar garden-court apartment called the Canterbury Arms, above Hollywood Boulevard at the corner of Yucca and Cherokee, a vile intersection that will forever repel the forces of gentrification. There were about 70 apartments in the Canterbury building. Its windows observed three distinct hubs of prostitution. Male hustlers taunted chicken hawks from the seats of a hotdog stand on Hollywood Boulevard. Real women and trannies, rival entrepreneurs, occupied catty corners of an intersection one block up from the boulevard. My first night in the building, gunshots were fired in the courtyard, and a pimp physically disciplined one of his wailing employees in the hallway not 15 yards from my Murphy bed. Juliet and I clung to each other, flinching with each new sound of terror. We had no phone with which to call for help.

Across Hollywood Boulevard, about a block and a half away, was an alley that led to an unmarked doorway. Concrete stairs descended to a maze of cinderblock rooms directly beneath the Pussycat Theater. These cavernous depths had been turned into the Masque, a nightclub with no bar, no refreshments, no booths or seats at all, no stage, just cement and brick, perpetually backed-up toilets and leaking bathroom plumbing crisscrossing the ceilings from the porno theater upstairs. Its proximity to the Masque put the Canterbury Arms at punk rock central. Blue-haired brats flocked to the building and soon occupied approximately half the units.

Once I began writing for *Slash*, I took a professional interest in the magazine rack. My attention would wander from the music and fashion titles and cross the line of indecency into the skin ghetto. *Hustler* was the biggest eyesore. No need to open the magazine to be offended by its boldly advertised "Scratch 'n' Sniff Centerfold," or the composite cover shot of a nubile model being fed headfirst into a meat grinder. Under all the bluster, the magazine's intentions were garbled at best. The huckster factor was impossible to ignore and difficult to discount. Attention-hog Flynt was in the news all the time, and he bought space on billboards out on Sunset Boulevard. My blue-haired friends and I would be driving back to the Canterbury Arms from shows by bands like the Cramps or Television at the Whisky a Go Go, and we'd see Flynt's handiwork, looming over the 3 a.m. traffic.

After Flynt was shot in the spring of 1978 you heard less from him. I was in a liquor store down the street from the Canterbury with a blue-haired friend named Ruff. While Ruff was stealing tall cans of Rainier ale, I squatted by the magazine rack and slid the current issue of *Hustler* under my shirt. Back at my apartment, I discovered the thing was filled with graphic photos of Larry Flynt in the hospital, focusing on his bullet wounds. Larry's wife was offering a $1 million reward for the name of the shooter. That money could have helped me out. I'd been inducted into the world of expensive narcotics. I did some dope in the bathroom, then came back to the sofa and the magazine and counted how many fixes that million dollars would provide.

The money was the only thing the magazine gave me to fantasize about. Deep inside the book was a photographic guide to sex positions. A guy who appeared to be gay posed reluctantly atop a woman with crisply styled hair. I had already figured out and tried all those sex positions on my own, as well as others.

Three punk girls who camped in the building came over looking for Juliet; at least that was their excuse for barging in. They caught me staring off into drug space.

"Are you jerking off in here? Is that why you spend so much time alone?"

"He's reading *Hustler*."

I couldn't believe I'd left the door unlocked. The Canterbury had devolved into a dormitory situation. Yellow-, orange- and green-haired kids popped in and out of one another's apartments as if we were all enrolled at one big mixed-gender sorority house. Juliet's three friends went through our kitchen looking for food, picked over Juliet's makeup table, then came back to me. I hadn't moved. I should have slid the magazine under a record cover.

"We hate *Hustler*."

"Alomar and Mohammed love that magazine."

Alomar and Mohammed were two among the many blacks who shared the building with the punks. A couple of white hookers had defected and joined the punk ranks, and their former boyfriend/managers felt it only fair that a few punk girls should put themselves out on the corner to square accounts.

"Alomar and Mohammed came down to Candy's apartment and brought all these *Hustler* magazines with them."

"Like we were supposed to just look at some photos of some black boy with a huge dick hanging it over a white chick's shoulder, and that would make us jump on our backs and spread our legs."

"Like we wouldn't be disgusted."

"You weren't disgusted, Laura. I was watching you."

"Alomar and Mohammed were watching you too."

"You didn't want to give the magazine back."

Laura didn't like the direction of the conversation and picked me to deflect.

"Look at him sitting there with his mouth hanging open."

I managed to lick my lips but couldn't bring myself to quite shut the hatch. Laura took this as encouragement and went on with mounting fury. "He's a fag jerkoff. That's the issue with the big black dick."

I protested and showed the girls the sex-position pictorial. "No, no. It's just this little white guy."

I thought I'd handled it pretty well, but Laura had a big mouth and so did the other two. They couldn't get out of the apartment fast enough. I don't know how long passed before Juliet came home;

could have been 15 minutes, maybe two hours. I'd spent the time contemplating getting up and locking the door.

"Laura and the other two are telling everyone that they caught you in here jacking off to gay porno," said Juliet. "Is that true?"

"You're asking me if it's true that they are saying these things?" My worst childhood fear was coming true: that masturbation would be interpreted as homosexual activity. I had no high left at all.

Juliet pressed her breasts together. "Why do you need something like that magazine?"

I wasn't so wasted that I couldn't fabricate an answer for her. "I thought maybe I could write for them. I think they pay a lot. *Slash* pays me nothing."

She was reluctant to buy my story, so I embellished, theorizing that if I could secure a *Hustler* flow of income, we could move into a place of our own, like in a duplex, and things might progress, and we might have a future.

A few hours later, I was in a car headed out to a venue in the Valley, a place called the Rock Corporation. The Go-Go's were scheduled to play. They all still lived at the Canterbury, and most of them still had their baby fat. About eight of us were crammed into the car, a big, late-'60s Ford. I was squeezed next to a guy named Black Randy. Black Randy was chubby, white, exiting his mid-20s. His teeth were oddly spaced, and he fronted a band called the Metrosquad, named after Police Chief Daryl Gates' elite tactical troops. His current hit songs included "Loner With a Boner," "Sperm Bank Baby" and "Trouble at the Cup," a rousing tribute to an imaginary uprising of the boy prostitutes who hawked themselves from the Gold Cup hotdog stand on Hollywood Boulevard. Randy had rehabbed once already, and he'd lived in New York. He claimed to have been friends with Dee Dee Ramone prior to the formation of the Ramones, and he had videotape to back up the claim. Black Randy knew the score.

The idea of career advancement at *Hustler* had grown on me, and Randy heartily seconded the notion. "I had a Dilaudid connection who worked for one of those magazines in New York. They're all the same. It's all Mob-run, so they give you half your pay in drugs. There's a girl there whose job is to come in early every morning and dice up the cocaine in your pencil tray."

Juliet and I pooled our last two unemployment checks, stiffed the Canterbury and landed an apartment in a residential district south of Hollywood. A Century City advertising firm hired Juliet to paste up presentation layouts. Making good on my contention that I intended to write for *Hustler*, I tailored a pair of sex stories to their "Kinky Korner" column. I meticulously printed the nasty scenarios on 20-plus pages of ruled yellow paper. If accepted, they would earn half a grand. I stuffed my work into a fat envelope, imagining several ways I would spend the money, and Juliet mailed it from her advertising agency. No response ever came.

Bullocks department store hired me as a proofreader in their newspaper advertising section. From Monday to Friday, I combed my hair, wore a tie and tried to pass as employable. One Saturday, Juliet and I were pronounced man and wife in a notary public's office on Wilshire Boulevard. Neither of us had been talking to our parents, and there wasn't much family living in L.A., so it was me, Juliet and two friends from where she worked. Right away, Juliet worried that she'd committed to the wrong man.

To encourage my writing career, she arranged a tryout with her ad firm. They suggested I put together a dummy campaign for something I was interested in. I created a brand of vodka that guaranteed it would make girls find a guy more attractive, and if not, he could take one more sip, and he wouldn't care. Juliet's bosses suggested I might have better luck elsewhere, so my hopes reverted to *Hustler*, and I occasionally studied an issue. Every time I picked one up, they seemed to have a fake photo shoot of girls doing it with some lout in a werewolf costume or dressed up as a space alien. I remember feeling ripped off by a pathetically prosthetic three-breasted centerfold and put off by a 50-year-old woman in a state of undress I had never cared to imagine. Was the shoot of the hairiest girl in the world intended to expand my notions of erotic stimulation? *Hustler* was more expensive than the rest of the stroke books. Try as I might, it was impossible to work up interest in a gold-plated, head-shaved girl supposedly photographed on another planet. The Tin Man, Cowardly Lion and the Scarecrow dangled their penises in the vicinity of a Dorothy look-alike's orifices, and I yawned. *Hustler*'s "Flash Before You Flush" contest, with its photo of the winner, an enormous turd coiled in a toilet bowl, convinced me there would never be another reason for me to pick up this magazine. But in 1983, LFP placed a help-wanted ad seeking an associate copy editor.

I folded the newspaper. The rest of the want ads fell to the floor. On Monday morning, I surveyed the view from my cubicle in the Bullocks newspaper-advertising section. Women dominated that particular sub-hierarchy. We males were outnumbered 30 to three, and the other two guys were dating one another. Incessant and petty infighting consumed half of my every day. I'd been promoted from proofreader. My management-adjacent job was to monitor the timely assemblage of the newspaper ads, coordinating the copy, the art and the merchandise availability. Basically, I was a snitch, responsible for ratting out whoever held up progress. No one was happy with my job performance. At home, Juliet had tired of my co-worker complaints. The guys my age where she worked owned starter condos and had plans for expansion.

I remembered Black Randy's conception of working at a magazine like *Hustler*. I pictured the girl whose job it was to come in early and prepare the cocaine. She looked good in my mind, far more attractive than the conniving, malingering and vindictive ladies at the department-store ad factory. Even Juliet, whose face drew taut and etched with hairline wrinkles whenever she looked at me lately, paled in comparison to the cocaine girl. So I called the number in the LFP want ad.

The *Hustler* Cover

THE MOST IMPORTANT page of any magazine, from a seller's viewpoint, is the cover. Before a sucker's impulse to buy can be triggered, his eye must be engaged by alluring photos, provocative snipes, boastful banners and alarmist blurbs. The consumer is led to pause and reflect that turning this first page will open a world of nonstop and complete gratification superior to all others on earth. The *Hustler* universe, as presented on the public face of its magazine, could be assumed to be a swirling orbit of available and playful women eager to dabble with irreverent, tough-guy iconoclasts in outlandish sexual adventures, the mere retelling of which might provide a lifetime of fulfilling fantasies for lesser men. Surely, there was room between those covers for me.

CHAPTER 3

Hired!

THE FIRST TIME I saw Larry Flynt in person set the tone for all future encounters. I'd been picking my fingernails in the reception area of his Century City office suites, 38 stories skyward. My interview for the position of *Hustler* assistant proofreader lay ahead of me. An array of Larry Flynt Publications was spread out on the coffee table that fronted the sofa.

A pair of floor-to-ceiling, ornately carved doors separated me from the inner world of *Hustler* magazine. Every time the doors opened and someone passed in or out of the sanctum, I tried to glimpse the exotic territory within. I also kept an eye on the receptionist, the only other human in the lobby. When she stood, I saw that she was hardly five feet tall. She had seemed bigger while seated. Big black hair, big dark eyes, big, tightly wrapped bust. Did she perceive me as some yokel who read a magazine like *Hustler* or who was fazed by such material? Her nostrils flared, and her fire-red mouth tensed. She spotted an approach from the elevator banks. A brick-shaped black man, huge like a professional athlete, pushed a gleaming, gold-plated wheelchair in front of him. The ebony mammoth scanned the lobby with the quick, calm thoroughness of a professional bodyguard. He discounted any threat coming from me and gave a cool nod to the girl behind the desk. She ignored him, directing her smile at the bodyguard's charge.

A figure of disconsolate wrath slouched in the glittering, precious metal chair. There was no mistaking the big-headed man in the golden chair for anyone other than Larry Flynt. Moony, pasty and waxen, his lumpy, drawn face seemed to be paralyzed in a pained rictus of displeasure. Without moving his neck, he shifted his clouded aware-ness from the big-hair brunette. A single pass of his glassed-over eye froze me to the spot. He was so doped up, I couldn't be sure he'd reg-istered seeing me. I felt like some cowardly character in a monster movie, holding his breath in the vicinity of the ogre, hoping to be passed over. This quaking reaction to the presence of an ostensibly crippled, massively medicated, spottily educated hillbilly would never wear off. Over the next 20 years, a sense of mild alarm and height-ened attention would accompany my every contact with Larry Flynt, even after he'd decided to like me.

I had no idea upon this first sighting that Larry Flynt would ever know my name, never mind come to depend on me like Hitler did Goebbels. A buzzer sounded, and the gleaming, golden wheelchair passed through the paired, carved doors into the promised *Hustler* realm. Released from the stupefying Flynt aura, I counted my bless-ings while waiting for someone from the personnel department to come and guide me to my interview.

This counting of blessings had been an idea floated by Juliet during the drive from our Hollywood apartment to Century City. My total previous experience of Century City was three days in a phone-sales boiler room, pushing low-quality office supplies to crooked purchasing agents. The towering office structures, monu-ments to affluence and ambition, made me feel shabby and out of place, even in my new jacket and tie. Juliet had acclimated to the monolithic ambiance in her few months as an advertising paste-up person. Her hair had grown out to her shoulders, a thick and lus-trous brunette, and she had taken to dressing in the manner of an account executive. Thin and attractively angular, she looked confi-dent, poised and in place behind the wheel of our 1971 Volvo P-1800, a classic sports coupe like the one piloted by Roger Moore as the Saint. We'd recently bought the car with our combined entry-level purchasing powers.

"Things are looking up for us," said Juliet, piloting the Volvo along a Century City parking ramp. She'd taken to flipping a strand of hair back behind her right ear when she felt she was making a pertinent point. "You're finally getting a job you'll like."

"It's just an interview. I'll be back in Bullocks this afternoon."

"Well, things are looking up for me. If you'd raise your career arc, things would be looking up for both of us."

"This is all easy for you to say."

She flipped the hair. "Count your blessings, Allan."

My blessings, the ones I could factor in the wake of Larry Flynt's chilly wheelchair tracks, were the inability of the woman behind the receptionist's desk to read my mind. The double doors cracked open, and another brunette, this one lighter and more animated than the receptionist, poked her head and torso into the lobby. She called my name. I pulled the knot of my tie out from my pulsating neck and followed the brunette's rollicking but narrow hips.

She had one of those guy's names, like Tommi or Bobbi, but there was nothing tomboyish about her. We walked in single file along an otherwise unremarkable corridor. We passed potted plants and a smattering of nonrepresentational art. I saw little beyond the brunette's pelvic twist to distinguish the place from an insurer's office. Still, being at *Hustler* and 27 years old, a current of sexual excitation prickled my nervous system. Once we'd arrived at her office, Tommi or Bobbi handed me an application. My thoughts throughout my teens and 20s were seldom far from sex. I fought them aside and concentrated on the mundane task of filling in my work history, schooling, home address, person to contact in case of emergency.

I handed the personnel lady my paperwork. Her melted-chocolate eyes visually caressed me, then I followed those frolicsome hips again as she led the way to the pen that contained the copy editors. The comma-catchers were situated in a long room with one glassed wall that faced west, beachward, overlooking the Century Plaza Hotel, where President Reagan stayed when he was in town from Washington. The copy editors, two guys—one with scraggly long hair—and two girls, evaluated me with mild disinterest. They wore casual denim and T-shirts. I'd gone Brooks Brothers for the event. The lead copy editor, the clean-cut guy, looked doubtful.

"Do you know where you are?" he said.

"Sure... What do you mean?"

"It's a specific kind of thing we do here."

He lifted a stack of printer's proofs off his desk and fanned them in my face. These true-color slicks represented the last chance to alter a layout before the pages went to press. One of the double-truck spreads held out for my inspection showed a painting of Adolf Hitler naked on his back. A girl child squatted above his chest and sent a stream of urine onto his belly. The remaining proofs were of a posed photo set depicting a blonde hospital patient granting sexual favors while she lay in traction with both legs in casts.

"Are you going to be okay with this?" asked the lead copy editor.

I shrugged, and with an effort managed to break off eye contact from the blonde in traction. "Sure, that's all fine."

"That's all fine?" said the taller of the copy women, squinting skeptically at me. She was blonde, early 30s.

"What's so fine about it?" said the other copy lady, about the same age as her colleague, but with sandy brown hair. Neither woman gave any hint of humor.

The long-haired guy snickered.

The lead copy editor handed over a clipboard and an attached manuscript page of a book review. I sat in a hardbacked chair, under the glare of the women, and circled typos, misspellings and grammatical flaws in the copy, inserting typesetting marks. Paste-up people and production editors wandered in and out, exchanging mild snippets of conversation. I admired their ease with one another while in the presence of the filth.

The lead editor let the taller girl grade my test. In the interval, no one seemed eager to say anything to me. I didn't want to just sit there and be awkward.

"Why are you hiring somebody?"

The woman looked up from grading the test. "Bobby's leaving."

Bobby was evidently the lead editor. I addressed him. "Where are you going?"

The sandy-haired girl answered. "He's going to the city desk at a newspaper in the Valley."

I couldn't fathom why someone would opt to leave this Eden that I was just now glimpsing. "That can't be as much fun as *Hustler*. Why would you do that?"

Bobby sighed. "You don't have kids? Wait until you have a kid, and you want to go to PTA or buy a house in a nice place where they have an owners' association. It helps if you don't work for somebody named Larry Flynt."

I doubted that what he said was true, but it was not my duty to wise him up, not if his departure was opening a slot for me.

The women finished grading my test. I'd missed three out of roughly 100 mistakes: a lowercase L used as a 1 in an address, which I pointed out seemed like a trick error; a necessary paragraph break, which I opined was discretionary; and a run-on sentence that the women would have broken into two and which I argued was a stylistic decision.

All four copy editors rolled their eyes, dismissing me right in front of my face.

"I suppose he should see Morgen," said Bobby.

Sandy-haired Chris, the shorter and less coolly dismissive of the women, led me through a network of corridors. We took a different route than the one Jimmi or Jerri had led me on, and I was exposed to a reality I had suspected and hoped for. The place was packed with effervescent women. A different delightful and consciously sexy female employee caught my eye at every turn until Chris deposited me in the office of N. Morgen Hagen, copy chief. How could a porno magazine need so many copy editors? Morgen was hovering at the 40-year-old cutoff, fit but imperfectly contained by a dark, pinstriped suit jacket and slacks, accessorized with an open-collar, two-tone dress shirt. The suit intensified rather than diminished Hagen's mien of the good-natured recreational brawler. His graying hair was unkempt; his clean shave was a few days gone; his milky blue eyes were absorbent and patient. Morgen scanned my test, then scanned me. He tried to dampen his admiration for how well I'd done. He put the test aside and paged through my résumé and employment application.

"Bullocks?" he said. He picked up a 64-ounce 7-Eleven cup and spat into it. He was chewing tobacco. "I bought this suit at Bullocks. I had to go to a wedding. How do you like it?"

"It's a nice suit."

His face showed that I was an idiot. "How do you like working at Bullocks?"

"I hate it."

His face showed that I was an idiot with a negative attitude. "You're Canadian? Do you play hockey?" He was visibly disappointed that I did not.

"Do my chances look good?" I said.

"Sure, sure. Well, don't blow up Bullocks yet."

I left Century City on the Number 4 bus. My mood fell as I stood and despaired of finding an empty seat. It was dispiriting riding away from those towering monuments, squeezed into a wheezing public conveyance, heading back to the no-fun zone of Bullocks.

Nothing has ever been easy for me, not even landing a job at *Hustler*. You hear esteemed sitcom writers discuss how they settled for a job at a tawdry magazine in their hungry youth. I gave it everything I had just to be considered for hiring.

About a week later, I was called in for a second interview. The people in Juliet's work environment were astounded that a second interview would be required for a job at *Hustler*. I scurried back to Century City and was met in the LFP lobby by N. Morgen Hagen. He appeared slightly furtive and was wearing the same suit and shirt as last time. He hooked my arm. We darted through the halls and cut behind corners. I sensed that we were avoiding somebody. We slid into an unused cubicle, and Hagen dropped his bomb. There was no need for me to be giving my two weeks' notice at Bullocks. "We've decided to go with someone else, a candidate who is on friendly terms with someone who is already on staff here."

Even at *Hustler*, you needed an in to get hired. This news would doubly astound Juliet's workmates.

After the winter holidays, I took proactive action, quitting Bullocks. I found a job earning 33 percent less as an editorial assistant at *Gambling Times*, a magazine dedicated to the proposition that wagering on sports and games of chance is a combination of art and science, has little to do with dumb luck, and might be pursued as a profession. I was writing captions for photos of championship slots winners and reading unsolicited fiction about desperate cardsharps gambling their souls with the devil. A few months in, a phone call came from Chris, the sandy-haired woman in the LFP copy department.

Morgen, she indicated, had taken a sabbatical in Ohio to stay at the farm of an old girlfriend. Perhaps he suffered a nervous breakdown.

No one knew when he might return. In the meantime, Flynt wanted to launch a digest-size fantasy letters magazine. Copy editors needed to be hired immediately. Chris and the taller, blonde copy editor, Jennifer, had broken into Morgen's office and rifled through his desk until they'd found my résumé. Would I come in and see them?

The job was offered to me by Chris as we stood in a hallway that was papered with blurred photocopies of pages from the current *Hustler* under construction. As I tried to comprehend what she was telling me about parking procedures and salary reviews, my mind reverted to the smudged images papering the walls. Twenty pages in a row were devoted to lewd, crowded advertisements hawking sex toys, skin flicks, penis enlargers, soiled panties and Karnal Komix. The temptation to move closer to the wall and investigate the fuzzy details of this intricate ad orgy was resisted. I smiled wanly to indicate I was still listening to my new direct-in-command. Avoiding Chris' eyes, I concentrated on her teeth, trying to block out awareness of the blood flowing through her lips. A surge pulsed in my penis. Which would be more humiliating: sprouting wood and being noticed, or popping the stick and having it go undetected?

Inappropriate erections would be the least of my worries. In the interim between my first interview and my hiring, both male occupants had departed from the copy pen. Chris and Jennifer, the two women from my initial visit, had been joined by Sarah, a brunette in the Mediterranean mold. Sarah had been on friendly terms with someone on staff back when she had been hired instead of me. Only in her early 30s, Sarah carried a prematurely matronly bosom. It was easily bigger than the combined heft of all other bosoms in the copy room. Sarah had an actual education, with a graduate degree and an applied understanding of grammar that trumped my theoretical grasp, and she had extensive experience at real magazines. I suspect to this day that the deciding factor in her hiring by N. Morgen Hagen had been those big tits.

Sarah knew that she'd beaten me out for the job, and she graciously lorded it over me. The other two women liked her less than they liked each other. Maybe Sarah felt that she needed an ally in the pen. She took charge of teaching me the points of house style and tried to instill a sense of mission. "Your responsibilities include ensuring that *cum* is used only as a noun (for semen and female ejac-ulate) and never as a verb ('to come'), that *porno* not appear where a simple *porn* will do, and that *blowjob* is always spelled solid, not as two separate words." She spoke as though addressing a select class of dedicated recruits. "The credibility of *Hustler* magazine depends upon such details." Sarah was a believer. The other two women, Chris and Jennifer, tolerated me.

For the first week, the copy ladies didn't let me do much work. The digests I'd been hired to edit had been held up in the design stages. The women insisted that I should spend my shift familiarizing myself with the collected works of *Hustler*. They insisted that under no circumstances was I to sign off on any finished boards in the box designated for a copy editor's initials.

"Why not?" I asked.

Matronly Sarah came out from behind her desk and settled into the chair adjacent to mine, a move that indicated serious knowledge was about to be imparted. "Allan, somebody will bring you a board they want to rush out to the printer, and it will have a copy mistake on it, and they might even know that, but they want to save their ass from being reamed for the material being late, so they'll pressure you to sign it off, and then when it prints with the mistake, you're fired."

I took this warning to heart, but tried not to let the anxiety it unleashed interfere with my studious review of *Hustler* past. For eight hours a day, confined in a limited space with three females, I sifted through page after page of America's premier sex mag. I saw photos of bald naked ladies, one frolicking on a sofa with a harlequin Great Dane, another being strapped into an electric chair. There were hun-dreds of amateur Polaroids focused between the splayed legs of gals-next-door from all across the hinterlands. Several pages were devoted to Jacqueline Kennedy Onassis sunning her bush on a remote Greek island. I tried to dissemble any signs of interest in what I was looking at.

One afternoon, Jennifer discovered that some type in a final gal-ley had been inadvertently sliced by a mat knife. This was before computer typesetting; the words and letters had to be manually past-ed into position on flexible cardboard flats by production artists who wielded razor-sharp blades. Occasionally, sloppy knife work resulted in damaged letters, such as what Jennifer had discovered. The look she gave me was not unfriendly.

"Allan, go and give this board to Barb and have her replace this word."

Barb was a paste-up artist in an art room to the side of the main paste-up pen. A bony chain-smoker, she wore flouncy harem pants, and she slanted her dyed-black hair across one half of her face, like a backup singer for Boy George. I found her easily, waited until she had finished her personal phone call, and presented the sliced type for her inspection.

"This word needs to be replaced," I said.

"I don't have any extra type from that job."

The extra type from the job (the typesetters always ran out doubles specifically so there would be extra type) was plainly visible, pinned to a bulletin board to Barb's right. "What about that right there?" I said.

"Do I have time to look through that?"

She opened a catalog of hairstyles and flipped its pages.

"Are you saying that I should look for it?"

"Be my guest."

"Well, here; hold this board."

"Oh, just set that on the table."

I placed the board that needed to be fixed where Barb indicated I should, on the corner of a seemingly unoccupied workspace. It would be only a moment before I found a replacement for the damaged word. An angry, high-pitched screech interrupted my search.

"Whose shit is this?"

The board with the sliced type whirred past my head. I turned. An outraged black man with processed hair and dramatically applied eyeshadow pointed a trembling finger at me. His lips were wet and shuddering. Roughly my age, late 20s, he was smaller than me, but also more rabid.

"Was that your shit?" he demanded. "Don't you see this is someone's workspace? Do you just come in and take over? Is everything yours?"

"How was I supposed to know?"

"Try pulling your head out of your fucking ass."

I turned toward Barb, cuing her to bail me out. Her eyes were widely innocent.

Back in the copy pen, I gave Sarah an abridged account of this interaction.

"That's Bunny. He works directly with Althea. You don't want to be on Bunny's bad side. Bunny and Althea talk."

"And what about that Barb?"

"Isn't she cute?"

That night on the way home from work, I moaned to Juliet. "I'll never make it through my first week."

"You're exaggerating, as usual. Let good things happen."

"People are telling me that all they have to do is say one word, and I'm flushed."

She flicked a heavy strand of hair behind an ear. "I'm sure you're imagining all this."

Was I imagining the frazzled and frenetic blonde standing over my desk and glaring down at me at 9:05 the next a.m.? I put aside the vintage *Hustler* I was perusing and tried to make sense of her incensed verbal stream. It was early for this kind of hysteria. None of the ladies of the copy pen had checked in yet.

"I need someone from copy to sign this off," said the blonde. "It was supposed to ship out last night, and now it's late, and heads shall roll, and you must sign it off."

"I was told not to sign anything off."

"Someone from copy must sign this off."

"Perhaps you might sign it yourself. Say you're from copy. Go ahead, I authorize you."

"Don't be surprised if I do."

She stalked out. I congratulated myself on handling the situation well. Obviously, she had no firing clout or she would have been less terrified of losing her job. Unless she had not been terrified but only high on cocaine. I let that thought drift away on its own and returned to my old-school *Hustler*. A large dark presence rushed up against the front of my desk. A swarthy and saturnine entity placed his hands on either end of my desktop and leaned forward. The wiry blonde stood behind him, relishing this shift in power.

"You're refusing to sign off this board?" This guy was big. He didn't need to introduce himself. I knew he carried weight.

"I'm not refusing."

"Then sign it."

"I'm not authorized."

"You're a copy editor, aren't you?"

"I only just started."

"If you weren't qualified, why did they hire you in the first place?"

The twitching blonde was having an actual orgasm, I'm pretty sure. Sarah slouched in behind her.

"Hey, Bill," Sarah said, seemingly unafraid of the intimidating raptor hunkered above me. "What's going on?"

"I'm being fucked around here by someone who's refusing to do his job."

Sarah physically intervened, placing her body between Bill and me. "Oh, that's my fault, Bill. I told him not to sign unless I was here. I got stuck in horrendous traffic. Let me look." She took the board away and signed it. As Bill and the blonde moved out, glaring back at me, Sarah sank into the chair beside my desk.

"Do you know who that was?" said Sarah.

I declined to make any of the obvious guesses.

"They say Bill parties with Althea, in private. Because Larry can't anymore. In fairness to Bill, they say the same thing about half the guys who work with Althea. But Bill's a genius. He invented the Scratch 'n' Sniff centerfold. You can't afford to be on his bad side."

Who else could I piss off? The only reason the Flynts hadn't taken a disliking to me is that they were both out of town. Neither Althea nor Larry had been spotted in the office since I'd been hired. Still, Althea's sister and her husband were around. The sister's name was Marsha, and she worked in supplies or something. She had been overtly friendly in passing, but her husband, Bill, held some nebulous position in corporate security, and I'd seen a gun jutting prominently from his waistband. I declined to acknowledge Marsha's overtures, a decision Sarah praised as wise.

I was afraid to leave the sheltering confines of the copy pen. To bide my time, Chris gave me a sheet of hundreds of off-color jokes that needed to be proofread for a magazine called *Hustler Humor*.

Here's a typical *Hustler Humor* joke: "The new student nurse was perplexed about bathing patients in bed. She said to the tough, old head nurse, 'When you're bathing patients, what do you do when you come to the genitals?' The hard-bitten old nurse replied, 'You wash them, same as you do the Jews.'"

It's hard to take these jokes seriously after the first couple of hundred, but I did my utmost. I handed the work to Chris and stretched out to bask in the glow of a productive day. Perhaps Juliet was right, and despite my paranoia I would come to feel a part of this vital enterprise.

A swaggering 40-something skeeve who'd been dipped in equal buckets of slime and smarm paraded into the copy pen. Greasy locks of dun-colored hair dripped down onto a polyester-blend collar that should have been buttoned at least one notch closer to the neck. This character's lips were curdled in a permanent, self-congratulatory sneer. He had those darting, leering rapist's eyes that give away the villains in 1970s exploitation cinema. Wafting clouds of sour cologne and cigarette funk shattered my feeling of well-being.

"Y'all must be the new proofreader."

The girls all bailed out as if on cue. I was on my own with this preening cracker bummer.

"Wait, proofreader is an arcane term. They call you all copy editors now, don't they? I'm Dwaine Tinsley."

He stuck out his hand. I had the feeling he might withdraw it suddenly if I made a move to shake, but I reached out anyway. His grip was damp and prolonged.

"I'm an artist," said Dwaine. "You're probably familiar with my work. As an artist, I sometimes surprise people that I also have more practical awarenesses."

In fact, I was familiar with Dwaine's oeuvre. He had created Chester the Molester, *Hustler*'s cartoon pedophile mascot. In a retrospective celebrating Dwaine's brilliance, the magazine had pointed out that Chester's antics were designed to provoke outrage and discourse on the topic of child abuse and that Chester had never actually been depicted engaged in a sexual act with a child. Chester was, however, commonly shown in post-coital bliss accompanied by one or more enslaved pre-adolescent females. Chester's creator spoke very slowly and deliberately. I couldn't figure out if he thought he was talking to a brain-damaged person or if he was just a retard himself.

"You know, I like to make the new people feel welcome. But I have some questions for you. Maybe you could step down to my office."

I didn't want to step down to his cell. I'd read enough prison novels to know how it worked. But I stood up and followed Dwaine's jail yard strut. He walked closer to me than he needed to. He wore cowboy boots and flared denim with a pressed crease. He was '70s at a time when to be '70s showed something other than retro fashion daring. Dwaine's creepiness was organic, developed all on his own.

He ushered me through the door of his office. There wasn't much free space in there. A triple-large woman had pushed the desk forward into the room during the disruptive effort of wedging herself behind it.

"This is my wife, Suzy," said Dwaine. "Larry just loves her cooking."

If Larry loved that cooking half as much as Suzy apparently did, he must have outgrown his wheelchair, which would account for his prolonged absence from the office.

"This is Allan," said Dwaine to his baking bride, "the new proofreader we was wondering about."

"You mean copy editor," said Suzy. Her smile was huge and it was brilliant, but it was entirely ironic. "Pleased to meet you."

"I'll be honest, Al. We like to take care of people," said Dwaine. "That's why we called you in here."

I felt that they expected me to thank them; for what, I couldn't tell.

"I want you to know that Larry reads *Hustler Humor* religiously, or irreligiously, maybe I should say."

"And he's a stickler for accuracy."

"We spend a lot of time up at the mansion, and he's often pointed out mistakes that he's found in the various publications."

"Although very rarely in ours."

"I'll get straight to the point, buddy. I want to save you the humiliation of being a scapegoat, but you'll have to take responsibility. This is your work, right?" He held up the galley of jokes that I had corrected.

"I read through those. Is something wrong?"

Dwaine simpered as if I'd tried to put one over on him. "Right here, in this joke, I put the word *affect*, and you changed it to *effect*."

"Well, I consulted a dictionary, and *affect* appeared to be the wrong verb."

Tinsley's down-home friendliness disappeared as quickly as a false sunrise. "Maybe you can check that dictionary again, after you change *effect* back to the correct word, *affect*."

He tossed the galleys at me. I thanked him and went back to the pen. What was it that I had not liked about working at Bullocks? They would never take me back. Sarah consoled me with sad eyes, but said nothing.

Rumors were abounding regarding Larry Flynt's whereabouts. He was alternately in a coma, in Mexico drying out, on suicide watch in a mental hospital and lying low back in Kentucky after having murdered Althea while she was in the act of partying with a subordinate. Late one morning, the entire editorial staff was called into the publisher's hangar-like office. Larry Flynt sat at the head of the room. Here reigned a totally different person than the dejected hulk who had been wheeled past me a few months earlier. His eyes had a shine that I could pick up at the back of the room. He overflowed with the glory of himself, and you were glad he did. Happy and expansive, he clowned with the insiders and intimates who clustered up front around his desk. His voice was steady, calm, loud, assured. The warm twang of his accent rang out with pleasure at being alive. He announced that he had been away to Duke University for laser surgery to sever nerves in his spinal cord that serviced the pain centers in his extremities. "Ever since I been shot, I've been in pain like I was being sunk into a vat of boiling oil up to my waist. Now I'm ready to pick up where I was when they cut me down."

A murmur of pleased speculation passed through the crowd of employees, rising to a solid round of applause, which Larry basked in, then bashfully cut short.

"We did a lot of things in them days, many I'm proud of, some were embarrassing. Mostly we shook up the status quo. Now, 1984 is right around the corner. It's time to shake things up again. Hold on to your seats. We're going to have some fun."

I, for one, was ready for the change.

The *Hustler* Table of Contents

HUSTLER'S TABLE of Contents is a sordid treasure map guiding the sensual explorer to rich stores of plunder and booty. Provocative visual snippets and evocative bits of wordplay are artfully arranged to best present the current issue as an important, well-rounded package of vital knowledge that is coincidentally populated by fun girls whose charming novelty will never dull. The *Hustler* components pimped on the contents pages will include the standards: pinup shots; inflammatory columns of reader letters; entertainment reviews; an advice section; a page of *"Hustler* Humor" jokes; and feature articles, with topics ranging from the intricacies of five-finger insertion ("Fist Fucking: A Cramping Twist," December, 1983) to the timely supposition that President Roosevelt disregarded advance warning of the Japanese attack on Pearl Harbor ("Explosive Truth About Pearl Harbor: The Story the Rest of the Media Won't Tell," January, 1984). If the reader is lucky, he may be directed to a special treat—perhaps nude photos of a normally clothed celebrity (Prince Albert of Monaco and kiddie model Brooke Shields, December, 1983), maybe a freak pictorial showing a pre-lop transsexual sharing her hefty penis and bolt-on breasts with a heterosexual couple ("Fruit of the Gawds," February, 1984) and occasionally an exposé that is touted to alter America's historical context ("The Bullet That *Really* Killed John Kennedy," May, 1984). Often, the table of contents promised more than would meet the eye. At other times, it could only hint at the full story.

CHAPTER 4

Fun in the Scum

LARRY FLYNT NEVER met an idea of fun that couldn't be improved with the addition of a network camera crew. Through the summer and into the fall of 1983, Flynt strung along the media the way a lesser marionette would play a sock puppet. The boss' prime-time antics added a current-events frisson to what was shaping up—in my head at least—to be the employment opportunity of a lifetime. Having shrugged off the ritual hazing following my hiring, I began to envision a career at *Hustler* as everything I'd yearned for since I'd crapped out of college. Here, if I played my lay right, would be a job that provided a creative outlet and perks—such as travel, exotic sexual overtures and stimulating co-workers predisposed to sharing their stimulants.

At age 27, I admit to being immature, impressionable and susceptible to fantasies of immediate and constant sensual gratification, but I have never been a full idiot, so I mentioned none of these arousing work considerations to Juliet as she steered the Volvo sports coupe along Olympic Boulevard toward the blocky Century City skyline. I smoked my wake-up weed, monitored three Darvocets as their warmth spread to the outreaches of my central nervous system and considered the daily routine ahead of me. Copy Chief N. Morgen Hagen had returned from his mental health leave and had overcome his initial disappointment at discovering me ensconced in the copy pen. He was still wearing the same blue pin-striped suit from Bullocks, more rumpled daily. Hagen's return to the scene drastically reduced hostile forays into the copy department by the company's roving predators.

"You know," I said to Juliet, "I've only been working in Century City a couple of months, and already I can drive in without wanting to puke. I thought it would take a lot longer to be comfortable."

"You're not comfortable," said Juliet. "You're stoned. I wish you wouldn't smoke that shit in my car. No one cares if you show up stinking like weed at the porn magazine, but I have a real job."

We were at a stoplight. Juliet stared over at me with a cold eye, pulled her hair back behind her ears and fastened it there with a tie. We drove on in silence.

I wondered what she might be brooding over. Had that icy glare been weighted with significance, or was I just tripping on pot? I hated smoking the shit, and really should have stopped. No one at work knew how dependent I was on chemical comforts. I felt less imperiled with Hagen watching my back, but not secure enough to expose the extent of my infatuation with intoxicants to my co-workers. The Volvo swooped deep into the underground parking structure, slotted into a spot, and Juliet headed off to the escalators without looking back. Was she jealous of my high? Or was she nurturing some other grudge?

I rode the elevator up to the Flynt suites. The elevator stopped smoothly and silently opened. A phalanx of broadcast journalists waited in ambush between me and the heavy, carved double doors leading to the Flynt cloisters. Cameras, lights and microphones tracked me as I crossed the lobby. Theoretical concerns about Juliet filtered on out into nothingness. I exchanged good mornings with the compelling, round brunette behind the reception desk. The door buzzed open for me, and I paused to look back at the lenses, the flashes and the booms, all held in abeyance. I slipped inside, where the reporters and camera people wished they could be.

The first order of morning business was to check the typesetting out-basket. I stepped into the closet where they housed the typesetters. Blonde Sheralynn, an angular, sporty rattletrap whose skinny behind had performed as a fill-in fanny on a half-dozen LFP magazine covers, was the only typesetter in attendance.

"Close the door," she said. "Quick. Lock it."

I complied. Sheralynn bent over a glass candy tray and resumed the fevered chopping of a white powder with the edge of her employee ID card. Her boyfriend sold the stuff, and she stole it from him.

"Did you see Larry on TV last night?" she said.

"Sure." This was not true. Juliet and I had yet to replace our television. I moved to take a seat in the chair next to Sheralynn's desktop where she slid a tubed $20 bill up her Malibu nostril and took a quick sniff. She handed the tray to me. I had a crisp piece of currency rolled up in my fingers without even realizing I'd taken the money out of my wallet.

"Larry looked good," said Sheralynn. "He talked good too. I think he's totally clean. He makes a lot more sense now that he's off drugs."

Cocaine residue dripped down into my throat, bitter and numbing. I thanked Sheralynn for the bump, grabbed the morning galleys and scooted back to the copy pen. My typo-hunting cohorts were percolating over cups of coffee. One good thing about working in a place with double-digit turnover is that seniority clicks in quickly. Jennifer and Chris had both moved on, which put Sarah in the lead editor's desk. She'd hired two new copy guys and taken them under her wings, which left me on my own. I sorted and distributed the stack of galleys to appropriate editors. I sat at my desk with a page of floating words flat out before me. I appeared to be concentrating on the copy, an illusion easily maintained while I calculated how many pages I would need to read before I could zip down to one of the ground-floor bars without rousing suspicion.

Sarah and the two new guys were discussing Larry Flynt's television appearance the night before with tall tales of Vicki Morgan, a beautiful and doomed California blonde who on July 7, 1983 had been bludgeoned to death with a baseball bat by her roommate, Marvin Pancoast. Pancoast was a moody sort who had made Morgan's acquaintance while the two of them were hospitalized at the same facility for depression.

"Larry Flynt is a pig in shit," proclaimed Sarah. "He's in his favorite place. The top of the news cycle."

Vicki Morgan had been a long-term mistress of department-store magnate Alfred Bloomingdale. Bloomingdale had been a kitchen-cabinet advisor to Ronald Reagan. Before the earth had been tamped smooth above Vicki Morgan's caved-in skull, a man described as a prominent Beverly Hills attorney, Robert Steinberg, was holding a news conference to claim that on the day of Vicki's interment, a well-dressed woman had come to his office and given him three video-tapes that documented sadomasochistic orgies. Alleged participants included Vicki Morgan, Alfred Bloomingdale, two high-level members of Reagan's administration and a congressman. Within the next 48 hours, Steinberg would claim that he had offered to turn the tapes over to President Reagan and would then report the inflammatory materials stolen from his office. Which presented Larry Flynt the opportunity to gather a pack of chomping news hounds and announce that Steinberg had offered to sell him the Vicki Morgan sex tapes for a hot million dollars. The news dogs out in the lobby were camped there drooling for confirmation that the deal had gone through.

"It's the Flynt law of thermodynamics," said Sarah. The two new guys were still so fresh that they would put aside their work and perk to attention whenever Sarah made one of her mock pronouncements. "No news void can exist in the vicinity of Larry Flynt for more than 16 hours without him expanding to fill the truth vacuum with hot air."

Neither of the two new guys harbored any hopes of seeing footage of Vicki yanking Alfred's chain and paddling his bloomy behind. "I don't think any Vicki Morgan sex tapes exist," said the more literal-minded of the two new guys. "I think Larry Flynt saw a chance to scam a million dollars' worth of publicity without paying a cent for it."

The other new guy harbored deeper, darker suspicions. "From what I've read in all these old *Hustlers*, Larry loves a conspiracy theory. I'll bet he ties in Reagan to Vicki Morgan's murder. I mean, look at this Pancoast patsy. He walks right into the North Hollywood police station and confesses? That's classic programmed drone syndrome."

I lit a cigarette and tried to block out their jabber. This was back in the days when you could keep a full ashtray at your desk. In approximately five minutes the cigarette would be smoked and, according to my calculations, I would have put in enough time on duty to wander off for 15 minutes. How could I concentrate with all these people yapping?

"Oh, shit," I said. "I forgot to go to the bank."

I hurried out to the lobby, put on a preoccupied face as I passed the news gatherers, and pushed the down button at the elevator bank. The tower that contained the Flynt offices faced a twin of itself. An underground arcade connected the two. Banks, a post office, a dry cleaner, a barbershop, a shoe repair and lunch counters lined the passageways between the two towers. One sumptuously appointed gift shop sold miniature bottles of hard liquor. Two restaurants had full bars. I strode into the Jade Garden and took a seat in the murky lounge. A juicer from the LFP art department, Frank, slouched in a booth at the far end of the bar, slurping a Pernod with a mineral water back. Frank spent as much time going to the bank as I did. He ran his fingers through his dark shag haircut, unable to decide if he wanted to be Jim Morrison prior to porking up or Warren Beatty circa *Shampoo*. Frank affected puka shell necklaces, chick-tight denim slacks and torso-fitted ribbed sweaters worn over tropical-print, collared shirts. He existed in a continuous low-grade Saturday night fever, as if punk rock had never happened. Only two or three years older than me, Frank's misfortune had been to peak in the early '70s. He had no strategy for maturing into the '80s, a dilemma that had befallen most of his sub-generation, and mine too now that I think about it. The '80s may seem harmless from here, but at the time they were a culturally harrowing era of noxious style and faux substance. How could I have not needed a drink? I craved a straight-out boilermaker, but without having downed a few first, I was too timid to order such a patently working-class libation in a Century City cocktail parlor. Plus, I lacked Frank's power base and had yet to develop a network of allies who would accept the stench of mingling beer and whiskey on my breath. I settled for a double vodka straight up. Legend decrees that such purity is undetectable to the olfactory sense.

Frank and I shared an elevator back up to the office. The doors slid shut, and we looked at one another as if surprised at having met.

"How are you settling in?" said Frank.

"Couldn't be happier. People couldn't have been friendlier."

Back in the copy room, chief Morgen Hagen splayed out on the sofa, hanging off both ends.

"Hard night at the mansion," he explained.

The mansion was where Larry and Althea Flynt lived under heavily armed guard. We underlings called their residence "the mansion," perhaps emulating the ringing terminology of Hugh Hefner's *Playboy* mansion. The *Hustler* homestead was more accurately a rather large house in Bel-Air. Sonny and Cher and Tony Curtis had been reputed to have lived in this large house at various times. Flynt, off drugs, had taken to throwing poker parties in the mansion's game room. He invited a few crucial editors to play along with his new radical friends, faded '60s luminaries such as writer Terry Southern and LSD guru Timothy Leary, whom the publisher kept around like pets. Usually no one lost more than a hundred bucks.

"I didn't get to bed until after four," boasted Hagen. "Came out 50 bills ahead. I had to drive Dennis Hopper home after it was all over, all the way out to Venice."

Easy Rider Dennis Hopper had either just hit the lowest point in his life during the summer of 1983, or else he was barely crawling out from it. I'd seen him slouching in the concessions room, flummoxed by a soda machine, pouring in quarter after quarter and belting the thing until a can finally rolled out for him. Hopper had agreed to direct a photo shoot for *Hustler*, a celebrity pictorial intended to depict his most cherished sexual fantasy ("What Is Art?" January, 1984). I blew smoke rings at my desk and might have dozed off. People made lunch plans around me.

"Oh, shit," said Sarah. "Your wife called when you were at the bank."

Privacy was no real issue. No one paid any attention to me. I called Juliet's direct line, and a male voice answered, saying "allo" in a feckless imitation of my wife's charming Franco-Germanic accent, the one she affected when she was mocking the parents of her childhood.

"Put Juliet on." I spoke in a flattened version of my regular tone.

"Allan, pal." It was Roger. He worked with Juliet. Roger wasn't exactly my wife's boss. In fact, he didn't even entirely work for the same company she worked for, but he had some authority over her. He was a TV writer "slumming in the mind-control medium of Madison Avenue," according to Juliet's version of how he described himself. Roger had shown an interest in Juliet's career and was directing her in producing storyboards for his latest campaign of 60-second masterpieces. I'd expressed skepticism about his intentions, but Juliet had assured me that Roger was married.

"What's with your boss?" demanded the committed husband. "Is he trying to get shot again?"

"Once should be enough for anybody," I said.

"If he keeps fucking with the government, they'll put him down for good."

"What are you talking about?"

"Well, you know that first hit was CIA-sponsored to shut him up on his Kennedy mission." In 1976, Larry had offered a $1 million reward for information leading to solving the shooting of JFK. Not long after that, he'd been shot himself. "You can add two and two, right?" said Roger. "Now he's telling the world he has Reagan's boys on tape? Believe me, Flynt has balls, but I'm not sure about the brains. Tell him for me to roll out in the bulletproof chair. You might want to invest in some Kevlar coating yourself, my friend."

"Interesting," I said. "Look, I'm returning Juliet's call. Can you put her on?"

"Hey, sport, I'll tell you what. She isn't available just now, but I wouldn't worry about it if I was you. I'm sure if she meant to say anything important, she'd call you back."

Concentrating on work was impossible. Luckily, lunch loomed. I'd been asked to join my copy compatriots at an authentic Korean-run deli in the open-air shopping mall a brisk block to the west, but I lagged behind. In the bowels below the building, I secreted myself in an unused utilities closet and allotted myself three lung-stretching huffs of hashish. Halfway through the second huff, a pair of nubile LFP editorial assistants, a black and a blonde, burst in upon my hideaway and pulled out a thinly rolled joint of super grass. I treated them each to a puff of hash, then we burned the J.

"You're a good dresser," said Monique, the black girl.

Down in the Century City utilities closet, I probably sported widewale corduroys and a long-sleeve dress shirt, tails casually out. Somehow I'd also taken to affecting English oxblood lace-ups. Where the money came from to buy them, I will never know.

"Does your wife pick out your clothes?" said the blonde, Susan.

"What makes you think I have a wife?"

"The ring?" said Monique.

"Most guys lack any sense of style," said Susan.

The two assistants and I stepped out into the sunlight of the lunch quad. For a moment, I envisioned a warm, fuzzy future. Then I spotted a familiar-looking guy in slacks across the quad, his tie flapping. Potted and round at the belly, shorter than me, hair fuzzy. Was that Roger? I'd never actually met the groom, only seen him wave a greeting to Juliet from a distance. These suit guys blend in with one another. He carried a cardboard food tray stacked high, nutrition enough for two people. I cut a beeline toward him to say hello, just in case it was Roger, just to be friendly, sort of like to network. Maybe we could do a double date, him with his wife, me with mine. This person, if he was Roger, refused to be engaged and scurried off in the direction of the building Juliet worked in.

I stood in line and bought my egg-salad sandwich and a bottle of beer. An older *Hustler* guy, almost 40, whom I'd so far avoided, sidled up to me. His name was Tom Connor. He was a holdover from Ohio, had been one of the early editors when Larry had started the magazine in Columbus and could still walk. Scuttlebutt painted Tom Connor as a survivor with a wildman past. A crisscross of scars on his forehead and one cheek indicated a history of sutures. Tom hadn't taken a drink or a drug in a number of years, and he showed it.

"You look fucked-up," said Connor.

How did he know? The two nubile editorial assistants scampered off into the noonday sun, putting as much distance between themselves and Connor as possible.

"My eyes get red when I read a lot," I said. "I'm a proofreader; so naturally..."

"Come over here and sit out of the sun."

We took a bench in the shade, and I decided that Connor was attempting to be friendly. I kept my beer in the bag in deference to his abstinence. Connor was one of the few long-term LFP staffers who had not threatened to have me fired during my first weeks. I resolved to attempt conversation. But I couldn't stop wondering if I had seen Roger. I spoke of that married man's theory of CIA complicity in the shooting of Larry Flynt. Connor was unimpressed.

"No one ever asks me," he said, "but I'm of the school that Humpty was shot by a Mafia marksman. You can't just start your own magazine-distributing company and tell the mob to fuck themselves." Shortly before being plugged, Flynt had tired of ponying up a huge chunk of *Hustler*'s newsstand take to the middlemen who controlled placement of titles on the sales shelves. He'd impulsively launched his own distribution network. *Hustler*'s circulation promptly plummeted, and then the publisher was dropped himself. "It's no coincidence," said Connor, relishing the sour irony, "that Flynt is limp forever. These are Cosa Nostra bosses Larry pissed off. They kept him alive, and they put him in his place."

I made some excuse about needing to resume work early and ditched Connor. I stopped in at typesetting, then went to the bathroom, where I came as close to actor Dennis Hopper as I will ever need to. As I wiggled my penis, Dennis stood at the adjacent urinal, wearing a striped, long-sleeve polo shirt and grimy jeans. His hair was listless and greasy. Subsequently, Hopper would flourish in a resurgent career based upon his powerful ability to vibe people out. None of that star charisma was in evidence on this early afternoon in the summer of 1983. Beside me slouched a flattened hipster.

I thought I smelled pot on the guy. In retrospect, the odor may have been oozing from my pores. Hopper stopped to wash his hands and the mirror caught him up. His was not the preening staring of an infatuated narcissist. This was the clueless wanderer searching the surface reflection for some glimmer of where the fuck everything had gone wrong. I rinsed water over my hands at the sink next to him, and he failed to register my presence. His lips moved. He had something to say to himself, but was unable to form the words.

Intrigued, I followed Hopper from the bathroom and walked at his shoulder along the corridor toward the soda machines. I thought I knew what Dennis had meant to tell himself, and I was willing to fill in. Still, I was surprised to hear myself hissing quietly, my face immobile, "You used to be somebody. Look at you. You had something. You threw it away. You're wasted to nothing." I spoke so low and slow that not even I could be sure I was talking. My delivery was as fleeting and slight as the voice of conscience. Hopper looked askance at me, then flinched forward again. "You ruined everything," I hissed. "You were loved. No one wants you anymore." Dennis' shoulders hunched tighter with each uttered phrase. He glared at me with quick, rodent hostility that soon melted away. A pleading to understand coalesced in its place. Hopper's eyes twisted. Was I pulling this stunt, or was he going crazy? Honestly, I wouldn't have been able to tell him for sure if he'd asked me.

He went to renew his battle with the soda machine, and I returned to my copy station feeling better than I had all day.

The two new guys were in there alone.

"Where's Sarah?" I said. "Did she die?"

"Hey, Mac, *Giant*'s on TV tonight."

"*Giant* what?" I said. "Don't call me Mac."

"The movie, with James Dean, Rock Hudson and Elizabeth Taylor."

"And a very young Dennis Hopper."

Sarah bustled into the office, flustered and bright-eyed. Her lips flapped, silently rehearsing an important delivery. The two new guys hadn't been on board long enough to recognize her huffing and puffing as the signal for hushed and total attention. I attempted to ward off her interruption.

"What time does the movie start?" I said, a meaningless question. I had no TV.

"Six o'clock."

I became conspiratorial. "So if we sneak out of here 10 minutes early, it should be a cinch to catch the whole thing."

Inadvertently, I'd given Sarah her cue. "Nobody's leaving 10 minutes early tonight. In fact, plan to have dinner at your desks. We're staying late. Larry's ripping the book apart."

"But we'll miss our deadlines," I said, surprised to be the voice of reason. "The entire package was supposed to have closed yesterday."

"He's Larry Flynt," explained Sarah. "He can do whatever he wants."

Larry Flynt wanted to tear out a chilling exposé on the evils of fluorescent lighting. The space would be used to accommodate a double-page screed from America's favorite atheist, Madalyn Murray O'Hair, and a five-page segment, including two sub-articles, on men who dress up in women's clothing, but are not gay. These manuscripts were being rush-edited as Sarah spoke, and each of us copy editors would be assigned one segment of the mass to shepherd through to print-ready form. In addition, each of us would read behind the others, a fail-safe support net to snare missed errors. I couldn't imagine this process going on beyond 8:30 p.m., an estimate I passed along to Juliet when I called to tell her that Sarah would give me a ride home.

"*Hmmm.* I've heard enough about this Sarah. I'll get a ride home with one of the girls here, and you take the car. I'll messenger the keys over. We have messengers running to your building all the time."

"By the way," I said, "did you call here earlier?"

"Two days ago I called you," she said.

I'm condensing this story as I'm telling it, of course. Not everything happened on one day, but it sure seems like it did, looking back.

"Well, what did you want?" I asked Juliet.

"Some creep here asked me to find out what you'd seen on those Vicki Morgan orgy tapes."

The typesetting machines crashed right in the middle of outputting godless O'Hair's sacrilegious guest opinion. Sheralynn had disappeared, but was finally located jabbering into a dead telephone. Progress dragged. Around ten o'clock, I accepted a small amount of powdered stimulant from a managing editor, purely for purposes of maintained alertness. Somebody up at the mansion must have been using the same alert dust; at 11 p.m., changes arrived on the O'Hair piece. A clarification attached to the drag queen story included an admonition that we in the copy department should "get it straight."

Some time after one in the morning, Morgen Hagen came to me with a wad of cash. He'd ditched the suit and switched to denim. "Mac, take your car over to 7-Eleven and bring back as much Coors as this will buy." I was honored to be given this position of trust. Before delivering the bulk of the beer, I split open the cases and secreted five cans. By the time I returned with the suds, half the staff had left. I guzzled a couple of cans, went down to the car and drove homeward.

Juliet had waited up. I excitedly babbled about the unprecedented cultural relevance of fusing atheism and cross-dressing within the pages of a single magazine. In my rush of enthusiasm, I failed to register that Juliet's attention fell short of my fervor. I took a wind-down smoke and a bootleg 'lude before crawling onto the futon. Rarely since starting at *Hustler* did I overshoot the mellow high and end up shit-faced and snarling. Certainly, Juliet must be appreciating this improved me? While floating in that nether grayness between altered consciousness and catatonia, I warmly regarded my sleeping wife and promised, *When I am with Juliet again, when time permits, I will be more attentive.* The power of my emotion roused me to a half-woken state, and I verbalized these vows within inches of my wife's ear. Juliet turned away.

The next afternoon, at a little after 5 p.m., just as I had cleared my desk and was contemplating the drive home, news came down through Sarah that Larry had killed the November "Publisher's Statement." The rough draft of a new salvo was being driven from the mansion and needed to be fine-tuned that evening. Also, aspects of the cross-dresser think piece had, upon reflection, galled the man in the golden chair. Didn't Flynt realize that while we nitpicked the November edition, deadlines for the December and January issues— big giant magazines—were fast upon us?

With his re-emergence as a media manipulator, Larry Flynt became a hands-on publisher, suddenly involved with every aspect of an editorial package that had hardly penetrated his fog for half a decade. Night by night, editorial shifts increased until an 80-hour workweek was a norm. Larry tore apart each month's magazine as it was being assembled. Entire sections were scrapped on the eve of deadline and beyond, with new pages hastily assembled and inserted. The magazine underwent a radical makeover. No more pedestrian profiles on baseball rebels like Billy Martin ("Baseball's Billy Martin," October, 1983) or lame cautionary narratives such as "Loan Sharks! How They Trap You" (September, 1983). The October 1983 issue gave notice: Flynt's opening editorial, "*Hustler* Is Moving Ahead," asserted that his goal was to provide "the most uncompromising, enlightening and titillating magazine you will have ever read."

On September 1, 1983, Korean Airlines commercial jetliner Flight 007 was shot out of the sky deep over Soviet airspace. On board was Congressman Larry McDonald, whose home district included the Georgia town where Larry Flynt had been gut-shot six years earlier. McDonald had been a rabid anticommunist and card-carrying John Birch Society member. Late one September night, I found myself reading the voluminous fine print of a faintly paranoid, oddly compelling editorial argument that raised the possibility that Larry McDonald had been on a spy mission over Russia when KAL 007 took Soviet fire. The rambling dissertation, credited as an open letter from *Hustler* publisher Larry Flynt, invoked Thomas Paine, the

Spanish-American War and the USS *Maine*. Flynt, or whoever had written this broadside for him, cited assumed subterfuges that had triggered various American armed conflicts, roping in the U-2 surveillance plane episode in which pilot Gary Powers parachuted to USSR soil and the Gulf of Tonkin incident that had preceded the Vietnam quagmire. As I read, I tried to imagine the mass of *Hustler* readers who had willingly endured a poli-sci class. I pictured the sum total of them comfortably convened in a single peep-show booth, with plenty of elbow room. Printing this treatise in the LFP flagship seemed like lunacy. I was relieved to be informed that Flynt had bought full-page ad space in the Los Angeles *Times*, the Washington *Post* and the New York *Daily News*, which is where this educative polemic ran. Then the December 1983 *Hustler* devoted 14 pages to reprinting letters from readers reacting to Flynt's paid editorial.

Right about the time of the Larry McDonald essay, CBS news magazine *60 Minutes* aired a purloined copy of an FBI sting tape that showed maverick automobile executive John Z. DeLorean exulting in the purchase of packets of cocaine the size of throw pillows. The CBS broadcast acknowledged that the video had been provided by *Hustler* publisher Larry Flynt. Suddenly the press corps had to treat the Kentucky cardsharp as if he might be for real.

I remember coming home in the late p.m., eager to give Juliet news of the DeLorean fallout. I took the stairs two at a time. Our living room was deserted. Behind the closed bedroom door, Juliet was already asleep. The kitchen showed no evidence of anyone having eaten any dinner at our house. Was Juliet on a hunger strike? Was she eating out, with someone else, someone she did not talk about?

In the mornings, on our way into Century City, Juliet and I hardly spoke. Often I slept until she had parked and dropped the Volvo's keys into my hand. I would wake up knowing that I needed time alone with Juliet soon, or we were headed toward a rough patch. At work, for a moment in October, while putting together the January 1984 issue, production slowed to an almost sane pace. The copy department arrived at a Friday night when only one person would be required to stay to all hours. Sarah offered to take the late shift and sent me home to nest with the wife.

At the elevators, I stood behind a pale, pockmarked apparition in black jeans and navy blazer. Dyed-black hair spilled out from a dark beret. He couldn't lift his finger off the down button. His name was Alec. I'd thrown up with him during my punk rock days. He should have been surprised to see me, but his demeanor was narcoticized beyond the possibility of being taken unawares. Alec was the dealer who'd sold singer Darby Crash of the Germs his fatal suicide hit a few years earlier. His pinned eyes took me in. I asked what he was doing on the premises.

"I was here to see Althea," answered Alec in muffled, measured enunciation.

"For what?"

"I delivered some documents."

"Geez, Alec. I hope you held a few documents back for yourself."

Alec's grin was sickly, self-congratulatory, self-loathing, conspiratorial and contemptuous.

"I just got paid," I said. "I know you have something left."

Alec drove an old station wagon with the side windows blacked out. It was parked under the Century City mall. We squatted back there and shot up portions of what was being sold at the time as China white, more accurately a garage-lab pseudo opiate. The rush was strong and similar to an incapacitating headache. Alec and I slouched and mumbled about old times and the massive quantities of dope consumed by Althea. I pointed out that the mall parking structure was crawling with security cops. Alec felt he should be cautious. Larry didn't want Althea doing heroin. If he were to find out Alec was supplying his wife with smack, the consequences would be dire. Alec dropped me at the Volvo, and I headed for Juliet.

I'd crashed down in the home living room by 8 p.m. I'd fallen asleep by nine, and the wife arrived sometime after. She was startled to see me, taken aback at first. Her posture seemed defensive, which was strange since I was the one guilty of being junked out.

"You're a little late," I said.

She checked a conciliatory impulse and brazened on forward. "You know I've been hitching a ride home from the office. When you're hitching a ride, you don't pick and choose the driving schedule."

"What does she do, this girl driving you home?"

"Well, actually, he doesn't work at my office. He doesn't work for us, he works with us."

"You're saying Roger is giving you rides home? And you dawdle on the way. How long has this been going on?"

"From when you started working late."

"But he's older," I said. "Married."

"He won't be married for long, not to that wife."

Juliet disclosed that she didn't love me anymore, that she loved Roger and he loved her. She and I were divorcing. It cost Juliet a lot to gush all this out, not as much as it cost me to absorb it.

"Why now?" I said. "Things are looking up for us."

"I'm going to bed," Juliet said, corralling her hair behind her ear.

Thank God I'd run into Alec. Still, drugs never help enough, especially not when you really need them. I felt that I might die. My brain throbbed, and I was unable to extract a single thought from the pained mess. I was experiencing an aggravated meld of OD and withdrawal. I could barely hold my head up through the pulsing nausea. To complicate my anguish, a knock came on the door. I stumbled across the living room and flicked on the porch light. Two middle-aged people stood uncomfortable but forthright in the pool of light. Their clothing looked vaguely foreign. I cracked the door. Up close, age had taken hold on these two quaint trolls. They were shriveled and gnarled, like European bonsai shrubs.

"We have come to see Juliet," said the man, his accent akin to Himmler's. The woman was flustered. She flipped her hair behind an ear. These two people were familiar, in a familial sense, although I was certain I had never met them.

I left them at the threshold and tapped at the door of the bedroom. I went in. Juliet lay wide-eyed, staring at the ceiling. Troubling thoughts had their way with her. Her new boyfriend was married too, like she and I were. Maybe Roger was less eager than Juliet to inform his spouse of her redundancy. Some aspect of the arrangement bothered Juliet. My job, as her husband, was to comfort her. I would have liked to help, except that I was vanishing right out from inside myself.

"Juliet. Someone's here to see you."

"See me?" She stiffened in alarm.

Did she imagine Roger's wife on our doorstep, wielding a carving knife? That's a picture I liked.

"Your parents are here."

She sat straight up, prepared to curse me for my idea of a joke. But she knew me. I had on the suicide face, grave beyond morbid levity. She pulled on a robe and brusquely motioned me to follow her into battle, exercising the uxorial imperative. Old habits, I guessed, died hard. I waited a moment, trying to imagine the existence of composure, then reentered the living room. Juliet had placed the folks in two hard-backed chairs. I joined her on the sofa. She introduced me to her parents. "This is my husband, Allan."

"Of course. We have met."

Our place looked goddamn abject, and I couldn't have appeared to be much of a prize. We strained for conversation, then the parents switched into their native languages. Mama addressed her daughter in wheedling, accusatory French; Papa barked in combative German. Juliet replied in muted, cowed French. I'd never known she could speak a foreign tongue, and a Romance language at that. What else had I turned a blind eye to? Juliet looked trapped. I could almost reach out to her. But I wanted to scream into the dour, judgmental faces of her parents that their daughter was a fraud. She was leaving me when I needed her most, when my life was finally turning around, when I had finally made progress at being a better human being. Juliet's hair fell forward from her ear, and she allowed it to curtain her face from me as she endured the parental barrage.

Suddenly she snapped at them: "Speak English. I will not have you speak anything other than English in front of my husband. Don't be rude."

The old couple started their appeals again, all abruptness and authority gone.

"Sweetheart," beseeched the mother, hands extended palms up in entreaty.

"My daughter," cooed the father, open arms begging an embrace. "My darling."

The parents had three free days, and they wanted to spend time with Juliet. She protested that she was very busy. "You did not warn me. You should have warned me. The letters you claim to have sent,

I have never received. I have made commitments this weekend that I cannot reschedule."

Juliet abruptly went back to bed. Once her parents had tired of sighing at me, they rolled their eyes one last eloquent time and let themselves out.

Juliet's weekend commitment? To vacate our apartment. While I smoked and drank, she and her new friends carted out everything that was worth more than 15 dollars. I refused to move off the futon, so they left it, but no forwarding address, no phone number.

The very next Saturday night, Larry Flynt staged a party at his large Bel-Air home to celebrate his candidacy for the United States presidency. Larry planned to run on the Republican ticket with a platform of free sex and free thought. Alone in the Volvo, I navigated west along Sunset Boulevard. Weekend revelers clogged the Strip, trawling in pairs and packs. Beyond the congestion, I wended through the soft, prosperous curves of Beverly Hills. The opulent homes to either side of the roadway contained, in my imagination, pudgy, fuzz-headed TV writers and their exotic young brunette girlfriends.

I handed my keys to the parking valet at Larry's Bel-Air party, still alone. Everyone else had somebody. All I had was the Volvo. I didn't even have a high. I was out of my element. I couldn't risk losing control on these meticulously landscaped grounds or in this lavishly appointed house. Warm, flattering lighting spilled down upon the guests. Everywhere I looked was a closed rank. Excited, bright-eyed women tossed sparkling quips to debonair fellows who batted them back with worldly confidence. Currents of mutual admiration ran high and swift, bypassing me. I felt the hot, green flash of aggrieved lack. I'd lost Juliet. She was at some salon with her TV writer, employing her fine-featured, smooth-complected beauty in the advancement of his profile. At a company party, especially at a *Hustler* company party, it is essential to have some covetable body near at hand who will attest to being available to bone you.

Handsome outlaw Dennis Hopper, sporty in a white motoring cap, stood in a doorway, entertaining a host of LFP executives. A classic California blonde stood poised and attentive at Hopper's side. On Monday, I would learn that she was Michelle Phillips, the skinny girl from the Mamas and the Papas. Here, on Saturday night, she was just one more indication of how far and how fast my well-being had slipped. I wrapped my hand around a drink and forced myself to sip judiciously, which eased my sad anxiety not at all. I wandered around the mansion and out onto the back lawns, too alienated to make eye contact, even with people I saw every day.

Monique and Susan, my black and white smoke pals, strode toward me, smiling, excited and very high. I relaxed.

"Hey," I said, "you two are just who I was hoping to see."

"Sarah says Jack Nicholson is here," said Susan.

"We aim to find him," said Monique. "And take all his drugs."

Their twitching haunches stalked off.

Inside Larry's study, I attached myself to a group in front of a video monitor. We watched a screening of the Flynt Presidential committee's first broadcast ad. The visuals featured hardcore sex. Larry sat in his gleaming, gold chair, wielding the remote control. He wore a T-shirt, jeans and Converse running shoes. A message across the shirt read, "Jesus is an Anarchist." Chipper and mischievous, Flynt explained the strategy behind the full-penetration production. In theory, the networks would be forced to run the ad uncut because, as an equal-time political message, its content was exempt from censorship. I finished my second closely regulated drink.

Larry's ad ran through a third time, and the group around the TV broke up, pairing off and strolling away, leaving me alone, as usual, and Larry on his own for what I perceived was a rare moment of semi-solitude. He gave me the green gimlet eye. If I were a hot chick, or had one on my arm, his look might have been softer. I lifted a copy of the January 1984 issue of *Hustler* from a stack provided for guests, stepped up to Flynt, thought better of introducing myself, and asked him to autograph the magazine.

"This is the issue that broke up my marriage," I said.

"How'd that happen?"

Flynt was quizzical. He really wanted to know how a simple magazine might destroy an eternal union established in the eyes of God and man. The simple truth, as I saw it, was that while assembling this particular edition of *Hustler*, I'd left my wife alone too many hours in a row, then I'd come home happy. Juliet had never known me to come home from a job happy. Obviously, in her mind, I must be banging someone on the staff. Larry graced me with a politician's polite, undivided interest, waiting for me to elaborate. I wagered that Flynt didn't know whether I worked for him or if I was a guest of a guest. I was better off retaining my anonymity. I said, "I'm just kidding. Thanks for the autograph."

I turned away, the skin on the back of my neck prickling, and I bumped hard into a grinning Dennis Hopper. It's a wonder I didn't break my nose on his teeth.

"Are you okay?" he said.

Was that mock concern? I would not be lulled by subtle sarcasm. I brushed past him, and a low, slow voice, like the disregarded tone of conscience, rose as if from a whisper in my ear: "You were loved. No one wants you anymore."

I made my way to the valet parking and waited while they brought up the Volvo P-1800. If only Juliet had been there, I could have drank like a normal person, secure in the knowledge that my wife would pour me into the car and drive me home. A woman, unattached, stood six feet away finishing off one last free cocktail while waiting for her car. We gave each other probing looks. She understood me, and that would never do. I drove along Sunset, winding into Bel-Air and Beverly Hills through bends of decreasing prosperity, cautious not to stray from the speed limit, finally reaching the neighborhood where left-behind people like me lived.

The *Hustler* Masthead

THE MASTHEAD IS that block of type appearing toward the front of every magazine, usually enclosed in a black-ink border. Akin to the credits of a movie, the masthead lists the names and job titles of every person who contributes to assembling the periodical. The most important players are listed at the top. Prominence diminishes with each successive entry, eventually descending to the lower rungs of insignificance.

A dozen strata of status and function were layered between Publisher and Editor Larry Flynt's perch at the top of the *Hustler* masthead and the fine-printed depths where lurked Associate Copy Editor Allan MacDonell. The names of researchers, studio assistants and production artists all merited a higher placement than that of the quietly toiling copy editor. The copy editor's esteem is built upon presenting the word of *Hustler* as competent, intelligent and credible. Almost every peg in the corporate structure was accorded a higher degree of importance than he who kept them all from appearing to be sub-literate buffoons. Security guards and receptionists carried more clout than a squinting nit-picker like me. Still, squatting as I did at the bottom of the totem pole, I was of the same tribe as the chief on high.

CHAPTER 5

▬▬▬▬▬

Code Pink

WHEN I WAS in high school, wallowing in stoner entropy, not once did any guidance counselor sit me down and warn me to bone up on my college preparatory curriculum, or risk one day looking up at the TV noon news and be assaulted by the image of my boss arriving at a federal courthouse with his ass and genitals swaddled in a diaper fashioned out of an American flag. Right on schedule for my 10-year high-school reunion, I slumped on a stool in a Century City sports bar where no one knew my name. I'd branched out from the lush spots frequented by LFP regulars. The office souses tended to embarrass me by loud-mouthed association. Still, there was no avoiding the contact infamy, not with television cameras tracking Larry Flynt as he was being wheeled into the halls of justice, Old Glory wrapped around his seat of ignominy.

"This fucker goes too far," said the bartender, taciturn up until then.

A drinker two seats away, who exuded the omniscient aggression of a personal-claims attorney, slammed his glass down and paused in mid-departure. "Don't worry," he said. "Someone will step in and stop him soon."

Larry's current troubles and air time stemmed from an audio tape pertaining to the John Z. DeLorean entrapment case. A followup to the video surveillance Larry had provided *60 Minutes*, this new tape purportedly captured United States government operatives threatening to kill DeLorean and his family if the automaker balked on a deal to import cocaine. Dangling the tape as a lure, Larry had drawn a discerning mob of real-world journalists into the skewed universe of Flynt. Reporters had crowded in among heavy, armed bodyguards at

Larry's mansion and strained to hear the recorded threat. The sound quality, an earful of painful static, provided a severe disappointment to the pressing newsmongers.

The federal prosecutor's office, listening closely, heard something useful. The Feds called Larry on his shenanigans and demanded to know where he had obtained the blast of white noise. Though citing journalistic privilege in refusing to divulge his source for the tape, Flynt was deemed to be in contempt of the court, a state of mind he openly admitted. As I lit a cigarette and contemplated the lunch menu, my boss was being compelled to appear at court and deliver a $10,000-a-day fine for the privilege of his scathing viewpoint. Larry, in his estimation, was being treated like a baby, hence the tricolor diaper.

The bartender turned out to be more talkative than I would have guessed. "Every time I turn on the news, this creep is going to court for something. What's he on trial for here? Is this some kind of obscenity bullshit?"

I answered as politely as possible. "Don't you mean to say, 'Another of the same'?"

The facts baffled me as much as they did anyone else. Larry was juggling courtroom dramatics in so many simultaneous cases that the details overlapped. Even his attorneys would have been hard-pressed to delineate them all. To complicate issues, the *Hustler* honcho had taken to firing his lawyers and representing himself. The self-defense worked fine while Larry argued his mental stability during competency hearings brought against him by brother Jimmy. Larry's counsel-yourself strategy flopped in front of the United States Supreme Court in defense of a libel case pursued by *Penthouse* publisher Bob Guccione's girlfriend Kathy Keeton. During the Supreme proceedings, Flynt had volubly interjected, "Fuck this court!" In case the jurors had missed his point, Flynt denounced the High Court Justices to their faces as "nothing but eight assholes and a token cunt." Subsequently, he rolled through my lunch hour in his flag-desecrating diaper. In truth, I wasn't sure if I should be proud of the lunatic or ashamed.

"I work for that guy," I admitted. "I'd like a double."

The bartender poured with an expert flick of the wrist. "On the house," he said.

I drank because I had problems. A miserable home life, the loss and indignity of wifely abandonment, that wasn't enough. Work had developed strains. For instance, the appearance on the 38th floor of rocker relic Frank Zappa had driven me to this distant sports bar. I downed my medicine and headed back to the war.

Zappa, the founder and conductor of '60s rock humorists The Mothers of Invention, had followed the examples of God-sneering Madalyn Murray O'Hair and celluloid rebel Dennis Hopper in contributing artistic commentary to *Hustler*. First, Frank had penned a screed touting free thought and individualism, "It's About Mr. Flynt," to be published in the January 1984 issue. Now, Zappa was micromanaging the layout for a grotesque and convoluted photo-comic sex fantasy, "Thing Fish," that would eventually consume 28 pages of the April 1984 issue at a cost in dollars and lost readers that would be comparable to Princess Cruises capsizing one-third of their fleet. I'd grown accustomed to Zappa scowling and whisking about the art room in a cable-knit, floor-length sweater as though the garment were some grand heraldic cape.

Some of the outcasts I'd picked zits with in high school would have thrilled at any proximity to Frank Zappa. There was no explaining the same Zappa-aggrandizing mind-set among the *Hustler* paste-up freaks. One vocal Frank-o-phile, an unreformed love child we'll name Crispin McMannis, drove a Volkswagen van into Century City every day from a shrinking hippie enclave at the blighted out-skirts of Venice Beach. Once in the office, Crispin spent altogether too much time on the copy-pen sofa, cradling a coffee mug the size of an oil can and engaging himself in sparkling conversation. Crispin and our lead copy editor, Sarah, considered themselves intellectual soul mates. Sarah had harangued copy chief Morgen Hagen until he'd forced me and the two new guys to move the Crispin-defiled sofa back into the pen from the hall where we'd dumped it hoping to discourage his visits. Sarah enjoyed her prolonged chats with the stridently positive, slightly crusty slug. He was creative and an old soul, a fact he broadcast by always wearing two contrasting colors of socks. On the day he landed the plum assignment of being the original Mother's personal production artist, Crispin looked as happy as if he'd just won a lifetime vat of patchouli oil.

"This is the coolest thing," he gushed.

Due to some failing within myself, I could not bear to see Crispin basking in happiness.

"Have you ever noticed how the word *cool* has almost exclusively come to be interchangeable with the word *crap*?" I said.

"How you can define working with one of the preeminent geniuses of the 20th century as crap is a bummer."

In the aftermath of Juliet's desertion, I'd had exactly one sleepover date, with a former Bullocks co-worker who kept her cable TV on all during our sodden attempt at sex. The tube was set on some Capitol Hill channel. I'd lain in the absence of an afterglow and watched tape of Frank Zappa addressing eight dour congressmen on the importance of unfettered artistic expression. Did he ever talk about anything else? The man who sang about eating yellow snow pontificated with all the rigid pomposity of a Nobel laureate in eugenics.

I squinted at Crispin along the barrel of my cigarette. "Personally, I feel that the only thing more boring than preeminent genius Frank Zappa's Senate testimony has been his music of late."

Crispin's cloudy hippie eyes clearly pitied me as much as I despised him or myself. "Well, in this country, Allan, despite its shortcomings, it's still okay for people to have different opinions." He stood with righteous hauteur, clutched his coffee tub to his heart and departed.

My pleasure was short-lived. Sarah, doing a final read on a late, crucial board, nitpicked a few lines of unaligned type, and she picked on me to take the slanted copy to the art department and have one of the creative technicians there straighten it. Sarah, in her mind, was my superior. I did my best to humor her delusion for the sake of Copy Chief Hagen's peace of mind. He'd given up wearing the Bullocks suit, except on payday Fridays. Generally he dressed like a minor-league hockey player on game day—rugby shirts, jeans and loafers or tennis shoes. The copy chief now chewed tobacco incessantly and carried a large go-cup that he filled with dark, frothy spit. I wouldn't have minded having a cheekful of dark, frothy spit at my disposal.

"Who's supposed to fix this?" I asked Sarah. "It was never finished because Connie was fired while she was in the middle of pasting it up."

"Take it to Crispin. He's always perfectly happy about doing extra fixes for me."

Though I asked him pleasantly enough, Crispin adjusted his John Lennon glasses and claimed to be waiting for a call from Zappa. The old creative soul could not take on a new task while thus disposed. Eight more production artists slouched at their drafting tables, their Exacto knives idle in the art room enclosure. Frank the art drunk tossed his shag and suggested that I was hyper, rigid and anal.

"Those lines are completely straight, just like the stick up your ass," he said, hardly slurring at all. He fingered a puka. "A little sex, if you could get it, let me suggest, might loosen you up."

Finally, Joop, a secretly gay Scandinavian whom I'd nearly flattened on a dope run when he'd stumbled out of a queenly bar and minced into the headlights of my Volvo, took pity and did the fix. I thanked him and quietly took my leave, hoping to exit without incurring another verbal barrage.

"Tell me," said Crispin. "I really want to know. What have you ever done with your life that you feel you can pass a judgment on preeminent geniuses of the 20th century?" He squinted out through his granny shades. "Who, precisely, do you think you are?"

The fact that I had no answer for them had sent me to lunch at the distant sports bar. I returned from my exile to the Flynt lobby. The crews of camera journalists had been supplanted by claques of low-fashion models. Many of these models could have passed easily for strippers. The eye-catching ladies had been rounded up to adorn themselves in sleazy plumage and sashay into court carting trash bags filled with crumpled $1 bills, total value ten grand, Larry's daily fine. The models were better to look at than the journalists had been, but the scribes and cameramen had at least glanced up and wondered who I might be.

Back in the copy pen, I despaired of experiencing low-grade happiness ever again. I dreaded the galleys on my desk. Juliet's departure had exposed the fragile emotional breakwater that separated me from the oceanic depths of all-encompassing depression. Perhaps insensitively, maybe maliciously, Sarah had assigned me a 5,000-word story on the Hemlock Society ("The Hemlock Society: Compassionate Suicide for the Terminally Ill," March, 1984). The

Hemlock people believed that when a person becomes too miserable for life, that sob sucker should be granted a dignified and painless method of snuffing himself. I was one or two mishaps away from signing up for Hemlock membership. The second article on my desk reported on the growing ranks of homeless Americans ("Address Nowhere: The Tragedy of Our Homeless Millions," February, 1984). Entire families were landing on the streets, in unprecedented numbers. Once to the curb, statistics showed, a loser had a window of three months to find permanent security, or a unique form of homeless psychosis set in, and there was no salvaging him. I teetered on a tightrope. I had no net.

I lit a cigarette and stared at the fluorescent lamps. A managing editor, Jim, popped in through the doorway. In his late 30s, blond, clenched jaw, eyes popping behind wire-rimmed glasses, Jim always seemed to be in a hurry to catch up with something that had left him in the dust. His attire might be mistaken for collegiate. Jim took in the room at a lightning-quick glance. Trails of white powder trickled down the front of his navy-blue V-neck sweater. He clapped his hands twice.

"We're busing everybody downtown to the Federal Courthouse for emergency picket patrol."

"What emergency?" asked Sarah.

"Last night they held Larry until he straightened out all his crumpled one-dollar bills and hand-counted them. Channel 9 News is on the way, assuming history will repeat itself. We need bodies to stage a demonstration."

Sarah screwed up her face, doubtful and slighted. "Jim, I can't help but feel that being paraded in public as a picket shill is beneath the dignity of the position I originally signed on for."

For two or three seconds, Jim attempted to appear unperturbed, but what was the use? "Christ, you get out of the office, ride downtown and stand around with friends. It's civil disobedience, plus it's fun, and you get paid. What about the rest of you spelling wizards?"

The two new fellows sided with Sarah. During the past few months, Jim had given me helpful portions of go powder when the work shift had stretched through the a.m. hours. Also, I wouldn't mind distancing myself from the tales of real-life misery on my desk.

By the time he blew around to me, Jim's breezy confidence had an air of desperation.

"What about you? Is picketing beneath you?"

"I have no illusions that I signed on for anything with dignity."

"That's my man," said the managing editor.

The best thing about picketing was that no one missed me when I slunk off under the pretext of looking for a bathroom and found a bargain-minded downtown bar. I stayed long enough to miss the LFP van ride home.

"Hey, snappy dresser."

Black Monique and blonde Susan sauntered along the sidewalk toward me. The editorial assistants bumped one another on every second step. Waning sunlight glistened off of their face-splitting grins.

"What happened to that wedding ring you used to wear?"

"It was a fake."

Monique and Susan showed no remorse for arriving at picket duty after all the picketers had disbanded. They broke into hysterical laughter and offered me a ride home in Susan's car. Monique climbed in the back beside me. By the time she and Susan dropped me at the apartment I'd formerly shared with Juliet, our faces touched in repose. Or maybe Monique had just passed out on my shoulder. Either way, her soft-lipped image lingered as I drank myself drowsy. A smoldering cigarette dangled from my fingers and fell into the cushions of the living-room couch. The smoke alarm woke me. I poured a tumbler of water into the sofa and put myself to bed.

A few nights later, after playing pool with her in a Sixth Street downtown bar, I lured Monique up to the apartment, and she immediately sniffed out the sofa. "This is how my cousin died. He died just like that. He burnt up the sofa and went up with it like a marshmallow."

"A chocolate marshmallow?"

"Why you want to make everything into something racial?"

Monique was not fat anywhere, but she was all-around much bigger than Juliet had been. Her arms were muscled like a man's, which troubled me until I slipped my hands into her pants and verified what I had been hoping to find. Her long, tapered black fingers played across my chest and shoulders. Her skin was dark and very smooth, except where marred by two thick, ridged scars. She'd been stabbed in the chest by one of her mother's boyfriends, and the fat remains of a cigar burn marked the inside of one thigh. Her cheeks were high, burnished apples that rose when she grinned, and she seemed to always be grinning, particularly when retelling the harrowing details of her adolescence.

Only about 22 when I'd met her, Monique had already been a murder witness, a sibling rape victim and a teenage prostitute. For therapy, she snorted coke and talked long into the morning, shaking her demons awake and engaging them in spirited badinage. The stepfather whom her mother had eviscerated with two shots from a bird gun. The older half-brother who had schooled her in the sexual arts as a seven-year-old. The bush men up in her hometown of Sacramento, lesser thugs who lurked in the shrubbery of the city parks while she plied her trade and only showed themselves as needed to calm unruly customers. The king pimp who ruled over this protective mob, a ruthless, sensual genius who had died from what Monique called infected blood. The characters of her formative years all came in for abuse and recriminations. I would lie naked on my back, aching for sleep, watching Monique's entranced performance. I might clasp one of her pink-soled feet to my chin, and still I would be a thousand miles from her. She was channeling, gone. It never occurred to me that dozing naked in bed with a person in the throes of cocaine psychosis might pose a risk or reflect on my own condition.

Moneyed stability was Monique's goal. She was a typing prodigy, having completed that portion of a secretarial course, and could rattle out 100 words a minute. The entrepreneurial striver had written a book, which she sold from ads in the back of teen magazines. The book was titled *Any Job Can Be Yours.* When a supplementary print run was needed, she photocopied the tomes on LFP's machines and shipped them out through the company mailroom. The book was 16 pages of affirmations and grooming tips, none of which Monique applied to herself. Her writing style, a mélange of instructive demands, echoed the cadences of her talk during sex. She gave detailed instructions throughout the act and critiqued each performance afterward. Perhaps this was the manner in which her half brother had taught her.

"You got to shave before you go down there. Your beard is too rough on my smooth skin. You're lucky I have this smooth pussy skin. A lot of black women, they all gnarly down here. Their hairs grow back into their skin, and it's all splotchy and rough. You're lucky, and you don't want to scratch up your luck with that nasty beard."

Despite the fact that I was sleeping with a black girl, and none of them were, the art department still refused to accord me my proper respect.

"What burns me up," I said to the two assistant copy editors, "is that 90 percent of the corrections we have the artists do are corrections of mistakes they made, and yet they never come to our office. We always have to track them down, and then beg them to fix what they fucked up in the first place."

"What I want to know," said Todd, the bolder of the two assistants, "is if these paste-up tools call themselves artists, then what word do they use to describe someone like Picasso?"

It was easy to disparage the artists from the safety of the copy pen. Carrying that justified arrogance into the art enclosure was a challenge. It was me against the room whenever I went in there. The layout geeks assumed that since I was outnumbered, I was also outmanned, a contention I refused to concede.

"Crispin," I might say, "you've just pasted in the same wrong type twice in these successive panels. What would Zappa say? You know he despises mediocrity and holds in contempt functionaries who revel in their own incompetence."

I would have Crispin where I wanted him, and then a wild card would be played. Either the drunken Frank would assail my seductive prowess, or the self-heralded genius of adult cartooning, Dwaine Tinsley, might be on hand to unspool a lecture.

"Al, buddy, what you will never grasp or understand is the workings of the creative personality. We in the arts, of the artistic temperament, are here to enrich the world with our vision. Me and Lar was talking about this last Saturday. Suzy and I took a skillet of biscuits and gravy up to the mansion. What we do here we do to honor the visions of the creators. That's why we need to keep the little needle-nose grinders around who can be bothered with what type is wrong and where the good type needs to go."

Back in the copy pen, assistant Todd wanted to know why I was fuming. He was from Chicago, half-Irish, half-Italian, and he had a philosophy.

"I'm calling up that Tinsley tool," he said.

Phone sex was the lewd marketeer's newest innovation. An isolated loser could dial up a juicy lass in some distant area code, and she would talk him to a climax. Of course, the gays had their version of the rotary connection, and prerecorded sample chats were available for anyone who cared to punch in the digits. Actually, the samples weren't entirely free, but the charge was nominal, and LFP, like most companies, had yet to install 976 filters. Todd dialed a gay phone sex preview, waited until the action heated up, then transferred the call to Dwaine Tinsley's extension. Every five minutes until noontime we took turns sending homoerotica Dwaine's way, secure in our anonymity.

At lunch we attended a party for Sarah, either to celebrate her birthday or employment anniversary. Company parties consisted of a meal and drinks consumed among a crowd of LFP compatriots, often conducted at the Century City Playboy Club, to which Hagen was a key-holder.

Sarah's party was held at the Avenue Saloon, a woodsy chophouse on an upper level of the ABC Entertainment Center. My recollection became increasingly vague as I sat and stewed, observing Crispin and Frank proposing toasts to the beaming birthday girl. By the time she blew the candle on the cheesecake, I was deep into my first on-the-job blackout in Century City. The next thing I know for sure, I woke up on my feet, standing at the head of the art department enclosure, having just concluded addressing the room at large. The ringing tones of my oration reverberated throughout the four walls.

From the artists' ruminative expressions, I seemed to have been talking for a while and had given them many nuggets of thought. Not a voice dissented or eye rolled. My pulse raced. Neither Crispin nor Frank dared to meet my righteous gaze head-on. I guessed that I had been presenting an argument, and I had won. This is the only blackout in my entire recollection of such aberrations that ever worked out to my advantage. I knew what had irked me about my art-room co-workers: their lack of professionalism, their can't-do attitudes, the buck-passing, the attempt to coast through the day with the least possible effort, an obsession with affixing blame rather than effecting solutions. These threads most certainly had been woven into the theme of my address.

Head up and proud, I bolted for the door. Hairy, gaunt and dead-pan, Frank Zappa stood against the jamb. How long had the Mother been lurking there? He clapped his hands, slow but steady, and held my eyes. As I squeezed past him, he nodded his head. I scanned him, hoping to ascertain that his applause was not ironic. Of course, I couldn't be sure. The sound of Zappa's clapping resounded throughout the art room. No one else was bold enough to pick it up.

As 1983 closed out, so did Larry Flynt's run of luck in the war between himself versus the world. Did the boss ever pause to consider the obvious ramifications of his actions? His stars-and-stripes-diaper stunt would not go unpunished. Two weeks after being wheeled into a den of federal prosecutors while swaddled in Old Glory, *Hustler*'s supreme commander was back in court to be arraigned on a flag-desecration charge. The hearing soured for Flynt, and he antagonized the presiding judge to the point of being ordered to undergo a psychiatric evaluation. Although no criminal charges were filed against our captain at the time of that fracas, a senior judge reviewed the proceedings and ordered Larry to appear a month later, in the middle of December 1983, and "show cause" why he should not be charged with contempt. Contrary as a point of principle, Flynt did the exact opposite of what the magistrate had ordered him to do. Rather than raise extenuating medical and emotional circumstances that might have contributed to his perceived misbehavior at the flag arraignment, LFP's steamed leader cursed federal judge Manuel Real and spat in his direction. Real interpreted Flynt's personified contempt as cause to pile up three-month blocks of prison time. With each additional 90-day stretch, our role model responded by shouting, "Motherfucker, is that the best you can do?" If the bailiffs hadn't taped his mouth shut and wheeled him immediately into custody, Larry might have gone on taunting the poor judge until he was locked away for 100 years.

An illusory calm descended upon the workscape for one-half of one day, but Larry refused to admit that he was gone. Two ominous words rebounded throughout the *Hustler* empire from lobby to toilet stall. "Code pink," the receptionist intoned over the intercom. "Code pink. Code pink."

Alarmed editors and executives bustled in bunches from closed-door caucuses, rushing into the halls and converging upon the executive conference room. All stood sheepishly around the long marble-topped table. Flynt's sneering drawl came piercing out of an amplified speakerphone situated like an oracle's globe in the middle of the vast table. The assembled minions were browbeaten and whipped by the high-pitched wheedle of the absentee despot. Hardened men were fired and jaded women were made to tremble by the force of voice alone. But the jailed maverick's remote control didn't last. Larry's phone access was reduced with each transfer of custody, from Terminal Island in Los Angeles to the Bureau of Prisons Medical Center in Springfield, Missouri, and from there to the psychiatric ward at the Federal Correctional Complex at Butner, North Carolina, where concerns more pressing than running a magazine (such as immense bedsores and playing practical jokes with his feces) weighed upon him.

Fiscally conservative factions within LFP were relieved to have the founder and editor locked away. Magazine covers that included a disrobed woman in bed with a pinkie-sprouting German shepherd (February, 1984) and a naked lady draped Christlike upon a Lucite cross (May, 1984) had been refused shelf space in statewide blocs, particularly along the reverential Southern belt. At Larry's whim, *Hustler*'s page count had swollen to 200 from 140, with no corresponding increase in revenue-generating advertising pages. Printing bigger, more expensive magazines and then not selling them sabotaged profits. Another ton of dollars had disappeared into Larry's side projects, typified by *The Rebel*, a lavishly funded weekly news magazine catering to conspiracy theorists. Among *The Rebel*'s more credible claims was a promise to connect the dots between Nazis and the JFK assassination, an assertion that attracted dozens of paid readers.

Aside from the summary dismissal of *The Rebel*'s staff, the most apparent change in Larry's absence was the arrival of an entirely new security presence at the office. As if our Century City skyscraper had been hit by a comet, drastically altering its climate, the shambling, overfed, down-home bruisers who had lumbered about as body-guards, drivers and wheelchair pushers disappeared into an overnight extinction. The next morning, the halls were policed by quiet professional-looking and—aside from their number—inconspic-uous guardians. These threat-assessing experts dressed in suits, ties and shined shoes. They could have been CIA station masters. Who had enlisted the sleek new mercenaries? Why had the old dinosaurs been let go? Sarah and Todd attempted to find out.

"Who hired you new guys?"

"Well, it's safe to say the company considered its options and went with us."

"Yeah, yeah, yeah. But who in the company decided on you guys?"

"Did Larry order this change from prison? Are you Jimmy Flynt's idea? Or Althea's?"

"Or has some cabal of editorial and finance bigwigs brought you in to stack their power base?"

"Just carry on as though we are not here."

"What happened to the old guys?"

"We were never part of that discussion."

Drug consumption became a stealth activity. I huddled in man-aging editor Jim's office with Susan and Monique. We'd pulled the shades, 38 floors up. Susan propped a chair under the locked door-knob, a duty that displeased her. "Not only do we have to hide from the Century City security cops and the straights on staff, we have to hide from our own protectors."

Jim could be philosophical. "This is what Reagan's son goes through ditching the Secret Service every time he wants to blow some sailor in a gay bar."

I snuffled a big glob of drug. Jim brushed a trace line from his sweater. We shared a camaraderie in Jim's tiny office. The four of us may have been united by nothing more than the fleeting bonds of chemical euphoria, but that was more than plenty of people ever had. Then the intercom put us all in a panic.

"All personnel report to the conference room immediately. All per-sonnel report to the conference room immediately. All personnel to the conference room."

The conference room was large, but not big enough to hold everybody. Latecomers spilled out into the hall and clustered around the doorway. I slipped between a pair of bodyguards, the old-school kind, and stuck my head through the door. The meeting had been called to order.

Althea Flynt stood tilting forward at the head of the long table. Her clenched fists banged on the marble slab. Her hair was punk-spiked, and she wore black leather. She looked like some urchin from the alleys of my recent youth, a tad older, but raging just as darkly.

"Some of you motherfuckers think you run this company. Some of you motherfuckers think this is your company. Some of you motherfuckers are going to have your fucking asses handed to you. None of you motherfuckers has the balls to be at the head of this company. You'll answer to me, I promise you this, motherfuckers. You think you have the big balls to run this company? I'll have those balls on a plate. Don't fucking look at me like you don't fucking know who you are."

There was no question-and-answer period. Althea blew out through a side door directly into the publisher's suite. No jokes were cracked in the wake of her departure. As a body, the LFP work force moved somberly back to our stations. The new security professionals were gone. Down-home diehards roamed the halls, exuding broad bravado. Their meaty eyes squinted out suspiciously. Did their primeval lizard brains intuit that I, a lowly copy editor, had been a part of the putsch that had made them obsolete, though only for a matter of hours? I tried to act happy to see them, but I'd never been on speaking terms with any of the bodyguards previously. Hostile skepticism repelled my overtures. Needing protection, I sought out Morgen Hagen. He lay cramped on the half-sofa in his office, stocking up energy for the night's hockey match. He skated three nights a week with guys half his age. I shook him awake.

"Morgen, what's with all this shifting of the guards? Should I be worried?"

Snooze interrupted, Hagen drilled me with a hoary eye and whizzed a stream of spit into the big cup. "Worried for your life? Or for your job security?"

"Let's start with job security and see how that goes."

"Just be quiet and keep your head down. They can't fire you if they don't know you're here."

I retreated to the copy pen and compulsively redoubled my efforts at sending prerecorded phone sex to distant extensions throughout the office. Flirting with disaster, I sent three in a row to Carol B. A brunette in the swinging-'60s mold, big of bust and hips, tossing a cascading frosted mane and with blended pastel cosmetics on her placid, round face, Carol was reputed to be dating Bob Dylan. She must have been about 19, with a very mature, fathomless surface. Dylan had been spotted picking her up in front of the building after work. Carol had confided that she would not allow Dylan any sexual favors, in consideration of his advanced age. She also claimed complete ignorance of his entire body of work. Carol had quickly become known as the angel of doom. Althea had selected her heavenly visage as the medium by which to deliver pink slips to disfavored editors. Althea was solidifying a reputation for being kill-crazy. Sending Carol out to slip in the knife was perhaps meant to indicate some slight notion of mercy. The smooth perfection of Carol's face made it impossible not to smile at her approach, even though her probable purpose was to dispatch you. Still, depths of icy malice lay beneath that coolly sweet exterior. Althea and Carol had been observed giggling as they plotted a surprise termination. I made a couple of direct hang-up calls to Carol, just so I could hear her honeyed California voice saying hello.

The savoring of Carol's sweet tones was cut short by the smell of rancid aftershave and stale cigarettes. I looked up; Dwaine Tinsley had abandoned his avuncular, down-home genius guise in favor of a psycho-eyed convict routine. Somehow he had deduced that all the gay-sex chatter he'd been hearing lately had originated with me and Todd. "You fellas think you're funny? Queering around is not funny, and it's not fucking brave. Larry won't find faggot talk funny, and neither will Althea. I fucking shanked punks like you two. Fucked them and shanked them." He adopted a bowlegged stance and glared at us as if we might be physically harmed by a mean stare. He kept the short-tempered eyes looking back over his shoulder as he walked out. We were stunned. Open-mouthed.

"How did he know it was us?" I asked.

"Maybe he really is a genius, like he says."

Days passed, more and less eventfully, moving into the Orwellian year of 1984. Carol B. herself was axed. Maybe she wasn't giving Althea any more affection than she had given Dylan, or maybe budget-minded Althea had concluded that sending losers packing didn't need a specialist. Anyway, I was sad to see Carol go, having anticipated every day to receive my first and final visit from her.

Monique did her best to dispel the Juliet void. Having offered to treat me to a night on the town, Monique borrowed $60 from her Avon funds, money that ladies around the office had entrusted her for the purchase of cosmetic products. Monique escorted me to a bowling alley bar on the east Hollywood back streets. Things went well until a random white drunk attacked her in our booth. Fifty-something and flabby, he probably hadn't been sober for a straight week since he was 16. He stumbled off his barstool, lurched across the intervening floor space and lunged across our table, diving for Monique.

"Why you coming in here, black bitch?"

This guy was acting like we'd stepped into a segregated enlisted men's club down in Biloxi circa 1942. His hands clasped at Monique's neck. I slammed a beer bottle down on his closest elbow, which broke his grip, then I repelled him, an easy feat in his uncoordinated state. The few direct punches I landed left a pleasant ache in the bones of my fists. His pals at the bar dragged him back to his stool, apologizing to us in a sneering manner that held us entirely to blame. The night was shaping up to be memorable and victorious. The attack had shaken Monique. She shuddered in my arms as we sipped a free round, and I anticipated a hero's welcome once I'd dragged her back to the pad.

My warm reverie chilled when I realized that Monique and a plump Mexican divorcée in the adjoining booth were making eyes at one another. The divorcee was in pleasant shape, with her hair bleached a rusty shade of red. She and Monique went off to the ladies' room. The longer they stayed, the deeper I stewed. I ordered another beer and drank it standing by the bathroom doors. Straining to hear, I detected an impassioned huffing from the women's stalls that could be produced by only one activity. I finished the beer and knocked back three quick whiskeys, breaking a promise to Monique not to drink any hard stuff. I sat draining another beer in our original booth. The two ladies finally emerged from freshening up. Their hair and clothing were entirely askew. What they'd been doing in the can was obvious to the entire bar. The cracker who attacked us cackled and gave me the finger.

Monique brought the bleached-rust divorcee to our table and introduced us. She and Monique had quickly become old friends, and they both seemed to have taken a liking to me as well. We stopped at a liquor store for two short bottles of vodka and gin, then piled back into the Volvo and drove to my apartment. No time had passed, and we had all squirmed out of our clothes. The divorcee's body was a revelation in natural pneumatics. The next thing I remember is waking up to a new day's sunshine with Monique half-dressed and ready to leave for work. The divorcee was outside waiting for a cab. My brains ached. Monique assured me that I'd had a great night, the night of my life.

Danger signs were everywhere. One morning I stepped into LFP's Century City tower and saw three out-of-place palookas milling at the bottom of the elevator bank. Two of the lugs were huge, with thick-knotted jaws and crooked, bulky noses. They wore bomber jackets, coarse canvas trousers and thick-soled work boots. The third skel strutted on stack-heel dress shoes. Barely five and a half feet tall, the spiv was the most menacing of the three. Jim, the coke-fueled managing editor, would later inform me that this guy was married to the sister of a prominent dead rock star and that he represented a consortium that was in silent partnership with Flynt's magazine concerns. The second that I put eyes on this uncouth trio, I intuited that they were headed for my place of employment.

I settled in with my spiked coffee at the copy pen. Susan and Monique summoned me to meet in the lobby and descend to the ground floor to smoke a bomber. I shouldered through a side door that led to the elevator bank. Monique and Susan stood next to the ladies' room and stared toward the carved doors at LFP's main entrance. The lobby was unexpectedly crowded. The preening man in the stacked heels and his two lugs stood in a tightly arranged group and made overtly innocent faces. Four cops held shotguns at parade rest and separated the trio from the heavy, carved doors. A fifth cop, evidently the highest ranking, holstered a pistol and yelled at a big-belly security guard who blushed and took refuge behind the receptionist.

"If you ever step between my men and a door again," bellowed the cop, "you be ready for a sucking gut wound. You might just be some bull-crap fat piece of crap, but some of the characters who frequent this place have a reputation for responding with real firepower, and we will treat you with that assumption."

I admired the officer's force of communication and succinct assessment of the situation, and I was drawn to him. The lawmen herded the bad men toward the elevator banks, all shuffling as one, followed by Monique, Susan and myself. We stepped into the elevator, between cops and creeps.

The lead thug, attempting to make good with the police, stood on tiptoe and twisted an impish grin. "Something of an overreaction, dragging you boys into a simple business arrangement," he said.

The lead cop refused to dignify him with existence. The subordinate cops were disciplined and kept zipped. Even I sensed the bite of tension. Every time the elevator stopped and the doors opened, potential passengers recoiled with horror. The lead thug leaned across me, smiled in a sickly way and asked tiny, blonde Susan, "Do I seem scary to you?"

She laughed. Four shotgun muzzles were holding at her eye level, pointing up toward the low ceiling.

As much to explain our presence in the elevator to the police officers as to appease the gangster, I opined, "By this point, the only people still employed at Flynt are those of us who haven't got enough sense to be scared by anything."

As the winter months passed and a barren spring arrived, I became acutely aware that elevators were red zones. One evening at quitting time, my mind dwelling in the hollow where Juliet used to overflow, I tramped through the lobby toward the elevator bank. If I'd been conscious of the present tense, I might have wondered why my co-workers backed away at my approach and no one else stepped into the car when I did.

"Hold that elevator," boomed a voice from behind. A beefy paw clasped the door and prevented it from sliding shut. Althea Flynt floated in. Her field of vision had been constricted to the size of a pinhead.

Althea slouched to the back of the box and slithered down the wall. A pair of giant, mullet-head bodyguards bookended her, but did nothing to prop up her slide. She was dressed all in some kind of early-'80s activewear popular among image-conscious cokeheads who wanted to give an impression of health awareness. Althea ruined that impression with a scraggly purple Mohawk haircut, abstract-expressionist eye shadow and a chain that connected a ring in her nose to a stud in her ear. This harried vision was a far cry from the firebrand who had slammed her fists down on a long, marble tabletop and menaced a conference room filled with slick Judases. The elevator dropped down a floor, opened, and three suits stepped in. They checked Althea with the black contempt that they would toss at any bum. It was easy to feel for Mrs. Flynt in this state. She faced the arrogant suits and responded to their dismissive sneers in a manner that justified you pulling for her: "I am you, and you are me, and we are all together," she sang in an opiated drawl. The words came out like a taunting curse.

All eyes snapped forward.

I felt as though Althea had deflated these suits for us both. With one snippet of the Beatles, she'd defended a lifestyle, a state of mind, a dereliction of reality.

At my one-year LFP anniversary party, held at the end of May 1984, my behavior was guardedly restrained. I'd implemented managing editor Jim's calculus of two bumps of blow for every one drink and endured the tribute without losing consciousness. Afterward, I joined Sarah behind the skyscraper stanchions to smoke an anniversary pinner, and she waxed sentimental.

"We were worried about you at first."

"You mean when I got hired?"

"When your wife left. But now you're doing great."

I had preferred to believe that no one knew the wife had left.

I started the Memorial Day weekend of 1984 on a slight bummer. On Saturday night, I attended a cocktail party, my most vivid memories of which are cadging diet pills from a pair of girls with weight issues, then the Volvo's speedometer wavering at 90 while I harangued God for having made a mess of my life, threatening to deliberately crash the vehicle for the chance to spit in my maker's eye. After that I remember standing beside my burning car, surrounded by Japanese vehicles that had been smashed into the shape of accordions. I assumed I was dead until the police arrived and slugged me in the face. They took me to an emergency room to be sewn up, then to the Hollywood substation to be booked for driving under the influence.

"We've got a celebrity here," the cops mocked, parading me to a holding cell. "This one works for *Hustler* magazine."

I had bail money in my wallet, but regulations dictated that another person arrive and take custody of me. The only free-world person who would accept my call was Monique. She arrived at 7 a.m. on a Sunday morning and signed me out. Her powerful rear flexed in lime-green hot pants. Monique's hair was half-braided, and half-crazy where she'd lost interest in braiding it. You couldn't call it natural. It was unnaturally wild. The cops didn't like her any more than the cracker in the bowling alley had. I signed papers, and an officer handed me a pair of box speakers that he'd pulled from the Volvo so they wouldn't disappear in the impound. I didn't recognize the speakers.

"These aren't my speakers," I said, carrying them off. It suddenly occurred to me that I was bare-chested. "What about my shirt? Where's my shirt?"

A high-strung cop bolted forward and popped into my face. "You just smashed up a car and put a whole neighborhood of civilians at risk, and you'll stand here whining, where's your shirt, where's your shirt?"

The Hollywood division had recently been in the news. A grand jury had been investigating charges that enterprising cops had been dispatching hookers out of this station and running a burglary ring. Two star witnesses, one a prostitute, the other an idealistic young policeman, had wound up dead, the prostitute with multiple stab wounds in her back. It seemed like all the cops in the station had come forward to shout their displeasure at me. "Just get out of here. Get the fuck out of here!"

Monique tugged me toward the precinct exit. "The police have enough problems without messing with your punk ass."

I was back on the job that Tuesday, cruising in along Santa Monica Boulevard on the Number 4 bus. Hagen drove me out to Culver City to pick up a copy of my arrest report. Some of the guys he played hockey with were cops, and he tossed back an occasional beer with them at a barroom they frequented. He wore his Bullocks suit for the purpose of an official call on a police station, and he left his spit cup out in the car. The suit had aged at least a year and a half since I'd first been impressed by Morgen's ability to overrule its civilizing influence. He'd had the garment pressed, and it made as dignified an impression as it ever had. Despite the stitches in my face and my furtive demeanor, the police were polite and efficient, a civil tone I attribute largely to Hagen's presence.

One reason for securing the arrest report had been to gauge my blood-alcohol level. The figure impressed Hagen. On the way back to the office, we stopped at a Baskin-Robbins, and the chief bought me a milkshake. We sipped in silence as we crossed the Century City quad. At the bottom of the stairs to the tower, Hagen paused and gave me offhand advice: "Think twice before you do something like this again. We can't afford to lose you."

He spit before I had a chance to respond and ruin everything.

Hustler Hot Letters

AN INTELLIGENT PERSON, smart enough to read, picks up *Hustler*. The first written narrative he encounters, under the heading "Hot Letters," is a supposed missive to the magazine from a putative reader, one who, like himself, prefers to remain anonymous. This mail-in reader regales the home audience with a report from the field that recounts the anatomical and emotional minutiae of he and his bong-buddy tag-team sexing a wickedly curvaceous female space alien in the Tennessee woods ("Unidentified Fucking Object," January, 1996). Though unlikely, this sexual boast is followed immediately by another so-called reader who details the equally fantastic experience of checking into a burn ward after catching a skilletful of sizzling grits flung by his wife, furious that the writer has "boned her tattletale little sister in the butt." Once hospitalized, the scalded cad charms an RN and nails her atop a female coma patient, who awakes under the oral teasing of the nurse, pulls out her dentures and treats the author to a vigorous gum-job ("Wet Nurse," January, 1996).

Intrigued, the new reader checks through back issues and discovers that the *Hustler* partisans who have preceded him seem to share a knack for lucking into extraordinary sexual adventures. The fresh arrival to *Hustler* might pause to wonder: what prompts the guilty parties to share these reader confessionals? If it were me, would I take the trouble to sit down and write out a detailed, 800-word description, or would I be scurrying off to plunge organ-first into my next outlandish and improbable foray?

CHAPTER 6

A Strange and Perturbing Reality

MILD JUNE SUNSHINE warmed the Century City quad. In the wake of my botched vehicular suicide, I'd crossed over to a state of abrupt purity: no more social opiates, medicinal cocaine, recreational painkillers or mandatory alcohol. A sparkling reality engulfed me, and a chunk of egg-salad sandwich adhered to my palate. I washed down the mulch with gulps of frosty chocolate YooHoo, straight from the bottle. I was like a fish plunged into an estranged medium—fresh, clean water. Never in my life had I been so bewildered in the middle of the day.

On this particular noon, my inability to process the world around me could be blamed on Pat Boone. All of sprawling Los Angeles was gearing up to host the Summer Olympic games of 1984. The Century City sector had devoted this shiny June day to staging a lunchtime rally for the USA swim team. The athletes stood grouped on risers, deeply tan in their red, white and blue activewear. The sun reflected off of smiles and sunglasses, and chlorine-bleached hair gleamed green. From where I sat on my customary lunch bench, the spectacle reeked of a high-school pep assembly. The emcee of this celebration was singing evangelist Pat Boone.

I chewed the last bits of my sandwich and crumpled the wrappers into a tight wad. I tried to remember having attended a high-school pep rally, but my wasted youth had robbed me of such pleasures. A conflicted bobble of emotions burbled up from the pool of suppressed feelings that, according to my recovery counselors, I had been self-medicating since grammar school. Sadness at having squandered my high-school experience swirled with anger for having acted a fool. Why had I been so stupid, sneaking around smoking hash oil and stealing *Penthouse* magazines? I should have been joining the math club and campaigning for student council.

I dragged myself away from the ceremonial viewing of the swim team. The last drops of syrupy chocolate from the YooHoo were powerless to sweeten the bile stewing in my belly. I stepped off the elevator into the LFP lobby. A pair of strippers awaited their appointment with the talent coordinator. I wended along the hall toward the copy pen. Porn workers buzzed on every side, laboring in the interests of a man who would never be praised by the good people of America. We on the *Hustler* staff were doomed to disgrace, and rightfully so. Gutter commerce united us in outcast shame. How could this bitter disappointment ever be borne without a stiff jolt of gin? I veered into the concessions room to buy a Baby Ruth and a soda.

There I stood face-to-face with a life-size cardboard cutout of Pat Boone. The two-dimensional representation leaned against the Coke machine, where I had passed him at least twice a day for three weeks. The beaming effigy had been constructed from a blown-up photograph of Pat Boone taken when he was a young Kentucky buck. Larry Flynt had a keen interest in Pat Boone, even more so than he did in most self-sanctified folk. Larry and Pat hailed from the same home state. So when an Appalachian trash-digger had approached Flynt with an excavated photograph that showed an exuberant Pat Boone standing fully clothed, but with his penis protruding through a hole cut in a shoebox held in front of his crotch, Larry bought the shot and ran it in *Hustler* ("Pat Boone Nude!" January, 1984). A life-size standalone reproduction had been prepared as a promotional item and was subsequently dumped in the vending room.

I looked down at flat Pat's penis shoved through a hole in a box. I pictured him fleshed out and swollen with righteous hubris on the bandstand 38 floors below. In the warm summer sun, Pat Boone had projected the moral equivalent of a squeaky-clean swimmer in the rivers of the Lord.

I lifted Pat from where he had been discarded and lugged him down the hall. The figurine was heavier than I had anticipated. The cardboard had been affixed to plywood, and the base was constructed using two-by-fours for ballast. My breath came heavy and fast. I shouldered Pat through the heavy, carved doors into the LFP lobby. Sweat ran down my flank as Boone and I rested waiting for an elevator. During our descent, I shielded his penis from the view of the car's other passengers.

Not wanting to be held liable for gouging the tower's marble floors, I sucked up and hefted cardboard Pat across the grand foyer. The revolving doors that spilled out into the Century City quad gave us some trouble. Boone's big two-by-four feet lodged in the pivot, but I dragged him through. Once in the open air, we broke a run across the crowded quad to the bandstand. Flesh-and-blood Boone's voice rang out in cheerleader mode.

A voice, raised and plaintive, pursued me from behind. "Allan, Allan, what are you doing?"

I looked over my shoulder. Sarah shoved forward through the crowd. Her bosom quaked from side to side in her agitated rush. We had spectators. Twin rows of open-mouthed gawkers stood in my wake. I hurried on to avoid reflection.

"Allan, stop," insisted Sarah. Her arms groped out in front of her as though reaching to hold me back. I hoisted the full-sized figure up onto my back, the way Jesus Himself would do it, and trundled forward. Pat Boone's last words of swim-team praise echoed off the encircling towers. I was more than halfway across the quad. My hope was to arrive at the risers a few seconds before Boone stepped down and entrench my position.

"Who do you think you are?" I would shout. "You present yourself as a blameless paragon. And for what? So those of us who fall short suffer like moral failures. Explain this, you dick-flaunting prick!"

Sarah's feeble imprecations faded behind me. The ungainly burden I carried on my back played havoc with my footing, and I tumbled face-forward. Plywood Pat smacked down on top of me and slammed my nose and mouth into the concrete. I stayed down for a minute. The pain topped out in increments. Rising back to my feet seemed like a bad idea. Humiliation coursed through me as I panted, but I had a mission to complete. A circle of skeptics stared down.

A heavenly visage detached itself from the crowd and stepped forward. She came to me like a savior, my Juliet, on lunch break from her advertising storyboards. This, I reflected, must have been how Christ felt, solaced in the compassion of his womenfolk after having collapsed beneath the burden of his cross. Juliet bent toward me.

"Here you are," she said, "drunk again."

I rose to one knee, protesting. My voice faltered, and I watched my ex-wife walk away. She never looked back.

Sarah's sandals slapped heavily on the cement as she finally reached me. She helped me to my feet and put on a stern front.

"Your nose is bleeding. You'll be lucky if you're not fired for this." My swollen upper lip throbbed like a fat leech. The real Pat Boone was long gone. Regaling the dispersing crowd with his effigy would be pointless at best. Sarah helped me lug the plywood cutout across the quad, back to the LFP tower, hiding Boone's indecent bit.

"Allan, you need to develop a better grasp of appropriate behavior."

We placed the dinged flat Pat in the alcove where he belonged. In the bathroom, I hurled egg salad and YooHoo and cleaned up.

On the whole, coming off of a lifetime of drugs and alcohol was less physically excruciating than the popular literature paints it. For the first several weeks, I shook out toxic sweat while riding the Number 4 bus to and from Century City. Headache and vertigo didn't last for more than a month, and the tendency toward spontaneous regurgitation subsided within 90 days.

Stoner buddies Monique and Susan were united in support of a chemical-free me. Their encouragement came from arm's length.

"You're still cool," said Monique.

I'd been telling her and Susan about my protective instincts being aroused while observing a sleeping woman on the bus. Tears brimmed above my cheeks.

"But you've become a little stranger than we can deal with," said Susan.

Acquaintances noticed I was jumpier than usual. When Sarah burst into the copy pen and blurted that Larry Flynt had been released from federal custody, my body jerked at the sound of her, and I doused myself with a cup of coffee.

"Look, Sarah, if you come into a room, and I'm here alone, and I'm preoccupied, it might be a good idea to make sure I've seen you before you start shouting."

"I'm sorry, Allan, that you've become intermittently spastic and that I neglected to take your condition into consideration, but

Larry Flynt is in this building, on this floor, and he's headed down to the art department."

Ruined shirt and all, I felt that Larry and I were emerging from parallel ordeals. I followed Sarah to the art enclosure. Hippie Crispin and drunk Frank glared at me with one suspicious eye each, but dared say nothing provocative. Nobody could be certain whether the absence of my medication would leave me less or more volatile. My stained shirt and I gravitated to the back of the room. The art sector always contained the best in foreign porno magazines, scattered about to be plundered for ideas. I blankly flipped through a fat glossy. After a while, I realized that it was a gay magazine, and I put it down.

Larry Flynt rolled in through the art enclosure door on a gurney. Paste-up and copy peons massed toward the front of the room. Taller than most, I had a clear view of Larry from three peons back. He looked pasty and beat. Dressed in a hospital gown, sheets wrapped tight around his midsection, he seemed half-starved. This gaunt apparition was wholly different from either the swollen, narcotically subdued toad or the manic trickster Flynt I had known. The most shocking aspect was that both of Larry's legs jutted out in full-length casts. The guy didn't walk; why were his legs broken?

We loyal employees filed forward to pay our respects. The boss limply took my outreached hand. "I'm glad you're back," I said. His green eyes drifted behind a reconstructed narcotic wall. Larry was there, but barely. The authorities had not sent back the same Larry Flynt they had taken away.

I was returning from 20 years of chemical digressions and felt like the same eight-year-old I'd been when I embarked upon them. While riding the bus to Century City, I sometimes observed a puffy-lipped blonde softly snoring when I boarded. Approaching our stop, she would rouse herself, stretch and look out at the world through morning girl eyes. Then her face would form its public mask. I stood back as the bus stopped, allowing her to step out onto the street in front of me, standing close enough to sniff the scent of her hair. The sleeping rider wore the burgundy jumper and white-lace apron that was the counter-girl uniform of the Boulangerie, a French-themed pastry shop. Her aspect as she walked off toward her job in this outfit was neither innocent nor pastoral.

Toward the end of summer, the sleepy bus rider showed up as a new hire in the LFP advertising department. The guy in charge of selling ad space had been buying his coffee and croissants at the Boulangerie and had been impressed by this girl Shelley's insouciance. I coolly awaited some circumstance that might thrust Shelley and me together, a turn of events that came indirectly as a gift from Larry Flynt.

Sarah had roamed from the copy pen, on a job interview, and I intercepted an incoming call.

"Larry's curtains are open," said a voice without identifying itself. "Go and see where your raise money is going this year."

I walked from my desk to a branch of hallway outside the thick-glass wall that fronted Larry Flynt's office. A multitude of art and editorial underlings had formed an orderly queue hidden by a bend in the corridor. I took my place behind the new girl from advertising, Shelley. Several curious employees stood ahead of us.

"I used to ride the bus to work," I informed Shelley. "I took it in from Hollywood."

She looked at me as though I might be trying to trick her. "Yeah."

"There used to be this girl who would sleep all the way in," I said. "I used to wonder how she managed to wake up at the stop."

Shelley turned crimson. "I'm from New York. In New York we always wake up at the right stop."

She suspected I might be weird, not a creep exactly, but odd.

"I'm a little embarrassed," she said.

Her turn came up, and she strode casually along Larry Flynt's glass wall. Heavy purple curtains draped inside the glass. As she reached the center of the drape, Shelley paused and looked into the glass. She jolted and then peered closer. She flushed red, shook her head and sauntered on, glancing back at me with a lopsided scowl. It was my turn. I tripped along the carpet until I arrived at the halfway point, then paused and stared into the slit where the curtains had failed to shut.

The light took a brief moment to adjust. A view of Larry Flynt's massive desk came clear. Perched atop the blotter, a lanky redhead, naked from the tube-top down, spread and lifted her legs. Her heels rested on the back of Larry's wheelchair. The boss' rounded shoulders could be clearly distinguished, hunched between her grasping thighs. The model's fingers wandered through Flynt's red hair. I was at a loss about how to feel. Had I expected to see Mr. Flynt reading spreadsheets and signing checks? I watched until Larry came up for air, just to assure myself it was really him in there. Larry's glazed face was oblivious and joyous, like a dog chewing into a bag of wet trash. I gave up my place to the next employee in line.

Back in the copy pen, I applied myself to writing a sexual adventure for the magazine's "Hot Letters" section. One of the editors, Ben, a thick-browed Harvard man with a well-used gym membership and a penchant for Western wear, had invited me to take a stab at authorship. He'd placed his ever-present can of Dr. Pepper on my desk. "What have you got to lose, MacDonell? Loosen up, naturally. We'll pay you for it. There's no other way a guy like you will get promoted at this company."

Initially, I'd been bashful about reading this type of florid sexual regaling in the presence of other humans, particularly females. Suddenly, inspired perhaps by Flynt's renewed vitality, I incorporated my most desirable co-worker into a sleazy narrative. I started off by setting the scene: my first-person character was riding the bus, and there was this woman, a blonde, who habitually snoozed through our entire transit. Her lips were forever moving while she dozed, and I wondered what she might be saying. If I could hear her words, would the murmurs give me insight into her dream life? I slipped into the seat beside her and stretched out my legs. Her voice came clear, up close.

"Take the keys out of your pocket," she said.

"What?"

"Your pants pocket. Take the keys out."

I removed the keys and transferred them to my jacket. Her hand moved out from under her coat, slipped into my pants pocket and gripped my penis. Her eyes remained shut; her breath continued to come in a somnolent rhythm.

The story wrote itself from there. In his Ivy League Texas drawl, Ben told me he was pleased and offered to buy me a Dr. Pepper of my own. I don't know where Ben came up with his hybrid origins of East Coast gentry and shit-kicking Southerner. He'd grown up Presbyterian in Pacific Palisades, not far from the Malibu-Santa Monica shoreline. Despite his confusion of pedigree, he was clearheaded enough to put in a check request for my bus ride story. It was the first paid prose of my life, and it unleashed a torrent. For quick Q&As or book reviews, I could reap anywhere from 50 to a few hundred dollars. I lost sight of everything, including Shelley, in my cash-grubbing frenzy.

Sarah found a new job, and on her way out she gave me a course in career advancement. She insisted that I should form a social bond with people in a position to assign me paid projects. In October I drove downtown to a Halloween loft party attended by a sizable work contingent. I hadn't worn a costume because I couldn't think of one. I picked out Sarah, with her hair frizzed out and powdered white, as Einstein. Storming Morgen Hagen skated by to say hello, in a goalie mask and full hockey gear. I felt conspicuous dressed as myself.

Something soft but solid pushed up behind me.

"Hey, buddy, take the keys out of your pocket."

"What?"

"You heard me. Take the keys out of your pants pocket. I don't want to be deflected by them when I kick you in the balls."

Shelley had a sweet grin on her urchin mug and a ring of garlic around her neck.

"I'm a virgin," she said.

This seemed unlikely, but I said nothing.

"Who the fuck do you think you are, writing sex fantasies about me?"

Up close, Shelley stood shorter than the impression I had received from her in line to view Larry. She carried a very large bust, and it helped her to project height. After giving the abridged history of herself, she asked for a ride home. She still didn't have a car, having moved west from Hell's Kitchen, and her boyfriend was working in San Diego.

We pulled up in front of her Silverlake apartment, and I left the car running.

"Are you in a hurry to rush home?"

I switched off the ignition, and we talked for a while. Neither one of us could break off eye contact or stop smiling.

"I can't invite you in. It's my boyfriend's place, and that wouldn't be right."

An awkward silence didn't last long before we were mouthing one another. Our hands joined the action. Mine pawed beneath her shirt and slid under the waistband of her pants. Shelley gripped my crotch and loosened both our flies. She sank below the steering wheel and christened the new car. Shelley was slick and smart—she knew not to insist on kissing me goodnight. I appreciated her discretion, and I drove home parsing out the Halloween hot letter I would write up for next year's October issue.

In the middle of the following week, Mr. and Mrs. Flynt circulated a memo directing all employees to join them in the conference room. Nervous minions filed in, ready for anything from mass layoffs to across-the-board pay cuts. A flaming birthday cake covered a large mass of marble tabletop, dedicated jointly to Althea and Larry. Her birthday fell on November 6th, and his on November 1st. Pale Althea leaned forward to blow out the candles. She wore a leather jacket that hung on her wire frame like a shell. Her hair was all one color—black—and the Mohawk was gone. It took her a few deep huffs to snuff all the flames. The effort seemed to steal her wind away. Althea was neither completely happy nor completely there. Larry rose up in the golden chair behind her, presiding over this melancholy birthday party. His eyes looked out toward the world from some pharmaceutical middle distance. He contentedly shoveled cake into his pie hole. His wife looked at the stuff as though it were a plate of lard.

I wandered toward the shadows at the back of the conference room, and I sighted a familiar crater face. Alec the heroin courier squinted out from beneath a beret set at a tired angle. Alec had gone peroxide blonde. I couldn't tell if his hair had tinged green from a bad chemical reaction or as a reflection of his complexion.

Alec lipped an unlit cigarette, which he slipped into his shirt pocket when he recognized me. "Allan, right? You're looking really good. You must be clean."

Why I stopped to talk to him, I don't know. "Good call."

"That's really great. I'm really happy for you. Are you sure you're not in the market?"

I looked at him, and I looked over at Althea. I was not in the market.

"I have extra. Very pure. By the way, I heard that chick Juliet is buying a house with some guy. Weren't you with her for a while? You sure you don't need anything?"

That night I gave Shelley a ride home. Her boyfriend was still in San Diego; she'd called down there and talked to him just at the workday's end. She snuggled up to me in the car and heated up my ear.

"Who was that dude in the beret you were talking to at Althea's party?"

Alec would become one of the first people I knew to die of AIDS. He had lost almost everything, but still Alec retained that ugly magnetism, that negative charisma, that rock-schlock shtick.

"I don't really know him," I said. "He thought he knew me."

"He looked like an asshole." That's what I mean about Shelley having discretion. Despite her negative summation, Alec's wasted appeal played upon her basest impulses, and she invited me up to her boyfriend's apartment.

The four rooms didn't contain much to define them as "his" apartment. Shelley's stuff was spread everywhere. A mattress was stacked on a box spring. I recognized the burgundy jumper and lace apron of a Boulangerie uniform near the bottom of a pile of clothes hanging across the bedroom chair.

I couldn't stop myself. "You know what drew me to you on the bus?"

"The fact that I was asleep and powerless to defend myself?"

"Aside from that. I fell for that uniform from the Boulangerie. I thought about it for days on end."

"Would you like to try it on?" She did a mocking Tuesday Weld thing with her nose and eyes.

She stood and modeled the outfit for me, but with no blouse beneath the jumper and no panties under the apron. I chased her around the bed for a bit. Shelley made the most of that Boulangerie jumper, and I was struck with an exultant thought: She's going along with it! "Hot Letters" do come true!

My drunk driving conviction had diverted me to an alcohol awareness program. I enlisted in supplementary support groups and found that I appealed to halfway-reformed prostitutes who were also attending the self-betterment seminars. Aside from Shelley, I was playing couch ball with a former freelancer of the infamous Madame Alex and with a pixie-junkie ex-streetwalker. So when Shelley cozied up to Ben the Harvard pornographer, my chagrin was mitigated. Ben stood four inches shorter than me despite his cowboy heels, but he claimed the status of an actual editor, and I slithered along as a mere proofreader. The sleepy, bus-riding beauty was a social climber.

I might have known happiness, except that an outbreak of whiteheads manifested upon the tender flesh of my pubic area. No matter how much I squeezed and prodded, the whiteheads wouldn't pop. I was perplexed by these hard, red-rimmed protrusions, but not alarmed, until a rash of them clustered on my penis. This development spurred me to drop my pants at a Century City dermatologist's office and be diagnosed with *molluscum contagiosum*. The eruptions were an STD caused by a virus not quite so inimical as venereal warts. They were the next worst thing. In the interests of civic duty, I felt compelled to alert editor Ben to the onset of these symptoms. After all, there was some overlap with Shelley.

I sat on the sofa in Ben's office behind a closed door. It was the Wednesday before Thanksgiving weekend. He had probably banged Shelley on that sofa. He coolly drank Dr. Pepper and eyed me over the rim of the can. He had one of those chairs that leaned back far enough that he was able to comfortably prop his cowboy boots on the desk. I felt self-loathing and would rather have kept my affliction a secret. I balked at going straight to Shelley. She might object that I was accusing her of being a carrier. My two ex-hookers were just as likely the viral sources. I explained all this to Ben, assuring him that I was casting no aspersions on Shelley. I'd seen them canoodling in the halls and on the quad. They might be settling into something serious.

"Still, Ben, you need to be treated, if in fact you're infected."

"So what are the details? How do they clean this stuff up?"

"They fill a syringe with liquid oxygen, put the point on your affected area, press the liquid oxygen down to the eruption, and burn it. The pinpointed area scabs up, and in a few days the scab falls off. Hopefully the eruption is all gone and scarring is minimal."

Editor Ben pointed his soda can at me. "Man, thank God it's not a wart, hey? Thanks for the heads-up, but I'm blemish-free. I'll show you my clean unit, if you like. I can't believe a scab-dick is sitting on my sofa."

Ben held himself in much higher regard than either he or I held myself. And though I didn't resent him for picking up Shelley, even though I hadn't quite finished, he was stung by my having been there first. His false East Coast cool prohibited him from admitting this pettiness, but not from acting upon it. Having mocked me as a scab-dick, Ben went on to spread news of my condition throughout the office. That should have made us even, but Ben could not leave low enough alone. He booted into my office and berated me for altering wording in one of his manuscripts. The wording affixed a physical description that matched mine to a character who liked to lurk in outhouse pits. I was the lead copy editor under Morgen Hagen, and I'd been given an office of my own. I shut the door when Ben stormed in, but he threw it open, hoping to attract an audience. He placed his soda on my desk.

"I wish you wouldn't set your soda on my desk," I said.

Ben had a rug burn on his elbow, and he picked its scab as he talked to me.

"That's grossing me out," I said.

"This?" He peeled off a big chunk of scab and dropped it onto my desk. "Put the adjectives back the way I had them, will you? You don't want Althea hearing about this."

He picked up his soda, swigged, and out he swaggered. I disposed of his scab, then sat stewing, staring into the hall. A ghost walked by. Actually, it was only Althea. She wasn't dead yet, just a preview of what she'd look like when she was. Her fragile limbs moved within a sheer, flowing periwinkle dress, and all traces of punkiness had been washed from her lank black hair and alabaster complexion. Aside from her birthday party, Althea hadn't been seen passing among the lowly workers in months. Here she glided, still living, and already a wraith of her breathing self. In the morning, we would hear that Althea concluded her stroll by remarking to LFP's creative director: "All I seen out there was a lot of dumb-looking people."

A memo was circulated on behalf of the boss' wife, two-part reply mandatory, instructing each of us to elucidate the exact nature of our duties. Secondly, we were to sum up in 50 words why we were justified for employment at LFP. The goal was to avoid being lumped in with the people who were dumb-looking. Under personal qualifications, I wrote, "I am the only person employed at this company who saw the Sex Pistols live."

Surviving the Flynt jungle for a year and a half was not a fluke. I could hold my own with any other brazen bastard on staff. I picked the latest batch of *molluscum* scabs off of my dick. They were small, each one about the size of a match head. I put half a dozen of the blood flecks into a glassine envelope and scouted around for Ben the editor. He would never apologize for mocking me and leaving his dirty, dried chunk of blood on my desk. But he would pay.

I picked up his Western-theme trail at the concession room. Ben bought a Dr. Pepper, snapped the cap, gulped a few swallows and headed to the art enclosure, with me and my scabs in his shadow. He tabled the Dr. Pepper can, the better to harass some poor tool lower than him on the masthead. I stepped up and emptied my envelope into the can. Then I waited. I engaged Ben in conversation. He gulped down a few big swallows and waved the can as if to underline his contention.

"You may have a point," I conceded.

Ben might later move on and leave me far behind. He can go ahead and win a Nobel Prize for literature, but I will never feel a tinge of resentment toward good ol' Ivy League Ben. The man has swallowed scabs off my penis.

Shelley dumped Ben at the entrance to the company Christmas party. He responded by being drunker than he needed to be.

"MacDonell, shake and make up. You should be happy," he said. "All she gave you was crabs. Look what she's done to me."

He pointed to Shelley. She wore a sparkling-blue, curve-enhancing gown and was parading on the arm of Ben's boss, a long-term managing editor. This guy had been with the Flynts pre-shooting and must have been making 90 grand a year. Shelley looked like a million bucks. Gazing upon her made me happy just to have known her. I extended my sympathies to Ben. He flagged down Frank, the art-room boozehound.

"That bitch Shelley raped me," said Ben.

Frank turned to me. "Jesus, how'd he get this drunk? He must have spent a fortune."

The main topic of dinner conversation was speculating upon what percentage of the exorbitant fees charged for drinks was being kicked back to the Flynts. As dessert was being served, Althea stood at the head table and wavered. Someone with talent and resources had spent several hours pulling her together. Larry slouched in the golden chair at her side, a soiled bib wrapped about his neck. Since coming home gulag-thin from prison, the golden chairman had put most of his weight back on. His eyes glittered from the far side of oblivion. A dazed moon expression seemed to say, "I know this woman. What is her name?" His wife announced that next year, if we loyalists worked as hard as we had the previous 12 months, we would be rewarded with a real party, presumably one that included free drinks. There she staggered, the multimillion-dollar addict spewing the gutter-junkie creed: I'll make it up to you next time.

"Next year, we'll really have something to celebrate."

"Maybe, baby, but it's hard to picture you being there."

Dwaine Tinsley and his teenage daughter had infiltrated two empty seats at the copy table. Dwaine's daughter would be old enough to start dating in another two or three years. Dwaine draped an arm over his daughter's shoulder and held her tight. His drink hand nudged my knee. "Isn't she pretty? Did you ever see a girl this pretty? Don't you look at her." She couldn't have squirmed free if she'd wanted to. It was a jail grip, the seasoned con's embrace of his reluctant punk. I wondered on which end of the prison love equation Dwaine had learned that maneuver. He squeezed his daughter's mouth between his fingers. Her pinched lips bulged out. "Did you ever see a prettier girl? I don't like the way you're looking at her."

Dwaine finished off a drink, gazed into his daughter's eyes and then seemed to consider the consequences of hitting me in the face with the empty glass. He stifled a belch.

"You don't see a little girl this pretty every day."

I edged away from his field of vision. "No you don't," I said.

The Hustler XXX Film Review

THE GREAT DILEMMA of the recreational masturbator is that porn flicks are so hit-or-miss. Not many predicaments are sadder than that of a randy self-flagellator who has endured the abasement of obtaining a full-penetration erotic entertainment, only to find himself on the edge of his futon, feeling futile and flaccid. One hand on the remote, he scans frantically through ill-lit, ineptly photographed, clumsily framed, grossly peopled scenes of rote rutting, hoping to find just three or four consecutive moments of sustained sexual intensity. The crestfallen consumer castigates himself for having believed the XXX hype, and swears for perhaps the thousandth time that he will never be fooled again by the false promises of a greedy industry built upon lust and illusion.

Where might this deceived innocent, and the many thousands of clueless mooks just like him, turn for guidance? Until recently, the connoisseur of the reverse-cowgirl position, of the double penetration, the monster shot and the gamete facial had access to only one voice of honest and frank expertise: The *Hustler* magazine XXX film review. At a publication where the deaths of statesmen, religious leaders, Lady Diana and Bob Hope were cause for unfettered mockery, the reviewing of hardcore sex films, what polite society dismissed as fuck flicks, was treated with utmost seriousness.

CHAPTER 7

Living Large Among the Dark Luminaries of XXX

BY 1985, I was on the fast track to becoming America's preeminent critic of contemporary porn. There were smut historians and archivists who might have greater knowledge of cumshot trivia, but no writer in the genre could match my viscerally evocative, flagrantly opinionated deconstruction of smut.

"In a way, Allan, you're like Dylan Thomas," said Entertainment Editor Oliver, the tall, thin big-brain who, as a favor, had given me my initial three XXX tapes to review. "God endowed Dylan Thomas with the ability to create these perfect distillations of the human condition, delivered with grace and brilliance. And you, God gave the ability to write the most florid porn reviews humanly possible."

My only drawback was that I possessed no TV or VCR. I was making hundreds of dollars every weekend watching tapes in Oliver's empty office at 40 bucks a viewing. The logical action would be to buy the necessary home electronics, but I'd taken up residence in my first solo apartment, and I was reluctant to spring for extras such as items essential to career advancement. My current girlfriend, one of the semi-reformed hookers who'd softened my fall from Shelley, owned a TV, but no tape player. Today, it is hard to imagine a time when VCRs did not saturate the American landscape, but my past deprivation attests to it. I began to find fault with the ex-prostitute girlfriend. She talked while she ate and expected me to answer while my mouth was full. She used hair spray. She had enrolled in a UCLA extension program for first-time screenwriters. If happiness were to ever come my way, I needed a different type of girl. The type of girl who owned a VCR.

I found Cora while sneaking out early from a North Hollywood Narcotics Anonymous meeting. Cora was Mexican, energetic and a trifle overweight, roughly my age, smooth of complexion. Her shiny blue-black hair was cut in an update of the style popularized by pinup icon Bettie Page. Cora taught junior high. Her biggest fear was that the school board would learn she had been buying bags of weed from a physically precocious but mentally stalled eighth grader who had been held back two years. "How could I help myself?" she said. "The little hoodlum has the best stuff at the best price. I'm trying to squeeze by on a teacher's salary."

Cora had quit the herb, but continued to funnel 10- and 20-dollar bills to buy the dealer's silence.

"You work at *Hustler*?" she said. I'd made that admission over cups of double espresso. "That's my students' favorite literature."

Flattered, I offered to provide magazines to pass on to the kids, which I thought might save her those 10s and 20s. She declined. Cora's Studio City apartment had two VCR setups: one with the TV in the living room that she shared with her roommate, Brice, a gay guy on relapse from Sexaholics Anonymous, and the other at the foot of her fluffy, down-comforted bed.

With Cora, I learned the time-saving habit of multitasking. One evening not long after our third date, I found myself eating Thai food from cardboard cartons on her coffee table, while auditing porn and receiving a handjob.

"It's different looking at smut with a pro," Cora said. She scooped noodles into her mouth with a single-handed flick of chopsticks. "Who's that guy?" She indicated a smirking, clean-shaven performer with a chiseled physique.

"That's Peter North," I said, proud to be teaching the teacher. North was renowned for the girth of his unit and for the copious splashes of wad that jolted from his penis at orgasm. Peter North shot more ejaculate than three average stunt-dicks combined. Cora received this information with a bemused expression. She cleared her mouth of noodles and wiped her lips on a napkin before speaking.

"Usually, when some guy brings porn over early in the relationship, it's because he's trying to work me into a three-way."

Eventually the routine must have bored Cora, although she never told me so. Cora was an educator; her preferred mode of communication was to teach a lesson. She and I were stretched out and rolling around in bed. I'd caught up on my load of review tapes. This might have been the first time we'd ever hit the mattress without a video playing. Cora's flashing eyes burned slightly brighter than their usual glow.

"Allan, I have a treat."

"For me?"

"It's a porno. You'll find it interesting."

The cassette was in the machine and ready to go. Cora, I realized, had been looking forward to this treat as much for her own pleasure as for mine. She hit the play button and moved in for a big kiss. Men filled the screen. My attention was partially deflected as Cora drifted south, licking down my chest. The blue-cinema stud I knew as Peter North struck a pose on the cathode box, flexing his biceps and turning his waxed nates to the camera.

The flick's opening sequence credited Peter by the name Matt Ramsey. His hand fell down by his thigh, drifted off to his side and stroked a penis not his own. It took a moment for me to register the inconsistency. At first, the vision of Peter North onscreen with no women in sight fascinated me, in the way that an ape would if it were speaking English and writing checks.

Peter North spread his Matt Ramsey butt cheeks, and Cora's mouth fastened onto my prick. I reached for the remote control, wanting to stop the pictures, but teacher had placed the device out of reach. Peter North's face scrunched up in a rictus of ecstatic Matt Ramsey agony. The camera cut back to North's ass. A dick even fatter than his own shoved into the clench of his sphincters. I trembled in the presence of a shattering myth. Cora attempted to slip an oiled finger up my chute. What next? Was this crazy broad going to suggest a threesome with her roommate, Brice?

That weekend I broke down and bought a TV and VCR of my own. Soon after, Cora graduated to a guy who was attempting to turn a taxidermy hobby into a livelihood. In our last phone conversation (I'd left a box of videos at her place and was wheedling to retrieve them), Cora insisted that she was trading up from me with the animal stuffer. I refused to give her the satisfaction of agreeing.

A whole new self-confidence and sense of purpose filled the void that formerly I had bloated with drugs and alcohol. This improved identity was based largely on writing reviews of porn videos. I cranked out between six and 20 reviews a week, sometimes scratching out three different synopses of the same tape for three different magazines. My stable of fake names expanded from Christian Shapiro to include Max Cara, Hakim Whithers, Kurt Blume, Victor Battle, Aron Cope and Alex Marvel.

The first video star to shirk my acquaintance was splendidly robust Taija Rae. Taija was adored for a plush, firm roundness and a slightly protruding underbite that pushed out her puffy lower lip in an insolent pout. Taija graced the LFP offices to negotiate her cover appearance on *Hustler Erotic Video Guide*, an auxiliary Flynt publication dedicated to the parallel universe of porn. Entertainment Editor Oliver brought Taija by my office for a quick hello. At Taija's approach, an excitement seized me, such as being reunited with a long-absent, cherished lover. I'd shared many private and pleasurable moments with Taija Rae. I failed to realize that she had shared nothing with me. She stood in front of me, shorter than I'd expected and far prettier in person than on the video screen (a common phenomenon among XXX starlets).

"Wow, it's great to see you." I gushed.

"Thanks." She curled her lips as if she were accepting my apology for having accidentally soiled an article of her clothing. Rather than wait for what I might say next, Taija turned and went into seclusion with lanky, big-brain Oliver.

Upon initial contact with a porn girl, the illusion that she and I shared a sexual history never failed to disturb my perception, even after I had met dozens of them. My one-sided infatuation with Tori Welles was typical of the emotional fiascos that befell me. A classic Southern California brunette, Welles strutted into my imagination while strolling across the floor of the 1989 Consumer Electronics Show (CES), an annual convention held in Las Vegas, Nevada. At CES time, a XXX trade fair runs in conjunction with the mainstream event. Owners of mom-and-pop video shops, their numbers swollen by mobs of registrants supposedly attending the legitimate CES, throng the aisles between booths displaying fliers, posters and sleazy box covers. Many XXX companies enlist near-naked sex actresses to man their exhibits. The glamour-pusses autograph glossies and pose for souvenir photos with long, long queues of businessmen on junkets from points as remote as Boise and Kyoto.

Tori Welles stood out in this crush of glitz and chumps by exuding a force field of sexual brilliance. Complexion the color of cinnamon or bourbon, brunette mane of body and bounce, flaunting the defiant cheekbones and chin of an urchin empress, the sublime Ms. Wells stepped with the self-assurance of the lifelong stone fox. Her clothing—a tight black miniskirt, heels, form-fitting top—was nothing beyond the norm of a sharply dressed shop girl in a basic San Fernando Valley mall. But wait. Tori flashed a smile, and her eyes sparkled with a sleek, sensual ferocity, like a caged she-panther who has just come into the realization that with one leap of her glistening, muscled loins, she will have escaped her cage and will be on a rampage of joyous bodily mayhem.

Tori seemed to stroll to the bathroom every 15 minutes. Either she had a bladder condition, or she was rubbing her nose for a reason. There was no use talking to me while Tori was on the move. Upon first sighting, I had yet to see Tori in a video. She was that new; she hadn't even had her implant surgery yet. Showcasing an unknown girl might have seemed like a risk to whatever video company had sponsored her trip, but hundreds upon hundreds of attendees had a reaction to her that was identical to mine. We were all hooked. Of course, being less of an idiot than the teeming masses, I knew not to approach Welles while among a multitude of disposable mooks.

I attended the CES convention as the editor-in-chief of *Chic* magazine, which was positioned as a marginally more sophisticated offshoot of *Hustler*. As soon as I had returned to the Beverly Hills home office, I assigned myself to write a celebrity profile on Tori Welles.

Our first conversation was tough. I pressed the telephone hard into my ear. Only a few Tori videos had been released. My reviews, written under the protective pseudonym Christian Shapiro, had earmarked Tori for the sex-star stratosphere. She pretended not to have read Shapiro's coverage. Nonetheless, on the strength of my *Hustler* connection, Tori agreed that I could accompany her on set, but she wouldn't be working for a few weeks. She'd had her boobs "bumped up" and had been advised to wait for them to heal.

I'd moved in with my first long-term girlfriend since my wife had dropped me. The new mate called herself Frankie and was English-born. We'd been together for two years and shared the top half of a West Hollywood duplex. Our living-room window opened to a view of the sky-blue modernity of the Pacific Design Center; it was the most chic address of my existence. My British soul mate was seven years younger than me and had arrived in California as a toddler. She'd gone to high school on the same Santa Monica campus as the Sheens and the Penns. Her accent was generally Malibu but shifted to a tony British lilt when special emphasis was required. I never fully determined if Frankie was to the manor born or only affected the tone. For certain, she was tall, dark, slim, sexy and inherently stylish, especially while naked. Frankie had traveled for a short time with the highest circles of early-1980s British pop-punksters. Her sophistication was easy and natural. She was also one of the most jealous women I have ever encountered. Her sixth sense for detecting straying affection, real or imagined, was like a rigged polygraph. I did my best to conceal from Frankie my excited anticipation of hounding Tori Welles at work.

Unfortunately, the final phone call setting up my morning meeting with Tori had to be made from home. While Frankie watched TV, I snuck into the bathroom with an extension phone and quickly dialed the starlet's number. A gruff male answered. I pictured renowned stunt cock Buck Adams. I'd been warned that Buck had shacked up with Welles; still, I hadn't expected him to be screening her calls. He passed me along, and Tori pretended to have trouble figuring out who I was. I was whispering so as not to provoke the extrasensory vigilance of Frankie. Welles verified our meet time and gave me directions to her apartment deep in the Valley.

I joined Frankie in front of the TV.

"Who were you on the phone with?"

"Just now? A girl I'm going to do an interview with tomorrow."

"Porn slut? I knew it. Where are you planning to do the interview? On the movie set? While she's sucking cock? I thought so."

That night, to reassure Frankie as well as to satisfy my own fired-up imagination, I was a particularly attentive and generous bedmate. My meticulous applications would be enough to send any woman over the brink, I reflected, even the high-voltage Tori Welles. My moves didn't quite do the trick on Frankie.

"You're pretending I'm her while you're doing all these extras," she said. "I could have predicted this."

Tori Welles lived in a vast, drab Valley apartment complex that could easily be converted into institutional housing. Her unit was behind three fire doors and down long expanses of windowless hallway. The place, at least the one room of it I was exposed to, was a mess. Floor, table, chairs, TV, all bore castoffs of chaos, mostly clothes. Taut butt straining the seams of stressed Levis, turbulent breasts bursting open the front of a white dress shirt, Tori checked her trollop makeup in one of the world's luckiest mirrors.

"Don't be too much of a bitch today," called a whiskey voice—presumably Buck Adams'—from the bedroom.

Welles hoisted two stuffed garment bags and lugged them to the door. I was hoping to get away without being grilled by Buck. Tori kicked the door open. "I'll be as much of a prima donna as I need to be," she swore with quiet conviction.

We ate breakfast at a '50s diner on Van Nuys Boulevard. Interviewing Tori was easy. I let the tape recorder run, and she did the same with her mouth. "Even before I had a name, I'm a bitch. But now with my name I can be a little more effective. Everybody has a certain game that they play to get what they want. They use the innocent way, and I use the bitchy way. I've always wanted to be the big shit around; so now I've found that in porn."

Her charm worked its magic. By the time we pulled up at the shoot location, I was wondering what I'd ever seen in Frankie. The set was housed in a failed movie theater down near the Crenshaw District. The place had been converted into an expansive and gloomy artist's loft, like an aircraft hangar with a kitchen and exposed pipes. A bogus bedroom, a fake fireplace and a spurious window had been constructed in one corner of the vast space.

"This would be the perfect place to hang yourself and have it be in the papers," observed Tori.

The makeup queen, eyes popping, remarked on the size of Tori's boobs. "Are they bigger again? How many times have you had them done?"

Tori was booked for a pair of sex scenes, one in a functioning hot tub, the other in a rigged-up conversation pit, couplings that she executed with professional aplomb. I bore witness from a medium distance, pen and paper at hand, taking scrupulous notes so that I would accurately transcribe the flex of her haunches, the tilt of her chin, the glaze of her eyes and the shimmy of her breasts and thighs for the benefit of the loyal *Chic* reader.

The loft's inhabitant owned a dog, a massive male Akita. The animal sniffed out Welles in her dressing room, a storage area cordoned off by a dozen bursting, black-plastic trash bags. Gnats hovered as Tori pulled on a pair of thick red socks. The Akita shoved his nose directly into the center of Tori Welles. One good whiff, and he leaped straight into the air, landing belly-first with his legs outspread. The love-stricken hound writhed on the carpet, glowering and slathering, with eyes only for Tori. The sad fact was that he probably had a better chance with her than I did.

Watching Tori Welles power through her moves was a reward in itself, but a bigger boost came when the cast and crew gathered at the lunch buffet during the lull between Welles' copulations. She joined her co-stars around an array of cold cuts and breads. I stuck with raw vegetables and fruits.

Paul Thomas, the director, cut in between me and the carrot sticks. Thomas was handsome, serious-looking, well into his 40s, a former video cocksman. Had he truly applied himself, he might have made a career of acting in television soaps. He'd slipped on the easier, slimier slope of hardcore sexual melodrama. The director wanted information. "Do you know this Christian Shapiro guy who writes all those reviews over at *Hustler*?"

"Never met him. He sends his stuff directly to Oliver."

My placid expression withstood the director's scrutiny. Thomas sneered as if taking a joke in his stride. "He calls me 'pompous Paul.'"

"That's nothing," said one of the girls. "He was writing about Bionca, and he said she was 'an acquired distaste.'"

The talent and crew guffawed at this cruel depiction of a common friend who happened to not be in the room. Paul Thomas exulted because Shapiro had termed a rival director's effort "a talky, pretentious plop of slop, a cancer on the body of sleaze."

Baby-faced stud Tom Byron, fresh from working over Welles in the hot tub, snickered. "The dude called Ron Jeremy a 'bloated, shitting dog star in an increasingly defiled cosmos.'"

Paul Thomas laughed despite resisting the impulse. "What does that even mean?"

Porn-level literates were quoting my bile word for word! The talent appreciated my trenchant humor! These unlikelihoods were Miracle-Gro to my ego. I was dying to reveal myself as the source of these splendid bon mots. Paul Thomas cut me off.

"Here's what else he says: 'It takes a special talent to construct a feasibly arousing adult entertainment, and Paul Thomas almost has that talent.'" Thomas' humor evaporated. He fixed his suddenly grave actors straight in the eye, one by one, then glared at me. "When I find out who that guy is, I'm knocking his teeth in."

I picked a shred of carrot from my incisors.

Tori went off to prepare for her second bout of video lust. The Akita tracked her every move. Finally, director Thomas insisted that the hairy beast be confined to an upstairs gallery. The animal's wide skull and hanging tongue lolled through a break in an overhead railing. Tori entered the ring of cameras that encircled the conversation pit. As Tori's partner crawled toward her spread thighs, the Akita wailed. Welles reached out and stroked her co-star's outcropping; the animal groaned and whined shamelessly. After penetration, the dog squealed as if its throat were being slit with every thrust.

The dog's vociferous protests would figure largely in the story I eventually wrote for *Chic* ("A Day in the Life of a Porn Star," September, 1989), and his actions played a leading role in the account I gave Frankie when I arrived to a cold and still home that night.

"Did he have a bigger hard-on than yours?" asked Frankie.

When the Tori Welles profile came out, Oliver appeared at my desk. The entertainment editor was tall, thin and mostly bald, so the slightest of skewed smiles achieved gloating. "Welles hates your story," he said.

"But I really like her."

"She feels you were disrespectful and that you made up humiliating details."

"Everything she said, I have on tape. Everything else I saw with my own eyes."

"Tori sees things differently. She claims that she punched you in the face in retaliation."

Any time the phone rang, it might be someone offering to make real Welles' imagined revenge. Mark Arnold, a puffy-eyed monger of lowbrow smut, tracked me down all the way from Chatsworth, deep in the outer Valley. Mark Arnold was a chubby nebbish who fucked amateur girls on video and turned some into pros. He later changed his name to Ed Powers.

"Look, I won't bullshit you," he promised. "Hurtful things are being written in your reviews. Bionca, for instance. Is it fair to keep harping on her teeth? You say she has no muscle tone and that her teeth are crooked, and it's just not true. Anyway, she's getting braces.

"The point is, you hurt her feelings on a very personal level. Look, why lie? I'm not hung like some of these guys, and sometimes I lose my concentration. I'll be doing a scene, and the girl will mock my penis in front of everybody. Do you have any idea what it feels like to have some girl mock your penis?"

Mark Arnold waited long enough to assume I'd conceded something, then went on. He invited me to a remote warehouse with visions of free sushi and a first look at his latest slop epic. How stupid did he hope I would be?

Entertainment Editor Oliver provided a voice of caution: "It's time you take responsibility for the venom you spew."

Was I overdue to "own my actions," as the therapists say? That's what Frankie had been screaming while driving off with all the good stuff from our duplex. Perhaps my life would have meaning and substance if I assumed accountability for my own behavior. Then again, I could seek a second opinion.

During my years as a XXX pundit, whenever I found myself in need of sage advice, I sought out proudly egregious porn director Gregory Dark. Saturnine, wiry and crazy-eyed, Greg gained his '80s notoriety as half of the nefarious Dark Brothers. The Dark Brothers' plaque shot to infamy with their first production, *Let Me Tell Ya 'Bout*

White Chicks (1984), the peripatetic adventures of a mentally chal-
lenged blonde entranced with black male members. Further titles
included *Let Me Tell Ya 'Bout Black Chicks* (1985), *Black Throat*
(1985), *New Wave Hookers* (1985) and *Between the Cheeks* (1985).
New Wave Hookers starred the illegal teen Traci Lords; *Between the
Cheeks* was declared obscene in an Alabama courtroom and helped
send Russ Hampshire (owner of VCA, the company that released the
Dark Brothers' output) to a year in prison.

My porn coverage extolled the genius of Dark Brothers produc-
tions. In return, Greg Dark smoked out my ego by hailing me as a
writer of unheralded genius, a cross between Damon Runyon and
Georges Bataille. My first contact with this adroit flatterer came on
the set of *Deep Inside Vanessa Del Rio* (1986), a fictionalized biography inspired by the world's most famous Puerto Rican sex worker,
on board to star as herself. Peons in the VCA art department had
secured me a part in the film. We carpooled one Saturday as dawn
cracked and drove for three hours, arriving at a sprawling, stalled
construction project deep across the Ventura County line. Every
porn shoot I ever attended was staged in a giant house that tottered
on the brink of foreclosure. I played Vanessa Del Rio's ex-husband.
Wardrobe decked me out in checkered pants and polyester. My lines
called for me to stick my head out of a doorway and lament that my
bride, Vanessa, had run off with our Great Dane, never to return. I
nailed the scene on the first take and ad-libbed, "I sure do miss that
dog." My pay was 50 bucks and all the salad, pasta and pizza I
could eat.

Naked lugs stood holding their paper plates in the food line,
pubes and penises wafting toward the buffet. My appetite waned. I
was feeling ripped off until the wardrobe mistress introduced me to
Vanessa Del Rio. Vanessa, a wide-boned, muscled-up dark woman
with an immense mane of black hair, brandished a formidable phys-
icality. She was swollen in the breasts, butt and thighs, and solid. On
the drive out, I'd been told Del Rio was considering a second career
as a pro weightlifter.

"When is *Hustler* doing a big story on me?" she said. A fluffy robe
enwrapped her points of interest, but the terrycloth did nothing to
dissuade my X-ray eyes. I was in the presence of a legend.

"I just played your ex-husband," I said.

Vanessa sized me up as being useless to her. She took her pasta to the makeup table. Greg invited my friends and me to stick around and watch the Latin from Manhattan perform as the centerpiece in a four-man gangbang.

Vanessa's four-guy supporting cast included semi-straight Peter North and a preening libertine who went by the name Marc Wallice. North seemed remarkably at ease in the presence of other naked men. Wallice, whose defining characteristic was a penis that curved like Death's scythe, spent the hours between shots outside in the driveway, dusting his Cadillac. Marc Wallice's lasting infamy would result from faking an HIV test while knowing he was positive and passing along the bug to co-workers. Vanessa emerged from the makeup area. Her flesh was squeezed into a black, lingerie-and-leather contraption that sectioned her like strung sausage. The quartet of stunt cocks milled about speaking in mocking Hispanic accents, casting aspersions upon Vanessa's virtue. They were oblivious to Del Rio's legend.

"Greg," Vanessa cried, "make them stop."

I noticed for the first time Greg Dark's striking resemblance to the common representations of Satan. The hollowed cheeks, the deep-cut eyes glittering with malicious mischief, the thick waves of oily hair coming to a "V" above the pointed brow; all this combined for a strikingly devilish effect. To his credit, the director sensed that a girl, even a professional of Vanessa's stature, can't be expected to jump straight into a gangbang. She needed foreplay.

An assistant handed the legend a wobbly black dildo the exact size and configuration of a policeman's billy club. Del Rio inserted the latex truncheon and pulled it out at Greg's direction. She crawled about in the orgy pit with the black appendage hanging from her haunches like a tail. Vaginal grip held the prong in place as Del Rio's hands and mouth fluffed three of the four penises assembled for her. My vantage point behind the perimeter of lights and technicians allowed me close scrutiny of the director's monitor screen. The camera zoomed tight on Vanessa's crotch. Her unhooded clitoris protruded to the size of an eight-year-old boy's penis, which was being fellated by the odd man out.

The four guys followed Greg's game plan and plowed into Vanessa, from all directions and for an extended duration. I was ready for it to be over sooner than the filmmakers were. At the end, the tumescent foursome stood one at a time and delivered the indisputable proof of male orgasm upon the quivering epidermis of Vanessa Del Rio. Peter North, the human grease gun, launched an even greater quantity of gunk than usual.

After the scene wrapped, but before Vanessa had showered, she and I stood side by side at a snack table. I swirled a carrot stick in a vat of onion dip, but couldn't bring myself to eat it.

Reporting on smut took me to many exotic locales far beyond the Ventura County line, including four expenses-padded visits to the Côte d'Azur. Every year, movie makers flock to the South of France for the Cannes Film Festival. Throughout the 1990s an impudent French magazine, *Hot Video*, hijacked promotional firepower from the Cannes establishment by convening in that quaint French port village for a coinciding festival of fornication.

In 1992, *Hot Video*'s dark, rotund publisher, Franck Vardon, and his minions inaugurated their Academy Awards of ass. Five days of porno trade fair would culminate in a black-tie ceremony where professional fuckers and the men who profit from them would step to the podium and accept statuettes for their efforts. Vardon imported 18 of America's most vaunted sex starlets to serve as festival-week camera fodder. A *Hot Video* charter jet touched down at the tiny Nice airport. Out spilled smut sirens Lois Ayers, Patricia Kennedy, P.J. Sparxx, Cameo, Lynn Lemay, Victoria Paris, Tonisha Mills, Jeanna Fine, Raven, Porsche Lynn, Madison and Sunny Foxx. Most of these subsequently obscure women were household names at the time, albeit in a certain debased type of household.

Vardon emblazoned a pair of cabin cruisers with *Hot Video* logos and trolled for news coverage through the crowded Cannes harbor. Yachts from all the richest ports of the world congested the Cannes waterways, but none of the others were carrying porn starlets. The girls dropped their tops at the fore decks, soaking up sun and teasing the cameras of photographers in speedboats running alongside.

Bleached blonde and surgically busty Sunny Foxx crouched aft in the same cruiser as me. A bandanna kept her hair manageable in the breeze. She'd just emerged from the head. "I checked the medicine cabinet in there. Band-Aids. But not even a Midol." Sunny always represented elegance over raunch, accenting her bikini with elbow-length gloves. Sly Foxx looked around to be sure no one was watching and stripped off a glove, plucked three Evian bottles out of the cooler with a single hand, then slipped the glove back on. Most porn girls considered the need for elbow-length gloves an off-limits topic, but in some ways Sunny was different than the ordinary porn girls. "I should have brought more of these goddamn patches," she said. "I had a doctor who offered to write a prescription for a methadone substitute, but I thought being here would be a good opportunity to kick, so I just went with the detox patches." She slid her bikini bottom aside to show me where the medication-delivery pad was affixed, right at the apex of her pubic bone. "I'll be jonesing if TWA doesn't find the bag where I packed my patches, but at least I won't run out of water." She squinted at the sun as if trying to force it to look away. "I didn't come to the South of France for ultraviolet poisoning." Her long fingers easily palmed the Evian bottles. She raised them to her mouth and shielded the world from a rankling series of coughs. "You're looking at my man hands. That's what your prick friend Christian Shapiro wrote about them. He says whenever they film my hand on a guy's cock, it looks like some other guy is jacking him off. People hate that."

"Not all people hate that."

She looked to see if I were humoring her. "Most people do hate that, Allan."

Sunny was one of the porn girls who had actually taken her college board exams. Also a top-ranked exotic dancer and a freelance entertainer at the one-on-one level, she claimed Jack Nicholson among her clients—but then, what L.A. hooker doesn't? The other girls straggled back from the bow.

"It's too windy up there," said a wispy, auburn nymph. "I'm tiny, so I was afraid I'd get blown overboard."

"None of us is going to drown," said Sunny. Somehow she'd fired a cigarette in the spring gale without setting down her cache of Evian. "You don't think these tits could ever sink, do you?"

Not all the girls got the joke. Some of the ones who did resented it.

"When I was a homely 10-year-old," giggled the tiny dancer, "I never thought people would be lining up to take my picture, and now people are paying scalpers $500 for tickets to the *Hot Video* awards."

"Five hundred bucks is chump change," said Sunny. "I can line you up to bring in three grand for a 40-minute hour."

"Really?" chimed three of the six ladies present.

Sunny squinted at me and coughed again. "All this is off-the-record, dude."

An L.A. madam had put Sunny in contact with a screening service in Cannes. The screeners took their percentage, and in return guaranteed clients and conditions. Not all the girls had experience turning tricks, or maybe they were being coy.

"What's the difference?" asked Sunny, playing the blowsy and brazen older sibling. "It's just like having sex on camera, except there's no camera."

"Don't the screeners need to interview us?"

"They know who you are. We're famous, honey. That's why it's three grand."

"Thanks for the tip, Sunny. But what do you get out of helping us?"

"My split comes from the screener's cut. I would never take anything away from you girls."

Everyone agreed that the arrangement was fair. Sunny handed out cards with contact numbers for the screening service. I wondered where she had kept those cards waiting.

The boat turned in toward the quay. Its companion craft sluiced through the sea beside us. The girls on the other boat had stuck out their time on the prow, thrusting their breasts forward into the heavy breeze like goose-pimpled figureheads. Their teeth gleamed in wide-lipped smiles. Sunny peered at the contingent of onscreen talent floating beside us.

"Look at the underarm fat on *******," said Sunny. "How can she wave her wings in the air like Big Bird when the flaps hang down like an old turkey neck? And how does ****** think that boob job makes her pretty? Until she has some work done on that beak of hers, she should stay home and peck grain."

Our boat bumped the dock, and Sunny jumped up before the ropes had been wound.

"Wait for me, Allan," she called. "I'll take you for a drink up on La Croisette. We'll cruise the Carlton."

Sunny boarded the *Hot Video* sister boat like a big-boob buccaneer and launched into her freelance trade pitch. Several girls secreted screener-service cards into their backpacks and tote bags.

We docked at a section of pier where mainstream celebrities and blue screen stars intersected. A staid female journalist stood to one side interviewing Spike Lee. The girls from the *Hot Video* boats, partially covered in cheeky shorts and summer frills, traipsed *en masse* toward the shore. Sunny clutched my arm and steered me away from the parade of *Hot Video* tarts. "Franck Vardon paid my way over here, but you know what? He can't match my day rate. I need to make 20 grand before I go home."

Sunny used her palm to cover a lung-searing cough. She stopped long enough to yank a long-sleeved jersey out of her tote bag and pull it over her head, stripping off the gloves and tossing them into the tote. She lit a smoke as we strode along the quays, away from the moored yacht, toward the Carlton Hotel. Sunny walked with fast intent through the dawdling Croisette tourists, like a girl on her way to cop. She hadn't always been strung out. She had dabbled in recovery culture for a few months. Her idea of proselytizing temperance was to wear an Alcoholics Anonymous medallion around her neck while being filmed with her heels up behind her ears. Even in her long-sleeve jersey and black jeans, she drew a lot of second gawks as we hustled along the crowded promenade.

She breezed up to the grand edifice of the Carlton and approached the lobby as if the proprietors owed her money. The Hotel Carlton Cannes prides itself on being *Le Palace des stars, la star des Palaces*. Evidently, the establishment was selective about the constellations that spawned its luminaries. A suave and implacable security representative blocked our path.

"Room keys, please."

"I'm here to meet a friend," said Sunny.

"I am sorry. Only persons accompanied by guests of the hotel are permitted to the lobby."

Sunny thanked the Carlton's guard in a way that convinced me of its sincerity. She and I retreated, passing the Carlton's outdoor bar, and shared a taxi out toward the hillside villa set to host that evening's porn-industry mixer. Traffic bottlenecked in the quaint boulevards of the old town, trapping us in a cacophony of blaring horns, revving scooters and a polyglot mass of whining and bickering. Sighing, clutching her gut, Ms. Foxx was feeling the indignity of having been tossed from the Carlton.

"Sunny, whatever possessed you to kick junk while working in a foreign country?"

She rolled her neck. "That stone-junkie trip went very ugly, baby. Savannah invited me for a weekend in Palm Springs, at that place where her boyfriend keeps her."

Any aficionado of E! True Hollywood Story will recognize Savannah as the picture-perfect, satin-soft blonde who had been a teenage companion to rock star Greg Allman before taking the porn world hostage. In July 1994, Savannah would commit suicide.

"Savannah can be such a cunt," said Sunny, coughing. "She acts so innocent. She knew I was strung out. Jesus, I taught her how to take the stuff. What did she think, I stopped?"

Savannah had refused to share her presumed stockpile of dope. The sugar-spun blonde claimed not to be high despite pinned pupils and incessant scratching. Sunny raged. She hadn't brought any stash with her, and she had no connections in Palm Springs.

"The selfish bitch. What did she want me to do? Go out and trick until I pulled a player who could score? I had no car and hardly any money. I was stuck out in the fucking desert, her prisoner, shitting for 48 hours while she stumbled around the kitchen scratching her pussy. The whole thing was a setup so I'd spend two days crapping myself and barfing, which was Savannah's form of passive-aggressive revenge."

Savannah was resentful because Sunny had refused to teach her how to shoot up. Eventually a hardened XXX fellatio artiste of the '70s New York era demonstrated the trick of hitting a vein to Savannah. The same woman had taught Sunny years earlier. "She indoctrinated a whole string of us into the sisterhood of the syringe." In the next millennium, this born educator would be a leading campaigner for safe-sex working conditions among blue screen talent.

The cab dropped us at Chez Porno, and we shoved in among the XXX contingent on a shady patio commanding a vista of cliff-dwelling homes. The women—sleek, sensual, mercenary—were grossly outnumbered by stolid, carnal, mercenary males. Greg Dark, looking more like Satan than ever, was sniffing out a brunette porn girl. She had natural tits and a knowing snideness that was attractive in a crass way. It was unclear whether she had a sexual history with Greg. She and Sunny embraced like lost sisters and immediately retired to the bathroom. When they emerged, Sunny was markedly more confident and energetic. She breached the crowd of alpha johns and it was as if she had ingested some chemical that unleashed a predatory instinct. She brushed against me while in pursuit of a tubby gray guy wearing a 40-grand Rolex. "No time to chat, baby."

Mark Arnold, the American performer/producer who a year or two earlier invited me to a deep Valley warehouse, was in the odd position of needing a haircut and hair plugs at the same time. Two girls I'd met during the *Hot Video* boating excursion joined me at the cheese platter. One of them was the woman Sunny had ridiculed for her underarm flab. She took angry, short bites out of a cracker. The cheese seemed okay to me, but it must have been bunk. None of the French dudes were having anything to do with it.

"Because of Sunny, these foreign fuckers think we're all prostitutes," said the girl with sagging arms.

Her companion was the tiny dancer girl, the formerly homely 10-year-old. She'd grown up to become a feather-light update of the hippie wood nymph. She took hold of my elbow. "If we stick around you, the tricks will leave us alone."

"Unless they think I'm your pimp."

The one with the flabby arms huffed cracker dust. "You, a pimp?"

Both ladies laughed. With a minimum of prodding, they spilled their biographical guts. Flab Arms was into S&M and came hardest when being spanked or having her nipples pinched. The most precious thing in life to Tiny Dancer was her daughter. Dancer was self-conscious about being pigeon-toed.

"I hadn't noticed." And why would I? She was a head-to-toe diversion, from her reddish-brown, softly falling tresses to her pert bottom and ballerina posture.

"Come here, walk with me. I have to pee."

Sure enough, her feet pointed in at about 45 degrees. She showed me how she waltzed her daughter around while the toddler stood on her feet. I went in with her while she peed.

"My baby's father is in jail, up in Colorado."

"That's too bad."

"Not really. I mean, how else would I have gotten away from him?"

Back in the Cannes party, the girl with the flawed underarms made a love connection with a financial component. She evaporated into the crowd. Pigeon Toes gave me the next chapter in her blue Hollywood story. She'd flown to L.A. to audition for a nude-modeling agency. The following weekend, one of the industry's leading porn actors had rented a U-Haul and moved her daughter and all their things out to Los Angeles from Colorado. "He did it because he was a nice guy. Not because he wanted anything from me."

The professional hard-on she named had a reputation for being a straight-up person. About five years later, while going through a divorce from a woman whose porn career was skyrocketing as his own spiraled, he took a pistol and blew out his brains in that woman's driveway.

My pigeon-toed friend and I hit it off in a lasting way. The next night we gravitated to adjacent seats during the awards gala. I'd hatched a scheme to extend my return plane ticket and call in to the office with some bogus lead about a burgeoning porn scene in Spain. I planned to rent a car and drive to Barcelona, stay a couple of days, take an overnight train to Paris and fly home from there. Pigeon Toes toyed with the idea of joining me on this four-day adventure. The *Hot Video* buffet was, contrary to expectations, excellent, but the awards presentations themselves were interminable and proper.

"Sunny Foxx looks sluttier than she needs to," said my new friend.

When the evening finally wore down, the pretty pigeon was obligated to return to the *Hot Video* chalet with their flock of girls. One final party was scheduled for the next evening, staged by Franck Vardon to honor a consortium of Italian porn producers and distributors.

I arrived 40 minutes late, not wanting to seem overeager. From the top of a stairway overlooking the garden setting, I spotted my object of fixation sitting at a table of American porn starlets, sucking in her lips. An empty seat separated her from the flapping gums of Sunny Foxx. I checked my pace, approached coolly and took the intervening seat.

The girl with the flabby arms was venting: "I feel like we're being auctioned off to these fucking Italians."

"They all want anal," said Sunny in a promotional mode. "They insist on at least one anal scene."

"I only like anal in my private life," said the pretty pigeon.

"You'll never make this kind of money in your private life," pointed out Sunny.

I asked the tiny dancer if she wanted to visit the buffet.

"Go ahead," she said, distracted.

I filled my plate with salad and chicken from tin bins. My seat at the table between Sunny and my fantasy travel companion was taken by an Italian. I had lost my chance to take Pigeon Toes on a Spanish excursion. She was moving in a different direction. Disappointment threw me off balance. As I moved closer to a castoff table on the far side of the courtyard, I recognized three hunched figures: Randy West, perhaps the oldest stunt dick currently working; Don Fernando, a second-tier swordsman; and Mark Arnold. His name had been upgraded to Ed Powers, and he slumped over his plate of greens like a giant gerbil. With my back to the table, I eavesdropped on Randy West in mid-anecdote: "I mean, everybody fools around, but every time I see him, he grabs my balls, puts his tongue in my ear and sticks a finger up my ass. I really hate it, except the money is so good."

How would I fit in with this conversation? I hoped to pass unnoticed, carry my plate of grub down the cobblestone streets to the seaport, jump in a taxi, head to the airport and fly home.

Mark Arnold hooked my forearm as I sidled past.

"Here's a place. Sit."

No one looked up from shoveling the salad. I took this lack of interest in me as a personal affront. With the perspective of time, something else—such as the Italians snatching up all the good girls— might have been rankling the players at the table.

Mark Arnold made a sweeping gesture from me to the other diners. "I want to introduce the table to the great Christian Shapiro." He spoke in a mock grand voice that I felt verged on overkill. "We here are all familiar with the work of the great Christian Shapiro."

Randy West, whom Christian Shapiro derided in unflattering, ageist terms, looked up briefly and grunted.

Don Fernando perked up.

"What is your name again?" he said. Maybe I was someone who could help his career.

Arnold silenced Don with a sneer and leaned in close to me.

"Remember when I invited you out to the warehouse for lunch?"

"No," I said. "I can't bring it to mind."

His shoulders heaved, and his nostrils twitched, emitting a tight, contained wheeze. I've come to suspect that this snuffling was how Mark Arnold laughed. "Believe me," he said, "if you'd come out there, you'd remember it. And it wouldn't have been a happy memory."

I marveled at this improbable schmuck. He'd changed his name to Ed Powers, and reinvented himself as a multimillionaire. He wasn't smarter or better-looking than me. His penis was just as puny as mine. Why was I such an insufficient self-starter?

The *Hustler* Articles

ONLY A MORON would try to convince a friend or loved one that he had sneaked a *Hustler* into his bathroom for the sake of reading the magazine's articles. One quick pass through Larry Flynt's flagship reveals the enterprise for what it is. Unlike *Playboy*, where teasing pictorials seem to be included as an afterthought to pseudointellectual stimulation, pages upon pages of gaping *Hustler* models are splayed in brighter-than-life pink, vividly defining the purpose of the publication and the intention of the consumer. The stories in *Hustler* give the reader an excuse to keep the periodical in his hands until he is again ready to use those mitts on himself.

Hustler led the printed world in coverage of sexual profiteering (typified by "My Beautiful Balloon: Testing the '97 Model Blow-Up Sex Dolls," June, 1997) and of libido-based lifestyles (for instance, "A Family's Affairs: Two Swinging Generations of Open Marriage," May, 1998). The monthly "Sex Play" provided couch-bound access to intriguing fetishes (start with "Humping Stumps: The Limbless and the People Who Love Them," February, 1997). *Hustler*'s relationship coaches dispensed how-to guides for threesomes ("Two's Company, Three's a Wow!" December, 1989), quickies ("Fun on the Fly: Defending the Fast Fuck," January, 1994) and fail-safe philandering ("You're Cheatin' Smart: Getting Away With Getting a Little on the Side," December, 1995), while also declaring ground rules for the ongoing gender wars ("What Women Really Want ... And Should Men Give a Shit?" August, 1994).

At one with the historical moment, the magazine dispatched a literary prostitute to post-Cold War Germany, where she commemorated the falling of the Iron Curtain by being the first free-world hooker to market her gear in East Berlin ("Eros East Germany—Selling Sex With Dolores French," August, 1990). An atomic alert on the black market for nuclear terror tools ("Bargain Armageddon: Who's Paying and Who's Selling in an A-Bomb Spending Spree," October, 1993) and a wake-up look at ubiquitous militant Islamists ("The New Crusade: Islam's Holy War Against the World," April, 1996) were presented years before mainstream media tied up the same threads. Conversely, conspiracy theories never touched by a reputable news source were published with all the gravity of the *Congressional Record* ("Sirhan Sirhan: Hoffa's Hitman?" February, 1990, and "Unsafe Sects: CIA Connections to Mind Control Cults," July, 1995, to name only two). The feature articles defined what passed for reality in the world of *Hustler*. The trick was to remain in that shifting sector where *Hustler* reality and the outside universe overlapped.

CHAPTER 8

"Don't Be a Nerd."

NO UNIVERSITY IN America could have prepared me for a day behind the features desk at Larry Flynt Publications. Mere weeks after my promotion to the position, I have a visitor. A self-proclaimed three-tour Vietnam veteran occupies the sofa in my office. Dressed in worn Levis, a muscle shirt and engineer boots, bald on top, he has more facial tics than I can count without staring. His eyes swim in his skull behind bent, wire-rimmed glasses. My hand throbs from where his grip has crushed it. He perches upon the front edge of the seat cushions, poised like a Doberman. Only the desk separates us. He glares at the door. "Does this thing lock?" he asks.

"The door is secure."

He looks at me as if I don't know the meaning of security. In truth, I've forgotten what freedom from fear, danger or anxiety might feel like. A big knife has burst the sheath on my visitor's belt. The fingers of one hand drummed on his twitching knee. His other hand paces along his belt line to the hilt of his knife. I curse the receptionist for having walked this risky character through the double security doors and into my office. In a scary whisper that compels me to lean forward, placing my throat well within the slay zone, the vet claims to live in a halfway house where the springs of the sofa prick him and inject him with a serum the CIA has concocted to enhance his vulnerability to radio waves that are directed at a receiver implanted in his brain. He shows me hairline scars on his skull. "They did this during my last stay at the V.A.," he says.

His hand returns to the knife. He wants his story told. My objective? Move him out of my office before fresh kill signals are radioed in. First, I feign credible fascination. On a clean yellow legal pad, I transcribe the wild-eyed allegations. I assured the CIA pawn that I would collate his case in my files of similarly afflicted veterans and, once I had compounded all the evidence, present his story as the linchpin in an irrefutable blockbuster exposé. He seemed relieved to learn that he was not alone in his plight. We were friends as I walked him to the elevators and sent him south to the Century City Plaza 38 floors below.

I head back toward the protected environment behind the double safety doors. The receptionist smirks.

"You thought you'd killed me," I said to her. "Better luck next time."

Despite all my cringing on the inside, the Vietnam warrior had never seen me flinch. This gift for bald-faced aplomb had been developed under the sour pressure of *Hustler* cartoon editor Dwaine Tinsley.

The stale blend of Tinsley's cologne-and-tobacco wash usually preceded the arrival of his self-infatuated leer by a few seconds, time enough to blank out all authentic emotion from my face. Time and again, cornered behind my desk by the "cartoon iconoclast," I endured his soliloquies, delivered while the creator of Chester the Molester stood between me and the doorway, blocking my escape. Occasionally Dwaine would invite himself to "take a load off" and sprawl across my office sofa. Maybe Dwaine wore more than one change of clothes over the years, but I picture him in the classics: polyester and creased denim. Tinsley's holding-cell philosophy was expressed in semi-impromptu discourses that repeated common core themes.

"Larry thinks he knows what's funny. Thank God he found me, is all I can say. Any good cartoon he picks is one I suggested. When I do a cartoon edit with Larry, it's like psychological warfare. I stack all the drawings in the sequence I want, and I run a commentary that makes him pick my favorites. The test of a great idea is to make Larry think he thought of it first. Placement is everything.

"Where we situate the cartoons in the magazine, that's a science. Specific material goes on specific pages for specific reasons. I don't expect you could understand all the reasons behind the place-ments. But, Al, you can know that nothing I do is random."

Tinsley intuitively knew that I loathed being called Al. In the kindest of all possible interpretations—not mine—Dwaine didn't realize that he meant any harm. He came up to the offices only when he had unavoidable tasks to perform. More accurately, his pie-baking wife Suzy had tasks to perform in his stead. Dwaine sim-ply could not abide that uneasy feeling of being in the proximity of productivity. If by his example and influence, he could render some-one else useless, if only for an hour, then he had done his bit to make the universe conform to his usage.

I could take advantage of hindsight and claim that ever since I'd witnessed Dwaine's drunken Christmas party pawing of his daugh-ter, daddy Chester creeped me out. The truth is, he creeped me out the moment I met him. Dwaine picked me to endure his lectures because no one who ranked above me would tolerate him. Pretend-ing to take Dwaine Tinsley seriously prepared me to contend with all manner of unstable sociopaths.

Acting creative director Tom Connor's distaste for Tinsley was strongest of anyone's at the company; Tom had known the skeeve longest. Connor would stick his battle-torn face around my door-jamb, having observed Tinsley's exit. "What did we learn from the publishing genius today?" he would ask. His jaw quivered. "One more publishing genius around here, and we're all fucked."

Connor's patchwork of scars—some inflicted by windshields, others in brawls—would whiten with fury within his ruddy com-plexion. He reeled in his outrage and wound tighter every day. Maybe a drink would have helped Connor loosen up, and then Dwaine would have died years ahead of schedule.

The last time I saw Althea Flynt alive, Dwaine Tinsley was lean-ing in my doorway. I had spent the previous 10 minutes trying to picture Dwaine entering unto death, and Althea's ethereal passing at the edge of my sight gave me hope that perhaps I was succeed-ing. Dwaine had been cluttering my work space with self-laudatory plaudits, and had refused to take several hints that it was time for him to go. "Al, buddy," he said, "the artistic perspective is a rare and seldom comprehensible viewpoint."

Althea had seemed like a ghost the previous time I'd seen her, when her wraithlike defiance had inspired me to spike a rival's soda with scabs from my penis. In the intervening time, the remaining meat had been picked from Mrs. Flynt's bones. She could have been wearing a Laura Ashley ensemble, and still she'd have looked like the late lady Keith Richards. Dwaine loped after his benefactor's wife, spewing his treacly "Althea, hon" endearments and sweeping an arm out with the intention of enwrapping her shoulders. Althea said, "If you touch me, I'll scream."

Tinsley stood with his arm in the air, encircling the spot where his ego had been bounding along at his side. I turned away so that he could not be certain I had witnessed this humiliation, and Mrs. Flynt's fragile pins carried her toward her private office.

On a northern corner of the tower, overlooking a lush country club and the handsome, craggy Santa Monica Mountains, Althea's office had been kept intact for many vacant months. Pencils were sharpened and light tables were lit, as if the absentee occupant might swoop in at any moment to reestablish her prominence within the company. I'd stepped out of my office to avoid being boxed in by Dwaine on the rebound. Idle curiosity—of the morbid variety— impelled me to loiter where I could observe Althea. A dire resolve pooled within the depths of her dark eye sockets. Those eyes, sunken and hidden, had a far-seeing quality, focusing way out there on the other side of life. Tom Connor stood to welcome Althea, and she brushed past him. She recognized him as a type, not an individual: He was the type of person who might reasonably expect to be alive six months in the future. The very fact that Althea willed her shell into her office illustrated her grim determination to carry on, a determination to carry her into the next life.

At one time she was the highest-paid female magazine executive in America. Here she sat behind her desk, a spiky head attached to a framework of hollow twigs. She lifted her chin and surveyed her domain with lost black sockets. A hand like parakeet bones reached out for the speakerphone. Her body pitched to the side, her head dropped down, and she vomited into a wastebasket. It looked almost as if her skull had tumbled off of her shoulders and fallen into the trash bucket. Connor went to help her and motioned me away. I returned to my office. Within a few minutes, a female assistant and a man in a suit I didn't know hurried past, and Althea was being propped up as she tottered out of the office. This is the last time I was aware of her stepping foot on the premises. She hadn't even hit her mid-30s.

Once Althea started to deteriorate, corporate legend decreed that she had caught the AIDS bug from a legitimate surgical procedure and not from years of slamming dope in shitholes all across Hollywood. Celebrity profiles referenced a tainted blood transfusion during a hysterectomy at the Century City Hospital, and an oft-repeated quote had Althea insisting, "I don't share needles. I may be a junkie, but I'm a rich junkie. I can afford my own needles."

My question is, where's the stigma in being generous with a needle? Granted, sticking to your own works will provide limited health benefits, for yourself and for others, but there is nothing noble in being a snob about it. Such an attitude is contrary to the *Hustler* way. The overriding editorial imperative at *Hustler* was not to be a snob and never to look down on the little man. We were akin to Jesus in our acceptance of sinners and sluts.

Tough, tightly-wound Connor in particular was Christlike in his willingness to mingle with persons of impaired virtue. He did his best to convert me to his charitable viewpoint. A married couple had contacted him, former lawyers in their early 50s and mid-40s who, in pursuit of an honest living, had purchased a legal brothel parked alongside a desolate stretch of Interstate 80 in the northern wilderness of Nevada. The wife, on the theory that she needed to know the business from the bottom up, had strapped on a mattress and pitched in. Connor insisted that he would do her, given the opportunity. I tried to interpret whether or not this meant he had done her already. Tom had called me into his office to share the good news: I would be traveling to Battle Mountain, Nevada, to research an article on proper behavior in a place of prostitution.

"Cathouse Etiquette: In Which Our Well-Mannered Correspondent Goes to a Bordello and Can't Get Laid," credited to Christian Shapiro, ran in April, 1987. I did not know that I would not get laid when Virginia and Chuck Barrett met me at the Reno, Nevada airport. The Barretts were friendly and happy to see me. He was strong-jawed and keen-eyed, conventionally grayed with a healthy, wind-burned visage. Chuck seemed stocky and solid, maybe because Virginia stood long and lean beside him. Her wavy, reddish hair draped well below her shoulders, lustrous like a college girl's. The Barretts made an attractive pair. I could picture them chairing a meeting at my father's real-estate association.

We bundled into Chuck's tiny propeller plane for the hop from Reno to Battle Mountain. My *Hustler* credentials accorded me the place of honor, up in the copilot's seat. Sitting aft, Virginia offered me a drink. I selected a juice, and looked back out front. A stern row of mountains had risen up from nowhere. Was this to be my end? Splattered like a bug across their severe granite countenance while en route to sport at a godforsaken whorehouse? Neither Chuck or Virginia panicked. I sucked down grape juice and watched as the plane's wheels scraped the ridge.

After they put the plane to bed, the Barretts drove me from one end of Battle Mountain to the other. Their complex boasted two separate brothels, the Desert Club and the Calico Club. Each establishment was constructed of three large trailer homes that had been placed side-by-side and welded into one big domicile. A bar occupied the reception area of both trailer-built contraptions. The girls' rooms and work quarters were scattered behind. One pool of workers serviced both places. When I first met them, the girls—Tracey, Cabelle, Charley, Raven, Valerie and Anna—were bustling around the kitchen table, clearing off remnants of dinner. Anna, a diminutive native of East Los Angeles, had a quick, tentative smile. Cool, lean and black Tracey teased with her playful eyes. From Florida, Cabelle was a mocha-mix with an insolent, droopy gaze. Charley was the bouncy blonde li'l sis of the bunch, not yet outgrown her baby fat. Big, country girl Raven was a chestnut mare of a woman, and Valerie was sleek and urban, more like a racetrack filly.

"You must be hungry," said Virginia.

Chuck stepped up. "We're taking you to the best restaurant in town."

Outside, the wind blew unfettered across the high plains. The sky was distant and brightly starred, and the ground was cold and barren. We ate chicken-fried steaks and meatloaf submerged in thick gravy at a truck stop, the only restaurant in town. Somewhere around the Calico Club's kitchen table, in the presence of the six working girls, I had stopped functioning as a journalist. I should have been asking the Barretts if they'd been swingers before deciding to become whoremongers, and what the kids thought of mom and pop's new venture, but I'd lost my sharpness.

The couple drove me back to their personal trailer to "unwind." Chuck seemed to be telling me that I was welcome to take the proprietress for a free spin. This offer further threw me off my game. Creative Director Connor's plan was for me to remain on the Calico and Desert Club premises for a long weekend and gather my impressions. Virginia Barrett was attractive, preserved, long, pleasant, but I was barely 30 years old. My fantasy pool was stocked with catches my age and one third younger. How would I gracefully explain a lack of arousal? I had no means by which to sneak away in the middle of the night. Virginia suggested I take a seat, and indicated the sofa. Where had Chuck gone? I grabbed a chair. I didn't want to get trapped on the sofa. Was the lighting dimmed to facilitate a mood? Or had the generator stalled? Virginia offered me some expensive alcohol, but booze wouldn't help. I couldn't bring myself to directly address the situation. Eventually, Virginia seemed to arrive at the conclusion that my personal preferences might lie elsewhere. Though crestfallen, she presented me a gift certificate, granting me one tumble with the girl of my choice. On the house. Any additional tumbles could be had at a discount.

Virginia and I walked across the crunching tundra back toward the warm lights of the Calico. Chuck met us at the door. When informed, by a glance, that I had decided to hold out for one of the girls I'd met around the kitchen table, Chuck's visible disappointment was identical to what I'd seen Virginia display.

In fact, I don't know what the hell was really going on up there on Battle Mountain. In possession of a cathouse gift certificate, I admonished myself to use it wisely. Which lucky gal would be the one for me? Wearing their on-duty lingerie, the ladies of the houses clustered around a CB radio and took turns luring in truckers with promises of free showers and no-pressure conviviality.

"Breaker 1-9," said country cousin Raven. "Who's ready for that coffee break and shower? This is Sweet Pea at the Desert Club."

"I'm ready for a pussy break," crackled a white-line wit.

"Lord, I hate crude people."

In the background, Jane Fonda's prostitute flick, *Klute*, played on a cracked portable television. I lurked at the bar while the independent contractors socialized and waited for a long-haul pilot to come in. The girls worked in 10-day or two-week shifts, on call 24 hours a day. In a way, doing a stint was like a short prison term, but the inmates kept a good face. The bartender had been one of the favorite bed laborers on the premises, but had fallen in love and now only worked pouring drinks. She passed a hand in front of my blank gaze.

"What will you have?"

"Give me a grapefruit juice and club soda."

"One of each?"

"Mixed."

"What does that do for you?"

Tracey, the lean, teasing black girl, drew me into a game of poker dice. We played at penny stakes for more than an hour. She had a lazy smile, easy eyes and a cute space between her two front teeth. She filled in the rules of the house: "If a girl drops a cigarette or money on the floor, it stays there. Money on the floor is money out the door; kick it aside. A cigarette can be stepped on three times, walked around, then picked up. Otherwise, leave it down there for good luck. No cut roses in the room. Change is never picked up."

About eight grapefruit juice and sodas into the night, I croaked out that I'd like to visit in Tracey's room. She acted surprised and flattered that I had chosen her, which enhanced my ease. Tracey's room was only big enough for a surprisingly narrow bed, with a bureau beside it and a washstand at its foot. Frilly curtains closed off a window that looked to the pitch-black outside. A few framed family photos stood on Tracey's dresser, and a pair of plush animals hugged one another upon her pillow.

Tracey had me stand and drop my pants at the washbasin. She looked up from the bed, smiled grimly and gripped my penis, pulling it to either side. She rinsed out a fresh cloth and washed me down.

"Wait a minute," she said. "What's that?"

She'd spied a bump, an eruption so small and far back on my groin that my immediate impulse was to argue it was not there.

"I don't know what the fuck that is," I said. But I knew. My Century City specialist had wielded his wart-searing liquid oxygen and assured me I was clear! I thought I had known humiliation before. Tracey began washing her hands with surgical quality soap. Steam rose from the basin as she scrubbed. This *molluscum* pimple was a leftover from the outbreak that had provided me the scabs I'd put into a rival editor's Dr. Pepper.

Once her hands were cleansed and dried, Tracey was sympathetic, but firm. I was cowed, or I might have asked to at least see her naked. We went back to playing poker dice at the bar, and my embarrassment soon wore off. Hearing of my plight, the other girls wanted to see what my particular taint looked like. These women expected me to expose myself in what was more or less a place of business. For the next half an hour, they insisted that nothing could make them happier than to gaze upon my personal parts. Reluctantly, I lowered my pants in the bar and pulled out my unit. The working staff all crowded around on their knees, in their public lingerie, placing their faces down below my scrotum to peer up at the tiny viral bump. Somehow, their scrutiny—nonjudgmental and sympathetic—made me feel comfortable with my penis and my sexuality and myself—with who I was at my core—in a deeper, more profound way than I ever had before. So that ended okay. Not that everything does.

On page six of the October 1987 *Hustler* is a cartoon drawing of a urinal and toilet stall, provided and placed by Dwaine Tinsley. A fractured graffiti rhyme scrawled upon the toilet stall reads: "A tisket a tasket / Better use a condom / Or they'll bring you / Home in a casket."

Facing this cautionary poem is a full-page photo of Althea Flynt, paying tribute to her life, bearing the inscription IN LOVING MEMORY 1953–1987. Althea, weakened by narcotics and the AIDS virus, had drowned in her bath water during June of that year. Her commemorative page had been rushed into the October issue. The specific reasons behind the specific placement of the memorial photo and the adjacent doggerel were beyond my understanding, but as Dwaine had said: "Al, you can know that nothing I do is random."

In November, Larry Flynt's birthday rolled around. There would be no dual celebration this year. The editorial and business staffs assembled in a wide hallway just inside the double security doors. Forewarned of Flynt's approach, we huddled around a giant cake placed upon the empty desk of a fired editorial assistant. Larry's chair, golden and gripped by a towering black handler, eased in through the doors. "Surprise!" shouted the crowd.

Flynt might have been startled, but the reaction would be a long time reaching his inert, pained face. The trickster Larry who had announced his Presidential bid in an animated mockery of government and media was long gone. A slumping mass filled the chair, Humpty Dumpty put back together again—but with a million-dollar dope habit. I tried to meet Flynt's gaze as he rolled toward the celebratory cake. His flat eyes gave almost nothing back. Still, I sensed Larry far below the surface, sedated and stationary in the silt at the deep bottom.

The birthday well-wishers stirred and twittered. The stripper had arrived. Typical of her breed, she was falsely buxom and topped with a helmet of brassy hair. The dancer moved with the grace of a second-string tackle. She plunked her cassette player on the desktop next to the cake and pressed play. Strip bar music blared out, and her big hips swung into action. She spanked her ass, twisted her neck, stuck out her tongue and salivated on her behind. The crowd cheered. A lane formed in the surrounding mob—leaving the stripper at one end and Larry at the other. Flynt's wheels were locked. He had nowhere to roll. Dwaine Tinsley leered, and his wife Suzy clapped her chubby hands. The chunky stripper flittered up to widower Larry, reversed herself and straddled the chair. Planting a foot firmly at each golden-spoked wheel, she leaned forward and thrust her buttocks toward the birthday boy's face. Her G-string wavered as she humped her hindquarters in Larry's chest. Nodding under the weight of the most powerful narcotics money can buy, Flynt denied the downward pull and lifted his quivering chin away from the stripper's satin-flossed anus. She lowered her can onto Larry's unfeeling, paralyzed, hopelessly limp lap.

Larry's mouth twisted, and his eyes tightened, sending a message up from the bottom of his pool. He was furious. Oddly enough, nobody in the hand-clapping, jeering throng seemed to sense that their boss was exuding a buzz-killing rancor. After the stripper squeezed out her high-volume, low-credibility orgasm, circulated among the onlookers soliciting tips and slithered away, the bodyguard stepped forward and wheeled Larry toward the privacy of his office. Flynt smeared at blotches of red lipstick planted on his face. The makeup could be daubed clean with a damp cloth; the smoldering malevolence would be harder to wipe off.

One introspective Saturday night, I shared a love seat with Frankie at a coffeehouse just south of the Hollywood city limits. The place was reputed to be frequented by Madonna. Frankie and I, in the full flush of our second round, had been fight-free for a month or more. Sitting next to my sparkle-eyed, black-haired girlfriend, I concluded we were the most attractive couple in the place. The urge to confide welled up in me, coinciding with the rush from my double cappuccino.

"Don't you want to ask me something?" Frankie said. Her smile was a blast of encouragement, as if she were a foreign language instructress, and I were a pupil of whom she had grown inordinately fond. Her sweet, pantomiming lips were trying to coax an exact and correct phrase out of me, but I had other things on my mind.

"I'm happy being the editor of *Chic*," I said, "but I know that I'm the guy for *Hustler*. They're going to make a change at *Hustler*. I sense it."

Disappointment clouded Frankie's fine-boned brow.

"Why can't you be happy with *Chic*?"

"I want to be lord of all things LFP," I said. "The company should have half a dozen sex magazines, niche books like for popular fetishes, and I should be in charge of them all. I could make enough money to buy a house."

Frankie seemed unaccountably discouraged. At the mention of purchasing a home, her lips plumped up in annoyance. She tried to maintain the façade of benign interest. "What's your first step?"

"It wouldn't hurt if Larry Flynt somehow realized I was alive."

"I know how you feel," she said. "Why don't you take me into consideration with your house-buying plans?"

Driving back to my place, Frankie became very British and high-toned. She went home without coming in, and I was left alone to mope and mull. How would Larry Flynt ever notice me?

Tom Connor arranged the introductions. He tapped me to interview *Hustler*'s founder and publisher for the 15th anniversary issue ("Larry Flynt: Hear Him Now," July, 1989), a little less than two years after Althea's death. I drove up the winding ascent of Doheny Drive, into the hills above the Sunset Strip. Flynt's house was set high among the weave of bird-named streets where George Harrison had written "Blue Jay Way." Obeying protocol that had been dictated by Larry's secretary, I knocked at a side door that opened to the service porch. James, the monolithic, black and casually friendly bodyguard, led the way through a laundry. Two bulked-up German shepherds abandoned their vigilance at the dryer and prodded me forward with their snouts, shoving me into the living room. Antiques and *objets d'art* that Larry had accumulated during manic European buying sprees cluttered the floor space. The shepherds and I maneuvered along a narrow footpath through thickets of Tiffany lamps. We cleared the most congested area, and James shooed the dogs away. He knocked at an open bedroom door and stepped inside.

"Allan's here," he said. Did this mean that Larry knew my name?

A brunette woman, shy of 40, boldly dressed in a sheer, form-fitting skirt and blouse, bustled from the room on heels that were steeper than modesty would permit. The brunette clutched a palette of fabric swatches. James ushered me forward.

The boss sat propped up in bed. The tight lapels of a green silk robe were pulled close to his neck, setting off the yellow-emerald glimmer of his hooded eyes. Larry's face had fleshed up since the gaunt prison days, filling out in a meaty, broadly pleased, vaguely preoccupied look. His attention seemed to be monopolized by a big, muted TV tuned to a news channel. I moved forward and introduced myself. Larry returned my handshake with hardly discernible enthusiasm. His chin indicated a chair beside the bed. I sat there and set up my notepad and tape recorder. The brunette woman breezed back in. She stood on her tiptoes whipping a tape measure across the width and height of the bedroom windows. Sunlight streamed in and profiled her hips and bust through her sheer blouse and skirt. Larry's eyes lazily but thoroughly observed the play of shadow and skin. He caught me looking.

"I hope you've brought some tough questions," he said. "I don't want you to be a pussy."

"We'll do our best."

"You'd better test that tape recorder. What would we do if it wasn't working?"

I rewound the tape to play back. The brunette grinned in passing and twisted out again. Larry replicated the contour of her haunches with his gem-encrusted fingers. "That interior designer?" He lifted a glass of water. Ice cubes rattled with the shaking of his hand. "I'm banging her."

Maybe I appeared skeptical. After all, paraplegia tends to crimp even the most ardent womanizer. Larry laughed, and his green eyes sparkled. He set his drink down without spilling, a miracle. Oddly enough, I could picture the designer lady going for him. I switched the tape back to record, and Larry revealed how he had come to realize that he still had sexual feeling. He'd been lying on his belly, watching a porno on the same big TV that was muted behind me, half dozing. Larry claimed that a series of multiple orgasms had brought him abruptly awake. "I reached down, and there was cum all over my legs, up by my thighs. But I was only partly hard."

Thus encouraged, the man who "used to screw 18 to 20 women a week" had sought out a specialized urologist who sold him on a penile implant, the top-of-the-line model. Two silicone rods had been inserted into Larry's corpora cavernosa, the paired venous chambers within the penis that are essential to erectile function. Larry needed only to squeeze a subcutaneous bulb, and the cavities filled. Through applied bio-hydraulics no woman was safe from the Flynt charm. I congratulated Larry on his good fortune. He furrowed his brow as though considering offering me a chance to view the thing. Before Larry could make up his mind, James stuck his head into the room.

"Ruben's on the phone," said James.

"I'll take that," said Larry.

I didn't have to ask, "Ruben who?" Ruben Sturman had been the target of federal probes for decades. Originally an operator out of Cleveland, purportedly mob-backed and firebomb-tested though never convicted as such, Sturman was one of the biggest porn catches on the FBI's wish list. Years after this conversation, the smut pioneer would be locked up for tax crimes, escape from prison and be recaptured. Just being in the same room while someone else talked to Ruben Sturman might result in a co-conspirator charge.

"Should I wait outside?" I said.

Larry waved a dismissive hand and wedged the phone between shoulder and ear. "Yeah, Ruben," he said. "Sure, I feel pretty good except for the fucking you gave me yesterday." Larry's dissatisfaction had to do with a price negotiated for bulk repackaging of unsold copies of *Hustler*. Despite the fiscal pain, Flynt retained a cheerful air, I suppose due to ruminating upon his penile implant. If the mechanism had been operating two years sooner, he might have been more welcoming to that birthday stripper.

After he hung up on Ruben, Larry seemed open for anything. I reminded him of the day he had been rolled through the LFP offices after being released from the Federal Correctional Complex at Butner, North Carolina. He'd been imprisoned at Butner for contempt. When they'd let him out, his legs had been in casts.

"How in fuck did you manage to break your legs?" I asked. "I mean, it's not like you could have tripped and fallen down the stairs."

He laughed fondly, at himself. "I have problems with authority ... You'd think I could learn to get along."

He'd had a particular problem with an ungentle Butner medic who took delight in abrasively cleaning Larry's bedsores. Larry expressed his displeasure by chomping down on the guy's thumb and nearly biting it off. Federal marshals hurried in to subdue the patient. In their haste, they broke his legs. Larry savored the memory, clearly as impressed as I was by his cursed obstinance.

While the boss gloated, hulking James carried in a huge strawberry shortcake on a tray. The dessert was drenched in raspberry sauce and had been driven up in Larry's burgundy Rolls-Royce from Michel Richard Patisserie on the outskirts of Beverly Hills. This was the rich life. James set the tray and the entire cake across Larry's lap. Flynt's arms encircled the five-story confection. "I hope you brought some for Allan," he said.

"We saved a tiny piece for him." James glided out and returned with my slice—about a third of a cake balanced on a platter. The stack of glaze and strawberries tumbled sideways as I perched the plate on my thighs. I've never liked strawberries, but what could I do? I took a bite, and sweetness rushed through my body. There were another 50 mouthfuls to go.

The cake deepened Larry's mellow mood. He forked chunks of pastry and candy-coated fruit into his mouth, working his jaws in a circular motion. Strawberry juice seeped down his chin. Bliss spread across his wide face. He gave me a conspiratorial squint and surrendered to a luxurious garrulity. My boss confided that he might be married again, sooner than anyone would have predicted. He unraveled a story about traveling in Thailand and meeting a 12-year-old Thai virgin. If I heard him right, and could believe what he said, he'd trekked up-country, made the acquaintance of the girl's parents, met her extended family and won their approval.

Won or bought? My mouth chewed, and I drifted out on a short-cake cloud, only eight bites into my snack.

Larry claimed to have plans for this preteen virgin, a scheme that he assured me his lawyers had guaranteed was airtight. Rather than bring her directly to Los Angeles, the wheelchair-bound groom would take his child bride to the Central American nation of Belize, where the age of marital consent was said to be the lowest in the western hemisphere. Once legally wed, Flynt asserted with a gleam, he would be free to return to L.A. and set up a household with the new Mrs. He licked a stray pink crumb from his lips.

Let me hasten to point out that these nuptials never came to pass. Larry, let's be realistic, was fucking with me. As Flynt concluded his story of Thai romance, I rose out of a sugar crash and realized that my recorder had shut off. The tape had run out. My mind posed two questions: How long had the tape been off? And had Larry known the tape was off? Before switching cassettes, I quickly back-checked and determined that my audio had cut out precisely when the strawberry shortcakes had arrived. I looked up to see Larry openly smirking at me.

"Always be prepared," he said.

There was no point in asking him to run through his pedophile bombshell again. Career advancement at LFP, on the basis of bonding with the boss in sugar indulgence, didn't look good. Feeling doomed and queasy, I asked if there was anything our conversation had missed, if there was any message Larry would like to give.

"Yeah," he growled. "Don't be a nerd."

I rose to leave, trying to project any image other than dork, geek or dweeb.

Larry called after me, "Hey, and Allan? Next time you go out to do an interview, bring some tough questions."

Hustler Bits & Pieces

ACCORDING TO CLICHÉ and the recognized geniuses of cinema and literature, satire is best wielded like a rapier, used to carve up deserving targets with finesse and precision. Pointed humor is a high-minded wit's deftly drawn equalizer. The lordly buffoon, the self-satisfied fraud, the common hypocrite, the professional prig and the raging demagogue, all are susceptible to the swift blade of finely-honed irony. These same louts are also vulnerable to the blunt trauma of bludgeoning parody as applied by *Hustler*'s "Bits & Pieces" section, where over-hyped personages of the day are commonly portrayed with invasive genitals grafted upon their likenesses.

Celebrity bashing—it's one vice the common man can indulge that celebrities are discouraged from dabbling in. At Larry Flynt Publications, an ambitious editor gains nothing by sucking up to publicists and courting the hot actress of the month. Even the smuttiest of mainstream personalities flinches at stooping to *Hustler* level. Comedian Andrew "Dice" Clay, widely admired for characterizing persons from the sub-Asian continent as "urine-colored," developed scruples rather than voluntarily appearing in America's Magazine. If Dice was worried that *Hustler* exposure might tarnish his image, imagine the trepidation of all those famous people who aren't scumbags.

We in Larry Flynt's bullpen resented being shunned by the exalted media stars. We envied their privilege and riches. Admittedly, we were small-minded, insignificant and malicious, but did no other media outlet recognize that celebrity fixation had reached pathological and epidemic proportions on the American airwaves and newsstands? The *Hustler* brain trust felt an imperative to teach, to illuminate, to provide a dissenting wail in the vast chorus of groundless approbation that awards greater value to name recognition than to actual achievement.

Fame-inflated egos are such easy and gratifying targets. To resist pricking them is futile. In the May 6, 1994 London *Times*, then-wed Richard Gere and Cindy Crawford financed a full-page open letter to assert their "basic rights to privacy," to flaunt their support of "difficult" causes such as AIDS research and treatment, and to admonish the media to be "responsible, truthful and kind." *Hustler* lashed out appropriately ("A Personal Statement to Richard Gere and Cindy Crawford," December, 1994). Our response read, in part: "Fuck you. You buy up valuable space meant for real news to announce that you do not plan to divorce and will not stop your lucrative participation in some of the most insipid entertainment ever foisted upon a gullible and chronically disappointed public. No one gives a shit about you.

"You demand your right of privacy when you've devoted your lives to getting your fat faces on as many magazine covers and in as many shitty movies as possible instead of, say, working as missionaries in Tibet. So fuck you again."

All of this firing-at-will came with a price: The "Bits & Pieces" Curse. The Curse was first noticed by a cheeky editorial assistant, Kristen. Reasonably stable and well-adjusted, she had moved to Los Angeles from Pennsylvania to find work in the public relations sector of her academic major. The content of *Hustler* offended and saddened her. She tried not to impose her values on those of us who had none. One day, Kristen stepped to my office, asked for a private moment and quietly enquired: "Why do celebrities keep dying after you jokers make fun of them?"

"You're exaggerating," I said. She would move on soon, and I would not miss her. Although an affable and efficient worker, she was prone to stretching the unpleasant truth. Considering the vast number of glossy faces mocked in "Bits & Pieces," only a slight percentage had died.

Lady Diana Spencer provided the most prominent and troublesome Curse fatality. A "Bits & Pieces" writer had posed Di as a

spokesperson promoting a spurious brand of purge-inducing pota-
to chips ("What Will the World's Most Beautiful Bulimics Be Wearing
This Year?" November, 1997). A photo of the grinning princess was
pasted onto a stunt body clothed in streaks of self-triggered vomit.
This gag appeared on newsstands mere days after Lady Spencer's
August 31, 1997 vehicular demise.

Mild shame colored the next editorial brainstorm. One wistful
editor lamented that if the car-crash princess had been equipped
with gigantic fake boobs, like the porn stars wear, the augmented
bust may have functioned as a backup air-bag at the time of impact.
Within a quarter-hour, an inhumanly large pair of breasts were
superimposed upon an image of the miraculously saved princess.
She clutched a severed steering wheel in one hand and waved to
her subjects with the other. The headline read: "If Princess Di Had
Dow Implants, She Would Be Alive Today" (January, 1998).

Occasionally, staff meetings stalled out. Stumped editors
would gaze at ceilings, temporarily empty of bile or inspiration,
unable to meet one another's eyes. We all were given the chance to
stop and ponder, *Will the "B&P" Curse someday claim me?*

Of course it would; it already had. Once an idea for a cruel joke
presented itself, no matter how abominable, we were powerless to
resist carrying it out. This involuntary rush toward indefensible
humor was in itself a curse, a bane endured by each of us who
labored in the service of *Hustler*'s "Bits & Pieces."

CHAPTER 9

Top Dog on Slime Mountain

AT AGE 33, I had entered the LFP arena six years earlier and had expected every intervening day to be fired. But somebody, presumably Larry Flynt, had noticed a decline in the quality of *Hustler* and a corresponding improvement in the content of my magazine, *Chic*. I was bumped up to the top job at *Hustler*.

All I've ever wanted out of this life is to be a big shot. Prominence and acclaim, I believe in my heart, are rightfully mine. I feel underdressed any time I leave the house without them. But masthead eminence brought immediate problems. In October 1990, five days before Halloween, an outraged convenience store owner from Norman, Oklahoma, was forwarded to my phone.

"What were you thinking?" he yelled. "Where's your brain when you print these things?"

"What precisely are you talking about?"

"That article, that 'Mayhem Manuals.'"

The December 1990 *Hustler* contained a feature, "Mayhem Manuals: Killer Prose," that examined a burgeoning genre of do-it-yourself nonfiction—readily available survivalist primers that taught the rudiments of kitchen-sink explosives, improvised land mines, urban ambush, easy-to-mix poisons, killing people.

"Right," I said. "We ran that piece to stimulate an informed debate. We're not saying these materials should or should not be afforded First Amendment protection, we're merely suggesting a discussion."

"You haven't heard what happened to the kid."

"What kid?"

The text of the article quoted a passage from Richard W. Krousher's *Physical Interrogation Techniques* (Loompanics), giving instructions in popping out a detainee's eyeball so that the orb hangs functioning on the subject's cheek, unable to blink or look away as, "for example, you mutilate his genitals."

An eight-year-old Norman boy had been found semiconscious with his eyeball hanging on his cheek. It was unclear whether or not his genitals had been mutilated. The local sheriff was seeking a court order to pull the magazine off all store shelves in his jurisdiction.

"I can't tell you how I feel," I said to the store owner. Was I supposed to have anticipated this?

"We can't keep defending you guys if you're going to do this shit."

I had no answer for him.

Flynt's attorneys arranged a transfer of subscriber information to the FBI. The assault had occurred prior to the December issue's November 1st newsstand on-sale date, but after subscription copies had been mailed out. If the assailant had in fact followed the directions as seen in "Mayhem Manuals," he was a *Hustler* regular. Compared to what this phantom subscriber had done to that poor kid, I was relatively unscathed. Company executives, my shrink, lawyers and law enforcement had all assured me I was innocent of the crimes committed against that eight-year-old. All I'd lost was my pride at being appointed *Hustler*'s guiding voice.

I replaced Oliver, but he continued to make more money than I did, and he was hanging on to a large corner office. Walking the halls, on my way to the vending machines or to the bathroom, I felt scummy, underappreciated and stopgap.

A few crafty players, hedging their bets on the off chance that my promotion might endure, offered me special deference. Dwaine Tinsley made a show of speaking to me as if we were equals, and my name was near the top of the guest list for the *Rip* magazine anniversary party at the Hollywood Palladium.

Flynt launched *Rip* in the mid-'80s as a hair-rock fan book. Pearl Jam and speed thrashers Motörhead were among the anniversary headliners. Raven-haired Frankie and I, although living separately, arrived at the Palladium riding the special high that comes from possessing free passes to a sold-out event. Scraggly entrepreneurs badgered us for extra tickets as we walked through the parking lot. A blonde Valley kid with a red bandanna wrapped around his mullet sat in the passenger seat of a parked monster truck, the door open. He abruptly pitched sideways and efficiently puked in the slot between him and the next vehicle.

Frankie wore a rubberized stretch dress that clung to her long, narrow voluptuousness. Flat-heeled suede boots rose up over her knees. We stood in line to be searched at the entrance, and I gauged that Frankie might be a tad overdressed. Jeans and sneakers predominated on both genders. Off-duty Neanderthals patted us down, and we worked through the crush of rockers in the lobby.

I peeled off from Frankie and into the bathroom. Washing my hands, I stood next to a 20-year-old stick man. His hair dyed black and his face a pasty green, he stared into the mirror, sucking his cheeks between his teeth, drawing his fingers under his eyes, deeply regarding his pinned pupils. He abruptly leaned forward and puked into the sink. He straightened back up, took a deep breath, and walked out. I joined Frankie on the auditorium floor as some Seattle band, not Pearl Jam, played its wailful dirge. Two rows of tables flanked the main floor, and I wondered if seating had been reserved for *Hustler*'s new executive editor. I steered Frankie toward the booths. A girl in her 30s sat at a stage-side table and smoked a cigarette with an exaggerated nonchalance. She coolly leaned to her side and vomited beneath the table. She dabbed at her mouth and reapplied a line of blood-red lipstick. It was good to see that rock 'n' roll was still alive and vital, like it had been during my *Slash* magazine heydays.

The booths were all taken. Few, if any, of the girls in the capacity-crowded auditorium were as attractive as Frankie, who shimmered within the black cocoon of her form-fitting dress and over-the-knee boots. But then, all the other girls, bursting at the seams of their jeans and sneakers, were in fact not Frankie.

"I know what you're looking at," said Frankie.

"I'm trying to find Larry Flynt."

Bodyguard James' dark head and broad shoulders loomed above the head-banging mob.

"There he is."

Big black James pushed Larry's golden-spoked conveyance into the throng. Larry wheeled past a scraggy ring of well-wishers, his face blank. Frankie had never met the man who signed my checks. Here was her opportunity to dazzle and solidify my standing with the boss. James, who controlled access to the publisher, ushered Frankie and me to the chair and introduced us as "Allan, the guy who's running *Hustler*."

He raised his head. The cogs moved behind his eyes. Could he have forgotten that afternoon we shared in gluttonous bliss, gobbling strawberry shortcake? For about half a minute, Larry tried to focus and filter the information given by James. Frankie and I leaned forward, hands outstretched, like two beggars being denied alms. Then Larry turned toward the bodyguard. At some sign invisible to anyone else, James stepped forward with a ready syringe, opened the neck of Larry's shirt and fired an injection into the fixture planted in the boss' chest. Before he could turn his pie face back toward us, Larry nodded.

Back at the office, any meeting with Larry had the potential to end abruptly at injection time. Shortly before he resigned screaming, Connor shot out from a closed-door discussion with Flynt tight-fisted and fuming.

"You know what's fucked?" said Connor. "When the shit wears off, Humpty will remember all of what he half-told me before he plunged into netherland, and he'll fire my ass because the whole job's not done."

During crucial phone conversations, Larry's dope diction might slip at any second into a growling gurgle that bore only the vaguest relation to human language. I once asked the head *Hustler* to repeat himself for clarification.

"What's the matter?" Flynt had demanded, suddenly cleanly audible. "Cain't you fuckin' hear?"

I refrained from giving the first answer that sprang to mind.

Off duty, my girlfriend and I had degenerated to the miasma stage of conflict. Our bickering had grown insufferable even for our therapist. Doctor Joan—exquisitely cultured, rust-blonde—suggested that Frankie and I might better advance if we split up for separate sessions. Joan opted to stay on my case and refer Frankie to an "entirely competent" colleague. Frankie had accepted this news calmly and graciously, agreeing that individual work might fastest move the relationship forward. On the elevator down to the parking lot, she stewed. "What can you say in front of her alone that you can't say in front of me?"

"I don't know, baby. Don't you think you'd be more open if I wasn't sitting there?"

"I've been open."

The ride back to my place was rough, though largely silent. Frankie and I were better off taking separate cars, no matter where we went. She invited herself in, prowled my apartment and, as if by chance, happened upon a stack of my feature-writing clips. Her shuffle through the photocopies was a little too practiced, and her exultant reading aloud of my choice pronouncements rang of rehearsal. "'A man's penis is the antenna to his soul.' ['The *Hustler* Liar's Manual,' April, 1991.] The problem with you, Allan, is that you believe this shit you write."

"I'm messing around. I'm only kidding."

"Everything's a joke to you. Me and you, you're just kidding about us, right?"

She'd gone British in tone. "Where else are you messing around? Who are you messing around with? Will you be fucking that shrink next?"

Frankie balled her fists and ripped my feature clips lengthwise. She shredded the strips and tossed fluttering squares of paper to the ceiling. The confetti of shame whirled down around my head. My beautiful love raged at full volume. I tuned out the specific words. The landlady would come knocking in the morning. We went to bed about 3 a.m. (Frankie had the next day off.) I remained awake and vigilant. Where would I ever rest? The workplace was a trickster maze.

The company had been moved from the silver towers of Century City to a squat five-story block two miles east on Wilshire Boulevard. Dwaine Tinsley intermittently roamed the offices, dispensing sagacity and smarm. Exercising my executive privilege, I killed a full-page cartoon for space considerations. I hadn't expected anyone to notice the deletion of this superfluous page, but Tinsley's snarky smile oozed around the corner of my doorway.

"I hope I'm not troubling you, Mr. Executive Editor." Here Tinsley mocked me with a tip of the phantom hat. "Might I beg a moment of your valuable time?"

The trouble with America, I reflected, was that if I were to shoot this man dead, chances are a jury of my peers would convict me of a crime. Dwaine sprawled on my sofa, sucked at a tooth, rolled his eyeballs toward the ceiling and forthrightly insisted that Larry Flynt would notice and object if the cartoon quotient was short by one in any particular issue of the magazine. "Next time you're missing a cartoon," he said, "I don't know if I'll be able to protect you."

Personally, I doubted Larry would notice if his proper quotient of limbs was one short on any given drug-haze day, unless some helpful soul were to point out the discrepancy to him. I thanked Dwaine for watching my back.

In the middle months of 1990, a string of letters arrived from Jerry F. Stanley, a Death Row resident of California's San Quentin Prison. Stanley had been convicted of murdering his wife, twice. The first spouse he'd slain as a volatile young man in 1975, having caught her partially clothed in a parked automobile with one of his male friends. Jerry happened to have a pistol in hand at the time of this surprise. He pleaded out on manslaughter charges and spent three years in a minimum-security center. His three kids from that aborted marriage could not have been pleased when Stanley was arrested in 1981 for the murder of a second wife.

Bargaining out was not an option for the two-time uxoricide, and upon conviction he received a sentence of death. Stanley claimed to have tired of waiting for the state to schedule his execution. In his letters he promised to forgo all further appeals and to be put down at the first possible opportunity. He extended a front-row gas chamber invitation. I felt duty-bound to accept and arranged an interview with Stanley so that *Hustler*'s readers could get to know the man before we said goodbye to him ("Dead Man Talking: A View From the Gas Chamber," January, 1991).

For two hours in May of 1990, Stanley was allowed off of Death Row in the presence of three prison officials for two hours of questioning. An LFP lawyer and I had flown up to San Francisco late the previous afternoon and checked into a luxury Union Square hotel. My room had Egyptian linens, several telephones and a television in the bathroom. In the morning, I reviewed my questions for the condemned inmate while my attorney and I brunched on scones and farm-fresh omelets. The drive across the bridge was unrushed, with spectacular views. San Quentin Prison is nestled on a promontory jutting into the bay. Tidy rows of single-family cottages are clustered outside the penitentiary, with a view of the San Francisco skyline across the water. Sleek and bulky hawks circled and perched along the shoreline. No price would be too high for a piece of this real estate, except for the price paid by the men crowded behind the San Quentin walls.

We checked in at an admissions shack and submitted to a metal detector and a pat-down search. The lawyer had secured permission to bring in a tape recorder. A public liaison officer met us on the inside of the guard shed. Medium height and superiorly rigid in her posture, she spoke in a thick Scot's accent. Her vocation had been corrections for several years in South Africa before coming to America. She explained that the homes adjacent to the facility were largely occupied by prison staff, assuring me that the inmates walking among these homes in prison denim were in fact trustees responsible for general maintenance of the area and not escapees.

She escorted us past the gates into the prison proper. Looking in through a further set of bars, I sensed tiers forming in a vast hall of pain and irritation. A draft blew out as from the tomb, cold and fetid and unforgiving. I had neglected to mention to the LFP lawyer that two years earlier, when I was a mere features editor, I had conducted an interview with a former San Quentin guard, William Yount. In a gory exposé ("Prison Guard Tells All," February, 1989), Yount had seemed to implicate San Quentin brass in setting up would-be whistle blowers to be killed by psycho prisoners. This story was why I requested accompaniment by a lawyer in the first place. Once we'd stepped inside the walls, the limits of legal representation became obvious and unsettling. Wilding alpha energy ricocheted within the stone edifice. The posture of our public liaison officer remained perfectly rigid under this testosterone onslaught, and every single hulking guard or convict we encountered extended absolute respect to her.

"We'll be conducting the interview in this room to the right," she said.

Within moments, Jerry Stanley joined us in the utility room. He wore regulation denim accented with shackles and chains and was accompanied by two guards. We did not shake hands. The conversation took place from opposite sides of a wide, long table. The condemned was tight-lipped during the interview, his replies terse. The LFP lawyer sat at my side as I asked the killer about remorse, God, hell and sex behind bars. Tall, pale and graying, Stanley looked out through clear, blue eyes that darted and fastened. Despite his short-bitten sentences, the interview went smoothly. At the end, I asked: "Is there a moral to your story?"

"Sure. Don't lose your temper. It sure as hell isn't worth it."

Maybe three years following publication of my Tori Welles article, I had wrangled backstage access to an Aerosmith after-concert party when Frankie and I were a couple once more. We'd sworn off one another on at least three occasions, but had always slithered back together. I was impressed by how great we paired up in the midst of all those record-company lifers and Aerosmith hangers-on. The crowd paled in comparison to us, until porn star Tori Welles waltzed in on the arm of some dangerous-looking guy.

Welles passed within inches of my feckless smile and failed to recognize me as being remarkable from any other disposable mook. Perhaps Tori remembered the insulting content of my *Chic* article, but she'd become oblivious to me as a person. Frankie, however, had honed her ability to read my emotional weather.

"Who's that girl?" Frankie said. "What did you do with her?"

Life might have been easier if Tori and her boyfriend had simply shivved me. Frankie drove back to my place from the Forum auditorium in silence. She pulled her Mustang to the curb in front of my apartment, a one-bedroom dump on the flat outskirts of Beverly Hills, where three BHPD black-and-whites had their crimson roof lights flashing. Evidently, a car had been burglarized in the alley behind my apartment. A crime-scene investigation van drove up to join the black-and-whites. Innumerable cops kept passing through my field of vision, which was constricted by the silent accusations of Frankie's face. Frankie was beautiful, whether asleep or eating, watching a movie or flossing her teeth. And she was never more attractive than when she was furious. I dared not break eye contact. If I glanced off, even for the seconds it would take to tally the cops, she might take advantage of my relaxed vigilance and poke out my wandering eye.

"Why do you insist upon humiliating me?" Frankie said, reverting to a broadly posh English accent.

"I don't know what you're talking about," I said. The red of the police lights bathed her face in a wash of hysteria. She hit me, right on the nose. Her fist flew out again and landed directly on the button.

"Ouch! Why did you do that?"

"Don't play stupid." She pronounced the word *stupid* as though she were some villainous character played by Malcolm McDowell. Her fists came in a flailing rain. I deflected as much as I could. It's not like she packed a knockout punch. But she sure looked great.

"Get the fuck out of my car," she ordered, suddenly calm. I groped for the door handle and lost sight of her momentarily, which allowed her to lunge and clamp her hands around my neck.

"I should kill you," she shouted. Finally, she didn't look so good. The police lights had baffled me, but I became lucid, suddenly and uncharacteristically. I could easily break her grip if I were to shove her away or swat her arms. Then she could just as easily summon a policeman and claim that I had belted her with no provocation. The night had already descended a great deal from its apex during Aerosmith's encore. Was it destined to bottom out with me in jail? My breathing came harder with each gasp, and my head was throbbing. Frankie could squeeze much harder than she could punch.

A clank sounded on the car's passenger window, right behind my head. Frankie abruptly unhanded me, clasped herself and doubled over, bawling. I marveled at how adroitly the tears appeared. I rolled down the passenger side window. A cop stood there. His giant hand pinched my shoulder, softly. He bent down and spoke gently into my ear.

"Are you okay in here?" he said.

I entered my apartment under police escort, assuring the officers that Frankie had been only playing out a role.

Once I'd been to San Quentin and back, and choked by Frankie, only a select few at LFP were capable of spooking me. Jimmy Flynt, for instance. Larry's younger brother walked tall and broad. His bulk quivered within an aura of contained violence. I'd never heard of Jimmy harming so much as a flea. He cornered me during a party at Larry's house. I'd felt conspicuous in a crowd of wide-tie out-of-town distributors and family friends. Suddenly, the decks had shifted, and loose cannon Jimmy rolled my way. He held a drink, and his big finger poked me in the collarbone. "Do you think Dwaine Tinsley is funny?" he asked.

Was it a trick question? My mouth stopped short.

"I just don't think he's funny anymore," said Jimmy. He swirled his ice cubes. "He used to be funny. But he doesn't know funny from his ass."

I was afraid that Jimmy might broach the subject of what to do about Dwaine. Luckily, before Jimmy and I could advance to the proactive stage of the discussion, Larry was rolled into range. Larry made a sound like the clearing of phlegm.

"I wanted to talk to you about that too," said Jimmy. He fell in step with the golden chair.

"I wanted to talk to you about that too," I said, marveling at the genius of that response to Larry's incomprehensible mush.

The words "Mr. Flynt is on the line" never failed to make me feel more alive, a jolt of awareness along the lines of a mild electrical shock conducted through a penile catheter. One more time, I had Larry on the phone. His voice faded, and my stomach clenched. Through the raspy gargle, Flynt seemed to be asking about Dwaine. I latched onto every third or fourth word and tried to connect the dots. Had Dwaine made good on his implicit threat to poison the boss' pool of goodwill? I thought, *I wanted to talk to you about that too.*

But I said, "Larry, no one knows what the fuck goes on in Dwaine's mind."

No answer. A shuddering breath, then nothing. Had Larry hung up or had he croaked? What would I say when the newspapers tracked me down and asked for the dying man's last words?

I cradled the phone and wandered up to Larry's secretary. It was easy to charm Larry's secretaries. They deflected so many assholes per hour that simple courtesy made you seem like Cary Grant. I asked if I'd been fired.

"What makes you think so?"

"Dwaine's been badmouthing me to Larry."

"Dwaine? Well, who's listening, bub?"

Tinsley had been arrested out in the Valley. Within a day or two he would be arraigned on charges of sexually molesting a minor. The accuser was his own daughter, although her name and her relation to him were being withheld from the press. "The rest of it will be in all the papers in the morning. They'll identify him as a *Hustler* magazine editor. You're a *Hustler* magazine editor too, aren't you, Allan?"

"On the bright side," I said, "being charged with daughter rape should compel him to take a leave of absence."

The cuff dents had hardly worn off from his wrists when Dwaine overshadowed my desk. He was pissed and abandoned all pretense of being the mellow Southern fellow.

"You know, people say it's great to have a support group and all that fantastic horseshit," he said. "Can you imagine? So-called friends had the gall to come up and tell me they believed that I had not done it. Like there was ever any question that I would have done it."

I, unlike Tinsley's so-called support group, had the decency not to protest his innocence.

"You know Allison's a drug addict. She's my daughter, and I love her, but she's moving into dangerous territory. I'm just sad about the hurt she's putting herself through if this goes to trial. I'm just sick about the hurt."

Dwaine continued running the daughter down as a doper and a pathological liar. I accepted his assessment at face value. I pictured the father and the offspring in their stomach-churning embrace at the LFP Christmas party a few years earlier. No wonder the kid was stoned and scrambling reality.

I had my own concerns, and my mind drifted.

Frankie had discarded me for good after the choking incident, and life was a pale imitation without her. My sympathetic, sophisticated shrink suggested that Frankie was insecure because, in abandoning our life together in the duplex, we had stepped backward rather than forward. Perhaps if Frankie and I were to move in together, or become affianced, her behavior would stabilize.

XXX maestro Greg Dark received my Frankie lament at Kate Mantellini's, a sleek eatery adjacent to Flynt's offices. Greg's take differed from the shrink's.

"Dude, you drove a beauty of international proportions to a height of frenzied passion. She tried to choke you to death rather than lose you! Do you not understand what this means? You have been blessed with the pull. Only a very select percentage of the male population has the pull. Why be depressed? The pull is with you. Stick your head out of this booth. Are you oblivious to all the females we see when we look around here?"

Kate Mantellini's was studded with the kind of women who earn up to seven figures a year primarily upon the strength of their physical charisma.

"You owe an experience of the pull to each and every one of them," said Greg.

I felt better chewing down my double-cut pork chops with Greg than I had while driving home to an empty apartment from the shrink's office.

"I'm always sniffing," Greg said. His long, sensitive nose opened and scanned as if hoping to inhale a stray soul. "Every time a girl gets up and walks past me, I know there's a little air coming my way because of the turn of her body. I'm always trying to sniff her pussy, just like a dog. I flare my nostrils and breathe in, see if I can sniff her pussy. I've become conscious of this because some girl asked me, 'What's wrong with you?'

"I've been meaning to give you some advice." He twisted the edge of a recently sprouted satanic moustache. Greg encouraged me to exercise his olfactory principle while taking advantage of my position at *Hustler*.

"Where's the crime," he asked, "in claiming that you are auditioning porn girls for a feature layout and recurring column? You call them up, you get their numbers from your talent department, and you ask them to come in for an interview. Talk to them on the phone. Establish a rapport. These girls like to fuck, Allan. That's why they're porn sluts. Once they're across the desk from you, sniff out their pussies. They'll smell good. They'll know what you're sniffing at. If you meet with seven of them, three will be compatible."

"And then I could write an article."

"You could write a dozen articles, one a month. Believe me."

I did believe him, but I didn't follow his regimen. Calling in a different porn hooker every two days seemed too much like work, and work was strange enough with Dwaine Tinsley's family drama.

At wife Suzy's insistence, the magazine dispatched an editor to cover Dwaine's trial, intending to capture the full story of his vindication. Our courthouse observer reported Dwaine being painted in an unflattering light. The prosecution played a taped phone call between Daddy and a teary Allison. The father-daughter exchange sounded something like Dwaine was counseling his child to clam up and put all inappropriate incidents behind her. The father of Chester the Molester would have been better served hanging up on this phone call.

After Dwaine had been convicted of raping his teenage daughter on an ongoing basis, his wife Suzy—not the mother of the accuser—approached me seeking a written testimonial aimed at swaying the judge toward leniency during sentencing. While laboring over this plea for compassion on Dwaine's behalf, I paused. One question popped up: What kind of deluded miscreant requests a character reference from the editor of *Hustler* magazine after having lost a sex crimes case?

As the walls closed in on Tinsley, I was interacting with a higher profile of Death Row felon: corresponding with caged serial killer Richard Ramirez. During the 1985 summer of his run, Ramirez had been a nightly source of terror on Southern California television news, roaming the freeways, exiting long enough to slay and defile his victims, then jumping back on the highway to hell. Citizen vigilantes chased down the perpetrator in East Los Angeles, and the Ramirez trial turned into a 16-month freak show. Starstruck ghoul groupies filled the galleries and professed undying love for the murderer. Playing to the camera, radiating sick magnetism through aviator shades, Ramirez drew a pentagram on his palm, made what were interpreted as Satanic gestures and nonchalantly slouched as if he were in seventh grade detention rather than on trial for his life. One of the female jurors developed a documented crush on the lanky drifter from El Paso, Texas, despite having voted to convict him of 13 murders committed with, in the words of Superior Court Judge Michael Tynan, "cruelty, callousness and viciousness beyond any human understanding."

I assured Ramirez that *Hustler* would be the only outlet on the planet that would present his story free of moralizing. One of his girl-friends visited me at the Wilshire Boulevard offices, took off her clothes for the *Hustler* talent coordinator and tested for a photo shoot. Our gracious treatment of this smitten lady predisposed Ramirez to meet. I flew to San Francisco armed with a tape recorder and a batch of questions, again accompanied by an LFP attorney.

At the jail, a burly guard led me away from my lawyer. I was told to stand on a spot within the impenetrable steel doors and wait. I tried to appear casual. Inmates in jumpsuits strolled past looking sideways. My lockup phobia broke out in a swarm of dizziness. I spotted Ramirez entering a glass-fronted interview booth. Immediately, I felt at ease. As this sense of security welled up, I realized it was twisted. The guy had snuffed more than a dozen humans, slashing, shooting and sodomizing his victims.

We said hello, shook hands and sat across from one another. A small writing surface separated us. Richard's attorney insisted upon remaining present and occasionally stopped the flow of conversation (such as when the Night Stalker discussed the joys of sneaking through other people's homes while they slept). Ramirez laughed at my jokes. We chatted pleasantly and openly. I took some Polaroid shots of him flashing his winning smile. The feature, "The Night Stalker Talks: A Q&A With Richard Ramirez," ran in the November 1993 issue. His girlfriend, the one with nude-modeling aspirations, unfortunately did not pass the *Hustler* screening process, but I was sending regular porn shipments up to Richard, so everybody was happy.

About a year after our meeting, the ever-resourceful Richard Ramirez managed to put a call through to my office. He mentioned a woman I had never met, another in his stable of lady devotees.

"She says you're going to exploit me. She heard you tell somebody you're going to take that interview and use it to screw me."

"I never said anything like that to anybody."

"You lie, Allan. You lie, and you die."

I don't like being called a liar, and the threat of eternal extinguishment also fails to amuse me.

"Richard, if I'd intended to exploit you, you'd have been exploited long ago."

Richard seemed honestly conciliatory for having upset my feelings. He stopped short of apologizing, but we were cordial by the time we hung up the phone. Yet another of Ramirez's enthralled women had told me of a prank he played at San Quentin. Anticipating a cavity search, he had folded a sheet of paper into a small pellet and inserted it deep within his rectum. The guards fished the pellet out, unfolded it and read the message: "Hope you like chocolate."

More than most famous people, the Night Stalker had a sense of humor about himself and his circumstances. Still, I decided, this was one celebrity we could refrain from bashing in "Bits & Pieces."

Hustler "Dear Slut"

ANY NEWSSTAND PERIODICAL that caters to readers in their reproductive prime contains its column of love-life advice. *Hustler*'s fount of carnal wisdom spouted from practicing porn star Jeanna Fine, a sassy oracle of erotic expertise whose anodyne and knowhow were presented in the recurring "Dear Slut: Jeanna Fine Tells the Fucking Truth."

Who better to dispense libido strategy than a mouthy bluescreen icon, the vigorously acclaimed star of such thighbrow fare as *Sexaholic* (1985), *Virgin on the Run* (1991) and *Slip of the Tongue* (1993)? Jeanna's views on the politics of seduction, the physics of passion and the emotional fallout of an incestuous three-way were sensitive enough for a woman, but loaded with plenty of the raunchiness a *Hustler* man loves. Pervert-friendly, gay-embracing, a magical performer of the deep-throat massage, Jeanna Fine had plied her expertise in 1,000 XXX videos, read all the fringe market self-help literature, achieved a four-digit score on her SATs, and had graduated from therapy. More importantly, she had an opinion on everything, a perceptive and compassionate point of view delivered in crusty language that was as inflammatory as it was informative.

For every kinky bind, Ms. Fine had a real-life answer, often surprisingly moralistic. What other sex worker would project the authority and integrity to caution a runaway sensualist: "Remember, true love isn't always about fireworks. After the rockets fade, there's still the matter of everyday life to consider." ("Dear Slut," November, 2000).

CHAPTER 10

Larry Flynt Straight Up

IN THE SPRING of 1994, I'd met the third lady love of my life. Self-employed in the fashion industry, close to me in age, housed in a hillside modernist box, the new soul mate was cosmopolitan, chic and connected. She appreciated my job for the intricacies of the deadlines and assemblage, for the edgy, almost-illegal content that gave me a quasi-outlaw slouch, and for the paycheck, which I'd finally bumped up to a living wage. Our relationship was at the stage where I wanted to be around her all the time, especially if she was wearing something skimpy. We'd been invited to a Silverlake Hills pool-and-spa party, and I was minding my own business in the hot tub, with the third love nestled between my thighs. Several guests at the party shared an immersion in recovery culture. One gay-male couple was employed at a prestigious Marina del Rey detox facility, a rehabilitation hospital that had made headlines weeks earlier when rock commodity Kurt Cobain had gone over its wall, caught a flight back to Seattle and shotgunned himself.

This pair of natty orderlies were recounting close encounters with Kurt. One orderly insisted that Cobain had appeared to be sincerely on the path to chemical responsibility. The other attendant claimed that he could have predicted that Kurt would have done exactly what Kurt did. Rather than argue the point, the synchronized couple deftly changed the subject.

"You'll never guess who we have in there now," said guy one.

His partner gave me a knowing wink. "But you should be able to guess." The water in the tub became a little warmer than I'm comfortable with.

"That's right," said the first guy. "Larry Flynt."

"Jesus," I said. "How does he do in group? Can anybody understand what he's saying?"

"Larry Flynt doesn't do group."

"He stays in his room. He has his bodyguard and his tiny nurse, and they stay in there as well."

My anxiety spiked as if one of the recovery pros had threatened to toss a hair dryer into the tub. I got out of the water and dried myself off. On one hand, I rooted for Larry to overcome the dope. On the other hand, job prospects had just become far more complex.

Flynt had made a pilgrimage to Duke University Hospital in March of 1994 for dorsal root entry zone (DREZ) surgery, a laser followup to a previous, partially successful severing of the spinal nerves responsible for continued physical agony. The man in the golden chair's autobiography, *An Unseemly Man* (Dove Books), posits: "When the pain was gone, I no longer had any desire to take drugs. I just stopped overnight, without any complications."

There are always complications. Any armchair addiction specialist can tell you that a recovering addict must find some new life focus to replace the primacy that narcotics have held. Otherwise, a vacuum will form, the patient's soul will be sucked into that vacuum, and relapse is inevitable. Luckily for him, Larry proved less ambulatory than Cobain and he emerged from rehab drained of narcotic traces. Grasping for a meaningful fixation to fill the drugless void, Flynt's focus tightened upon a point that seemed to center on me.

After his release from the Marina cloister, Flynt called a company-wide meeting. Loyal servants trudged into the halls and crammed into a conference room. I lurked toward the back of the room and cast weak scorn at eager workers who bellied up to the conference table, positioning themselves for optimum proximity to the king of LFP. The excited buzz faded as Larry was rolled in and his wheels were secured at the head of the table. Silence spread and touched everyone. The boss was changed. Purpose and determination animated a face that had been most often slack or grimly pained since Althea's death. People uneasily sought one another's eyes. Larry made a joke about the archaic mullet hairstyle of the person sitting to his left.

"I'll have it cut in the morning, sir."

"You must be bucking for a raise."

His voice was resonant and emotion-filled, each steady word distinct from the words before and after it.

"Last week I went to Westwood and saw a movie with my good friend Dennis Hopper. It was the first time I had been inside a movie theater in many years. Imagine never being able to go to the movie theater to see a movie." The commander's voice was clear, distressingly so. The precise enunciation matched his open, cloud-free eyes. Now, Larry explained, he was free to think beyond his discomfort. He was back, he announced, and changes would be coming. Big changes. "What I'm going to concentrate on is putting the edge back in *Hustler*."

The meeting broke up, and I passed Jimmy Flynt. Jimmy shook my hand. Was this a consolation shake or was he wishing me luck in surviving his brother straight up?

I sat behind my desk and stared blankly at the sunlight of the outside world. My assistant, Jeanne, came into my office and interrupted my empty meditation. Ten years my senior, Jeanne was the only assistant I ever hired who wasn't like a kid sister to me. Wiry and hyper, a middle-age pixie, Jeanne was happily failing to suppress laughter.

I met Jeanne Diamond after I had been named executive editor of the *Hustler* flagship. Carol from Human Resources poked her head into my office. I was auditioning applicants for a new assistant. The previous assistant had been fired following a screaming match in the halls. She had apologized and suggested we talk things through, but even counseling wouldn't have helped. I'd tried therapy with Frankie, and the process had gone nowhere, much like the search for a new assistant. Hence the sheepish look on Carol from H.R. We both knew that she should be doing a better job.

"Allan, how do you feel about interviewing someone older?"

"Like in her 30s?"

Carol winced. "Almost 50."

When my mother died, she was only 54. "Okay," I said. "I'll see her."

The angular, wise waif that was Jeanne Diamond took her first steps into my vast corner office wearing spike heels, dark hose, a bolero jacket and a black skirt that flirted with her knees. She flicked a nervous smile. Her eyes were dark and concentrated, flashing off sparks of mischief or emotion, and her back-length black hair was cut straight across her forehead. She carried a slim attaché, placed like a tabletop upon her knees when she sat. Jeanne's most recent bit was four years as secretary to the CEO of a Beverly Hills talent agency, a man so powerful that even I, the freshly minted big shot, was cowed by his name. If Jeanne Diamond could rise to the demands of that ogre, she could easily handle any fit I'd throw. She'd left the talent agency 18 months earlier.

"What were you doing during this last year and a half?"

She held a small breath. "My boyfriend became ill, and I took the time off to be with him while he died." She shrugged her shoulders and averted her eyes, then squinted at me with a look that said, *It's no more than what you would do.*

This woman possessed saintly, selfless devotion. Unless she was a consummate liar. Either way, she might prove useful.

She asked a question about company raises, and my evasion triggered her laugh. In a calculating mood, I might have been leery of a postmenopausal beatnik chick who felt free to tease me while asking to work for me, but I was relieved that she hadn't waxed all morbid about the dead boyfriend. We agreed that she would start in a week. We'd had good times, months and months with Larry in a fog, and now change was blowing in.

"Allan," Jeanne said, "the betting pool has you lasting between three days to five weeks. Do you want to buy a square?"

"Who's betting I'll make it five weeks?"

"Actually, nobody. I was trying not to hurt your feelings."

"Now is not the time for me to be putting my money at risk."

"You are wise."

My staff had finally gelled, a collection of contrary individuals, all talented, funny and opinionated. I visited each editor and art director separately and attempted to allay their fears. An important function of any leader is to instill a winning attitude. "Think of the situation as a battle," I said, "one that you are destined to lose because you are already dead."

It seemed like only moments later that Larry called me directly. No secretary instructing me to "hold for Mr. Flynt," no three-second delay during which I might gather a semblance of wits. Just a ring-ing phone, and then that eerily audible version of a voice that I'd grown to understand as permanently garbled: "Allan, pull your staff together and meet me in the conference room."

I could have asked Jeanne to round up the guys, but I extended the invitation personally. "It's time," I said, placing a hand upon each doomed trouper's shoulder.

Larry didn't keep us waiting long. He locked his gold-spoked wheels and ordered everyone to introduce themselves and state their job definition. The boss seemed satisfied with his foot soldiers as they relayed names and tasks. Next, Flynt asked what we used for news sources. The effect was uncanny. I understood every sin-gle word Larry said, for the first time ever. Still, it was as if he were speaking Martian. News sources? Our articles were about UFO date rape ("Alien Sex Crimes: Inside the Extraterrestrial Breeding Pro-gram," June, 1993) and how to talk to your girlfriend with the communicative efficacy of a pimp ("The *Hustler* Liar's Manual," April, 1991).

I took a shot at sounding capable and informed. "We read *Time* and *Newsweek*, of course, but we realize they are CIA fronts." Larry brightened visibly at "CIA fronts," and a few of the editors relaxed. I claimed we consulted the *Christian Science Monitor* for an alterna-tive view. I'd read up on Larry. He had once praised the *Christian Science Monitor* as among the country's few unbiased news sources. He seemed pleased at that paper's mention. The editors slouched into postures of alert ease. I understood at a deeper level that I must never relax.

As a matter of principle, I had never passed Nurse Liz without addressing her directly. My sly formula was to compliment her on a piece of apparel or hairstyle, then steer the conversation around to my admiration for Larry Flynt's integrity, his courage and his drive. In eager confidence, Liz would regale me with proofs of the man's bril-liance: he knew the names of all the politicians on cable TV; he was clean; he watched where every penny went; he treated his dogs well.

The magazine's talent coordinator—think of her as Eleanor—was either abruptly fired or had quit during a moment of pique. A proud-blooded Latina of South American descent, Eleanor looked down upon what she considered lesser Hispanics, particularly Mexicans. It is conceivable that she had taken umbrage at some slur from Liz Berrios (whose heritage traced to Mexico) and walked. I phoned Eleanor at home and asked if I could intercede on her behalf. She said no, and I turned my attention to determining who should fill the talent coordinator vacancy. The talent position is one of the most crucial spots in the organization, and Liz Berrios promptly claimed it.

Liz seemed to enjoy her new appointment and to exult in appropriating the creamy leather furnishings that had graced Jimmy Flynt's office. There was no need to make a mental note to stay on Liz's good side. I loitered in the talent office, pretending to help Liz during her transition. Jimmy's creamy, beige-leather chairs were among the most comforting seats I'd ever sunk into. While there, I furthered the conversation about what a forceful, great guy Larry was. Liz hinted that I did not know the half of Larry's largesse. She cut herself short, but she really wanted to go on.

"I think I know what you mean," I said.

"I can tell you. Do you know anything about Larry and that big porn agent in the Valley?

"Well, Larry said, if that guy causes me any problems, I just need to remind him that I work for Larry." Liz slid her elbows out flat on the desktop and leaned forward to whisper. Her chin nestled upon her clasped hands: "Once, a long, long time ago, the jerk took a girl that was supposed to model in *Hustler* and sent her to *Penthouse*, and Larry had his legs broken. That was the last time he caused any problems for anybody from *Hustler*."

Liz flushed with pride, as though Larry had snapped the agent's limbs expressly for her benefit. I acted as if Liz's telling were the first time I'd heard this legend of ceremonial fracturing, and I tried to give the impression that I was every bit as proud of Larry's fabled heroics as Liz was.

The leg-breaking myth was close to my mind as I sat across from Larry's voluminous desk and recalled nostalgically the days when his dope-weighted forehead had never been far from slamming down upon his blotter. Since emerging from the narcotic cocoon, he seemed determined to be displeased with me. As usual, Mr. Flynt dispensed with preliminaries.

"Are you familiar with the work of Frank Zappa?" he said. I nodded affirmative. "Then perhaps you know that he died recently. Frank Zappa always was a good friend to *Hustler*, and you really ought to have had something about his passing in the magazine."

"We did. It's on your desk."

The April 1994 issue contained a page dedicated to Zappa ("Frankly, He Gave a Damn") that commemorated the original Mother's contributions to American culture. The item ended with the line: "Frank Zappa will be remembered always at *Hustler* as a dear friend."

As Larry read toward those concluding words, I sat outwardly unfazed. Initially, my collaborative editors and I had outlined a mocking sendoff applauding the appropriateness of Zappa succumbing to ass cancer. We'd slammed together a merciless taunt at the departed's expense. Upon sober reflection, I had second thoughts and replaced the mean-spirited attack with the traditional sweet remembrance. Larry finished the Zappa obituary and fixed me in his emerald gimlet. He lifted a glass of water. The shaking of his hands made me cringe. If he sloshed water on something important, like a check, he might become even angrier. Larry thumbed through the magazine.

He turned to the "April: Fool Bloom" pictorial in the same issue. He held the pages up for my view. Pictures of April fluttered in Flynt's palsied grip. "What makes you think this is an attractive woman?" he croaked.

I tried to avert my gaze from the offending photos while maintaining eye contact with the offended publisher. The copy accompanying the model concluded, "For while she may not have a trick up her sleeve, it might be that April's sleeve is a trick."

"That's our April Fools' issue, Larry. She's not really a chick. At least, she didn't start out as a chick."

He grunted, neither one way nor the other.

My dilemma was how to bond with Larry Flynt. The answer came in a process that routinely sunders employer/employee relationships. We were named as co-defendants. Remember that displaced talent coordinator who had either quit or been fired? A single phone call from an LFP lawyer brought her back with interest. "Eleanor is filing suit for wrongful termination and sexual harassment."

"She quit. I asked if she wanted me to intercede on her behalf; she said no."

"Her lawyer says she was fired."

"I guess it's a perception thing. Too bad she's going down the sexual harassment road."

"What do you mean?"

"Well, she's vulnerable in that area." Eleanor had been a serial mocker. She'd made sex-based fun of co-workers to their faces and behind their backs. She had belittled the erotic prowess of others and had bragged in public work areas about her own sexual adventures, proficiencies, preferences and missteps. "I imagine the defense will make her look sort of bad," I ventured.

"That worries you?"

"Sort of."

"Maybe you didn't understand me. She's naming you as a defendant. You're being accused of harassment. You could lose your house."

"I don't have a house."

According to the plaintiff, I had ordered her to stand next to a window so that the incoming sunlight might give me a view of her private parts through her sheer dress. I was being accused of using a vulgar term for private parts. The supposedly vulgar term was "mound." In truth, my version of it, this woman had come to my office wearing attire I deemed inappropriate for office professionalism.

"That skirt is practically see-through," I had said, in my capacity as supervisor.

"Is not."

"Oh, it is. If you were to walk past that window, I would see your mound."

I'd wanted to say *mons veneris* but was unsure of the pronunciation. Believe me, mound is a far more benign term than those we—the accuser and I—generally bandied about to designate the female pudenda.

The second accusation was more serious. The plaintiff had come back from a week's vacation having undergone breast augmentation. She was sensitive about having indulged in the bump-up. The problem was, she worked at a company where a portion of the staff routinely was called upon to determine whether or not a particular candidate had benefited from surgical enhancement.

Photographer Randi Dench had come to my office to plead the case of some girls she had recruited as skin models. Randi Dench had spawned her ambitions during London's swinging '60s and had flirted and fucked at the fringes of '70s celebrity. Her autobiography, long out of print, had named names and dimensions. Dench's blab-all tome had alienated her men's-sophisticate benefactors, and she'd been reduced to shooting for magazines lesser than *Hustler*. I complimented Randi on the test shots and warned her not to bug Eleanor about a perceived increase in bra size. Dench, mindful of her reputation for bawdy exuberance, had immediately accosted Eleanor in an open workspace and bellowed, "Come on, Eleanor baby, don't be bashful. Show us those new tits!" This act had been cited as proof that I had created a hostile, sexually harassing workplace.

I knew something about how Randi's attentions must have made Eleanor feel. About a year and a half earlier, we had all three scouted prospective models at a world series of exotic dancers in Toronto, Canada. Randi had been drinking heavily, in her defense, but I had not, and her continual groping of my crotch and struggling to unbuckle my trousers while in crowded coffee shops had caused me no small amount of awkward emotions, much to Eleanor's delight. So the plaintiff's embarrassment might have been genuine, and I sympathized with it, but her case's merits were about as false as my letter of character referencing Dwaine Tinsley's sentencing.

The word *deposition* probably carries no visceral weight for anyone who has not endured one. The deposition tends to be a hostile event. Basically, two opposing attorneys and a noncommittal court reporter gather in a windowless room and combine their skills and training to put a civilian through a crash course in attack litigation. A veil of civility may be maintained. Under that sheer fabric of manners, anything goes. For eight consecutive hours, excluding a break for lunch, I sat stoic while a professional faultfinder assailed my character. His hair was the color and consistency of black shoe polish, and it fit awkwardly upon his skull. His front teeth protruded above his fat bottom lip and nibbled upon it like a pair of small, off-white chisels. I parried and repelled his aspersions. At day's end, I felt as though I had been standing for an entire work shift while being struck about the body with a sand-filled rubber hose.

I returned to work and found my assistant Jeanne so angry that she could not speak. Was something wrong at home? Had I said something? Her eyes filled with tears, and she would not look at me. Then she toughened up and tossed some crap around at her desktop.

I went to check with Young Bill the art director. "You didn't do anything to piss off Jeanne, did you? I've never seen her like this."

"Liz Berrios went monkey-shit on her."

"Why should the fucking talent coordinator go monkey-shit on my assistant?"

"She's the monkey. That's what monkeys do. Monkeys go monkey-shit."

Back in my office, with the door open so Jeanne could hear, I phoned Liz.

"Liz, I'm hearing reports that you were verbally abusive to editorial employees during my absence."

"Those people, you can't tell me those people were working right."

"They are my staff, and I am a demanding supervisor, and I don't have anybody here who I'm not satisfied with."

"I'm closer to Larry than you are, and he wants me to look out for his best interests."

"I spent an entire day taking shit from a rat-toothed lawyer in a bad rug for Larry Flynt's best interests, and I'm not happy to come back and hear that some self-appointed office vigilante has been harassing my staff."

Liz squealed like something out of the zoo, so I hung up. The monkey. As in, "The monkey is throwing another monkeywrench."

Most times, my strategy in presenting a conflict for resolution to Larry Flynt was to deal with a straight-ahead business issue, then mention the personal problem as though it were an afterthought. In the matter of Liz Berrios, I specifically addressed the issue of Larry's girlfriend running roughshod over hard-working, dedicated employees. I laid out my objections, respectfully, but insistently. I stressed that Liz's hostile meddling created an atmosphere where a basically well-intentioned person will become resentful, nonproductive and contrary. Larry watched me all the while until I stopped talking.

"I'll take care of it," he said.

I stood to leave, and he stopped me.

"Allan, I really want you to get along with Liz."

"So do I. And that's the only reason I'm mentioning the problem to you."

Liz cornered me soon after while young Bill and I were in the photo room selecting pictures with Larry. A bodyguard leaned against a light table ogling the images of open legs and squeezed cleavage that papered the walls. Larry's mood was positive, and he was praising the photos. Things were looking up, then the monkey arrived.

Liz clutched a stack of paperwork and gave Larry a peck on the cheek. She stood with an arm around Larry's neck. Their shoulders came up to my belt buckle. I said hello, and Liz responded brightly. She presented test Polaroids of a blonde for Larry's approval. Young Bill and I leaned forward to take a peek. Freshly scarred gashes marred the blonde's thighs.

"Jesus, who was she resisting?" I asked.

Larry eyeballed me. "What do you mean?"

"Those scars on her thighs. It looks like she fought off a rapist."

"It was her own pet!" exclaimed Liz. "She's an animal trainer. Maybe she can pose with some of her animals."

"Was it a tiger that did that?"

"No, it was a monkey!" shouted Liz.

I froze. Had someone divulged Liz's pet name to her?

"She has a monkey, and it's just like her child, but very excitable. You can't get the monkey too excited, because the monkey can scratch or bite, and that's what happened to her thighs. Right there." Liz reached out and touched my thighs where the monkey had bitten the prospective model's, high up near the crotch. Was Larry seeing all this?

"She couldn't stop the monkey?" asked young Bill.

"How?" shrieked Liz. "You can't hit the monkey!"

Halfway through the lawsuit from Eleanor, Larry purchased a black-glass death star of a building about a mile to the west, at the corner of Wilshire and La Cienega, and relocated his operation. A bronze sculpture of movie star John Wayne sat astride a well-hung bronze horse out in front of the structure. A dip in the occupancy rate of his new building worried Larry. He imagined that prospective tenants were being scared off by scruffy employees of the art and editorial departments. A dress code was established. Policy dictated that men wear ties, button-up shirts and slacks. Women were to present themselves in dresses or skirts. Denim was banished. Even with the magazine staff skulking about like ragtag Mormons, it was hard to imagine a young gynecologist or family psychologist hanging a shingle in the Larry Flynt building. Part of the problem was that Larry insisted upon cruising the elevators while wearing his pussy necklace. A medallion dangled from the necklace, about twice as large as a Mercedes-Benz hood ornament. Sculpted of platinum, gold and precious stones—diamonds, rubies, garnets, anything that reflects a shade of pink—the finely jeweled piece represented the folds and fissures of a life-size, open vagina.

Preparing for my testimony in Eleanor's suit, a pair of friendly attorneys drilled me on the accusations and their ramifications. The lead lawyer set the scene. "The plaintiff claims that Larry ordered her to enlist a male model to have sex with one of Larry's out-of-town business associates."

I sought clarification. "A male to have sex with a male?"

"Correct," confirmed the lead counsel.

His partner posed the question: "And you thought what?"

"I thought this scenario cannot possibly be true."

"Because Larry would never be involved with something like that."

"I don't see him facilitating a romantic evening for a homosexual. Anyway, it's so easy for gays to hook up on their own, why go through Larry? Furthermore, there are specialized sources for this type of thing, so if Larry were to reach out on the behalf of his friend, why sully his own company talent pool?"

"Plus," said the primary lawyer, "you know that Larry would never do something like that."

"Look, I've been told by a bunch of different people that Larry did some crazy shit. Some really crazy shit."

Neither lawyer asked me to elaborate. They switched the subject to Liz Berrios. They'd heard complaints. They were circumspect, dodgy perhaps, in their inquiries.

"Oh, you'll have some liability with Liz," I assured them. "She'll bring you some overtime."

The arbitration was staged in our law firm's conference room, an enclosure lined with windows that filtered the outside sunshine. The place was like a dark tunnel to me, a close, airless compartment with a tiny glimmer in the far distance. The opposing attorney's wet teeth gnawed upon his plump lower lip. A girl sat next to him. I assumed the girl was an intern to the rat-toothed attorney. When she spoke, I recognized the voice as belonging to the plaintiff. It was Eleanor. I tried to gauge how much plastic surgery she'd had since I'd last seen her.

The arbitrator, luckily, was a woman. It sounds egotistical, but women are drawn to me. What I mean is that, until they get to know me, women feel secure from loutishness in my presence. Eleanor's nasty accusations could not shake my confidence in the ability of this female arbitrator to peer into the clear, focusing lens of my transparent sincerity and perceive Eleanor's stories as greed-fueled fantasies. That's pretty much what happened. The toughest part was not being distracted by outside considerations such as *Can this opposing counsel imagine he's fooling anybody with that hair?*

When the verdicts arrived, not a dime of fault was assessed against LFP. As a reward, or because he'd decided to keep me on board and he wanted to watch me wield a knife and fork, Larry invited the wife-to-be and me out to dinner at McCormick and Schmick's, a fish place in the faux European opulence of Beverly Hills' Via Rodeo complex. We arrived at the appointed eatery about a quarter-hour after the appointed time. The wife-to-be stubbornly runs late. Big Doug the bodyguard convivially escorted us to where Larry and Liz sat. Liz adjusted a bib around Larry's neck. He polished off a cocktail. His hands were wobbling. The drink might have been his second. I opted for a club soda and grapefruit juice.

"What kind of magazine editor doesn't drink?" asked Larry. His voice was slurred from the alcohol. He would pose this question at many dinners through the years, and every Christmas his secretary would call me to the 10th floor to pick up an elaborate gift basket of hard liquor. Larry finished the appetizer course by slurping his soup directly from the bowl. Liz dabbed a napkin at his mouth. He smacked his lips and turned the conversation to the lawsuit. "They tried to make you look like a real scumbag," he said. "We would have settled; they just got too greedy."

Flynt gazed at the wife-to-be, then back at me.

"Where'd you two meet, at a dogfight?"

The wife-to-be and Liz Berrios had both grown up in the Montebello area, a Mexican-American enclave where boxer Oscar de la Hoya bought a house for his parents. Liz had attended an all-girls Catholic school, and the wife-to-be had run with gangs and loadies at Mark Keppel public high.

Watching his girlfriend relax in conversation with mine seemed to warm Larry to me. He divulged plans for reorganizing his holdings, including dumping his magazine-distribution company. Having eaten, the chairman's voice had stabilized, the alcohol slur completely gone. He asked how I liked being in charge of *Hustler*.

"Are you kidding?" said the wife-to-be. "He thinks he's a big shot."

Larry liked that kind of crap. "We usually go outside and have a *see*gar after dinner," he said. "Us big shots."

Bodyguard Doug fetched the cigars from a humidor the restaurant kept for Larry. The four of us settled around a table on a breezy veranda and fired up.

"That's a $50 *see*gar you're smoking," said Larry.

I would have preferred the 50 bucks, but I enjoyed the shared experience, much like when Larry and I had scarfed down those strawberry shortcakes while he told tales of child Thai brides. Larry smoked and mellowed, and he and Liz reminisced about lazing on the beach in the Cayman Islands.

"Doug takes Larry out in the water, and he just floats there, happy like a seal."

Larry and Doug both savored the memory. "Then we just lie on the sand and watch all the bodies," said Larry.

"We go a couple of times every year."

I thought they'd only visited the Caymans to spend time with all of Larry's offshore money. My face must have expressed some doubt. Liz was quick to dispel it.

"Really, it's the most relaxing, beautiful experience," she said. "You would have to see it."

Of course, I was keeping an eye on Larry, not too closely, my sight obscured by cigar smoke and good feeling. I saw his face expand, taking in the wife-to-be and me, and his mouth—I swear this is true although of course there is no way of proving it—his mouth half formed the words: "You two are going to fly down with us next time we go to the islands." Before his tongue could deliver his intentions, Larry's face and entire manner closed, alerted by the generous impulse to squelch his next action. Abruptly, he motioned to Doug, and the golden chair rolled away, into an elevator. Liz scurried behind, and they descended to the parking structure. The future wife and I waited for the next car.

"We almost got a free vacation," she said. I gave the cigar a last puff, then dropped it into a sand-filled cistern.

"Asshole of the Month"

IF A THINKING man were contemplating enlisting as a *Hustler* partisan, he must not be scared off by a burst of rabid confrontation. A fecal-tinged anger colors the *Hustler* worldview, a noxious shading of brown that is washed on every month up at the front of the book, under the heading "Asshole of the Month." The defining and defiant screed selects a fresh newsmaker each issue and pelts that person's deeds, motivations and morals, slagging reputation and record in the rankest sewer imagery imaginable.

Almost from the day of my hiring, I heard myself becoming the voice of "Asshole of the Month." Sally Corrigan, a twitchy blonde who had tried to have me fired during my second LFP week, had befriended me during the third. She sat with me on the Century City quad as I drank the last of my lunch. Did I have ambitions? Where did I see myself going in the company? I confided to flit-eyed Sally that I hoped to one day author the "Asshole of the Month" column. Sally clawed my thigh. "Write one about Larry and Althea, like as an audition, and I'll give it to Bill to pass along to them. The Flynts have an amazing sense of humor about themselves."

Even then, I smelled the trapped rat I would become were I to accept Sally's offer. I bided my time. Eventually, my proficiency with cruel epitaph and barbed simile were recognized. The poisoned pen of "Asshole" authorship was passed to me like a sputtering torch. In the decade that I pinched out "Asshole of the Month" columns, 13 per year, targets included politicians and their families, entertainers, religious leaders, sports figures, captains of industry and isolated screw-ups. In language always redolent of the cloaca, spouting a discourse so coarse that oftentimes not a single sentence could be recited in its entirety on airwaves or from pulpit, I did my utmost to elevate character assassination to the level of a septic art form. My accusations were precise and detailed, culled from reams of research, and impervious to litigation. I prided myself on composing fact-based smears more spiteful and vicious than any libel or slander.

CHAPTER 11

They Call Me
Mr. A-Hole

SPARKY THE RESEARCH director and I had been having problems. First of all, I didn't like the way he dressed. I'm taking you back to the days before Flynt's shirts-and-ties edict. Pot-bellied, bandy-legged Sparky's favored mode of work attire was the warmup suit. Athletic leisurewear had never fit my conception of passable office presentation, but I had no room to talk, being locked into a phase of jeans, T-shirt and $300 shoes. I clocked the arrival of my under-lings on a shiny, stainless-steel Tiffany watch. I calculated that I had witnessed at least 750 cumshots in the process of amassing the funds to buy this sparkling chronograph. Jaunty Sparky lugged his belly through the research door and wedged that bloated gut behind his desk 12 minutes later than would have pleased me. He unfurled a paper towel and laid out two fat crullers and a liter of diet soda. Sparky had recently moved from the crowded copy pen to the remote confines of the research suite, seeking solitude, autonomy and leisure.

One of Sparky's regular assignments was to provide candidate lists for "Asshole of the Month." His latest list had been topped by some minor-league football player who had grazed the sports pages for arriving late to practice. Larry preferred world-class villains. Sparky shoved a length of cruller into his mouth. His hateful, pinned pink eyes were slightly crossed. I slid his list of "Asshole" candidates under the second doughnut.

"This is the best you can do?" I said.

He chewed, swallowed, chewed. "If you want better, if it's not good enough, you can always look yourself."

"I am looking. I do look. I look every day. Right now I'm looking at you. You sucked up to people all around me in order to snake this job under me, and now you tell me that I should be doing your work myself?"

"You ask me for candidates, and you never use them. What difference does it make what I give you?"

I took a seat across from Sparky and assailed him as a lazy, stupid, impertinent, soon-to-be-sorry, slack and weak disgrace. I took him to task for his lateness, his lameness and for the fact that he creeped out all the women on staff. I laid on wrath in a manner too crass for me to repeat here. "I don't like arguing with imbeciles and shirkers," I said in summation.

Sparky didn't enjoy arguing with me either, at least not directly. Once I'd turned my back, he wired memos to two of my bosses warning that my interference in the research arena put the company at grave peril. These memos were kicked down to me along with instructions to resolve the situation. I picked up the phone.

"Sparky, do me a favor and trot down to my office."

I marveled at Sparky's presumption and agility. He'd dashed behind my back and leapfrogged over my head in a single rash bound. *Bold* or *gutsy* were not adjectives I could bring myself to use on Sparky or his strategy. *Short-sighted, thick-skulled* and *irritating*, those were descriptors I might apply. Sparky barreled into my office and plopped into a seat. He tugged the bottom of his sweatshirt to meet the waistband of his sweatpants, but the two hems recoiled from one another. I was pleased to see that Sparky, heeding an earlier directive, carried pen and paper with which to make notes. He also brought along a tape recorder.

"What's the tape recorder for?"

"I feel more comfortable with it."

"Is that more comfortable in general? Or specifically here with me? Do you take it with you everywhere? How about in the men's room? Do you record your activities in the men's room?"

He made a show of pressing the on button. In a calm, modulated manner, I launched the assault upon Sparky's failings. "I wonder, if you were to spend as much time on your work as you do on printing and distributing the football pool, do you think we would have these problems? Look at this football pool, typical of the football pool that you have prepared every week since moving from copy editor to research director." I held up the sheet and enunciated clearly and directly into the tape recorder's microphone. "You have each team's season record, you have the Vegas line, you have QB stats, away versus home winning percentages and pertinent injury reports. We see that you have the capacity for quality research and application. I also notice that you have no spelling errors in this assemblage. Do you photocopy your football pool at home or at a private copy center *en route* between your home and the office?"

Sparky had no answer for this obvious question. He addressed it by turning off the tape recorder. Here was my signal to amplify.

"You're a chickenshit," I yelled. "You're a rat-dick weasel and a suck."

Sparky recoiled and fumbled with the tape recorder. He switched it on, but I had reverted to being kindly and delicate in my words, almost scholarly. I presented a copy of the memorandum Sparky had written and assumed I would never see.

"You sent this memo over my head claiming that I, by giving you feature articles with facts to be researched by you, was exposing Larry Flynt Publications to litigation. I have an assignment for you. Of the numerous articles and 'Asshole of the Month' columns that I have marshaled to publication in *Hustler* magazine, I want you to tell me how many have resulted in lawsuits being brought against LFP. Hazard a guess."

He hazarded to guess that this conversation reflected dimly on him. Resigned, he again turned off the tape recorder.

I stood and leaned forward over my desk: "Zero, motherfucker. I have never had a story, a joke or an editorial attack sued. Why not? Because I know what I'm fucking doing, and when I ask you to research facts, I know what I'm fucking asking you to do."

Out came the tape recorder.

"So," I said, mild and kind, the benign mentor once more, "my question to you is, why did you send this memo? My feeling is that you attempted to circumvent me in a ploy to lessen your rightful workload so that you can spend more time on the football pool. Do you have any facts that would point me toward a different conclusion?"

He had none, but he did have a reason to shut off the tape recorder.

"You should have worn a wire with a concealed device," I said, the logical, patient, weary pedagogue. "Sparky, you can't win. That's why you were always picked last for any split of schoolyard teams."

Sparky's pink eyes blinked behind bristly pale lashes. Wordlessly, he left my office. He had the sunken-ass shamble of a guy who would save me the bother of firing him. Not all my personal interrelations were perfect, but I felt pretty good about where Sparky and I stood. My pleased reverie was interrupted by production coordinator Jeanne Diamond. I hired Jeanne into the company as my assistant. A better position had opened for her, with greater autonomy and more money. I suspected she took the promotion simply to be away from me, which bruised my feelings. Jeanne delivered a stack of internal schedules and blurted out an opinion: "Allan, I see you as someone who one day dies in a murder."

Did I remind Jeanne of a principled martyr along the lines of Martin Luther King? Or was she telling me that somebody some day would choke on my attitude and croak me? I followed Jeanne to her desk. "What did you mean just now, about me being murdered?"

Jeanne laughed and shuffled papers. "It popped into my head. I said it."

A selection of bitter retorts popped into my head. But I didn't want to wipe out her goodwill so I dropped the subject of my impending homicide and went back to sticking my nose into someone else's business. Jeanne's singsong aside—"I see you as someone who one day dies in a murder"—would rise like a fit of mental reflux over the following months. I became leery of Jeanne, despite her kooky efficiency.

Twenty-three months after being found guilty of sexually violating his teenaged daughter, cartoonish iconoclast Dwaine Tinsley's conviction had been overturned on procedural grounds. The prosecution let him skate with time served and, against all logic and expectation, the cloying voice of Chester the Molester's creator once more oozed out from the nearby LFP water cooler. Tinsley's arrogant and aggrieved whine, instantly recognizable, slithered through the hallways and into my office. There would be no avoiding him.

Rather than be trapped behind my desk, I moved out and approached the grating source.

Dwaine had recharged his jailyard stare during his refresher course in the pen. Two overweight girls—a toddler and a preteen—stood in Dwaine's grip. The older child seemed fascinated by the flow of the water cooler. These were Dwaine's kids with down-home baker Suzy. That marriage had dissolved while Dwaine was in prison. Informed gossips speculated that Suzy had changed her mind on Dwaine's culpability and severed all ties with him.

"Imagine that, Al. Me and the girls are a family now. Suzy's in no shape to take care of the little ones. It's sad and pitiful, but a man knows when to step up."

I sputtered. "It's great that they have you available to be home again." What I meant to say was more along the lines of: "Technically, dude, it's a criminal offense to bring children up to this premises, thus exposing them to the adults-only material that saturates the site. Furthermore, what the fuck insanity befell a judge to hand these two fattened innocents over to you?"

"Life's a funny thing," said Tinsley. "Al, we got us a nice cottage up on the hill in Cambria. You been up there? It's a jewel set along the central coastline. A real nice little arts community. Not like here in L.A. We got a hot tub under all the stars, don't we, girls? Well, it's a cute, quaint sort of town, but it's also got the local supermarket for miles around. I'll be off to buy my groceries, and I'm at the deli, and lo and behold, I'll be passing—less than an arm's length away— right by one of those Lompoc screws. I'm cool, buddy. You know old Dwaine is cool. But these tough-guy prison guards, you get them out in the real world like anyone else, and they go nervous on you." Dwaine covered a hand over each of his girls' ears and pulled their free ears into his belly. "It's like they don't have all their DOC buddies there to help them, and I might shiv the cocksuckers."

"It must have been hard for you up there," I said. "Inside."

"You know who prison's really tough for?" asked Dwaine.

Sure, I thought, *child-raping motherfuckers who prance around with bullshit attitude.*

Dwaine had other thoughts. "Celebrities," he said. "Famous folk should just stay the fuck out of prison. Christian Brando, Marlon

Brando's son? He was up there the same time as me. You know, Chris is the fella who shot his sister's boyfriend? Well, there was a bounty on that boy. He had to be put in protective custody. Hiding with the sissies and such. He couldn't step out on the yard with the big boys. If he'd dared to brave the mainline, I might have made a bundle."

"You mean, like murder him?"

"C'mon, Al. Don't act like we don't know each other. I'm just having fun."

He sauntered off with his roly-poly girls. Jeanne Diamond was covering the cartoon editor duties, so for the time being, Dwaine was out of an office job. That reprieve wouldn't last. Each new day brought Tinsley closer to being an on-premises pest again.

Jeanne Diamond's behavior went from odd to alarming. One day a little before lunch, she collapsed in front of a photocopier and was wheeled from the building by a craggy pair of handsome paramedics. Despite Jeanne's mugging and joking while on the gurney, Larry's fiancée assumed that the fall was a stunt foreshadowing a lawsuit. Through lunch and into the afternoon, Liz and her assistant stalked the halls and tried to quash a get-well card circulating among Jeanne's friends, convinced that if no attention were drawn to the incident, it would revert to having not occurred.

Envelope and card were secreted hand-to-hand throughout the editorial department. By the time the surreptitious goodwill package reached my desk, two days had passed, and Jeanne had returned to work, acting as though she had been to Cancún on a short adventure. I wrote her a note and passed the contraband greeting to the next Jeanne Diamond fan.

Maybe a week passed. Jeanne and I stepped into an empty elevator. A lurking H.R. co-worker waved and hollered, "How's the health, honey?"

Jeanne gave the grin and a thumbs-up. "I'm great. Everything's great."

The elevator doors shut us in. She sagged against the wall. "Let me tell you, Allan. If you're ever in this situation, most of the people, you're better off telling them nothing real. Thanks for signing my card. You're a funny man."

I had written, "Is there no limit to the lengths you will go for attention?"

Jeanne Diamond's fainting was the result of rampant lung cancer and complementary brain tumors. I organized a fund to purchase a medicinal herb not covered by our HMO, and Jeanne called to thank me. She would be entering the hospital in a few days, and she would not mind if I dropped by.

Jeanne's impending demise was not quite the most startling news. Young art director Bill and I were trailing Larry's wheels from the photo-edit room when Liz Berrios sidled up to me. Her posture conveyed a reticence and vulnerability that I hadn't seen in a woman since the Sadie Hawkins Day Dance in junior high. She looked up at me, way up at me, with fervent and misty eyes.

"I just want you to know that I really do appreciate working with you." Her voice quavered. "I respect your abilities, and I recognize that you are a valuable contribution to *Hustler* and Larry Flynt Publications." She handed me an envelope.

"Thanks, Liz. I appreciate this." I folded the envelope and placed it in my suit pocket. The days of T-shirts and jeans were long gone. I'd taken to wearing suits and sport coats of European design. If Liz's envelope contained a check, I might use it toward purchase of a Dries Van Noten chocolate-striped textured-wool blazer.

In the privacy of my corner office, I was disappointed. I'd been handed a letter of apology.

TO: ALLAN MAC DONELL FROM: LIZ BERRIOS

I AM AWARE THAT WE HAVE HAD PROBLEMS WORKING TOGETHER IN THE PAST. I WOULD LIKE TO APOLIGIZE [SIC] FOR ANY CONTRIBUTION I HAVE MADE TO THESE PROBLEMS. I WISH TO EXTEND MY APOLOGY AND I PROMISE TO MAKE EVERY EFFORT TO WORK TOGETHER WITH YOU IN THE FUTURE.

SINCERELY,

LIZ BERRIOS

Liz was handing out these personal disclaimers like dance cards. The photographers received the same note, same wording, that I did. The fact that I was not the unique recipient of Liz's amends failed my special needs, but I consoled myself: At least I was off her hit list.

I went to see Jeanne twice; that's as long as she lasted. My mother's leukemia had taught me that I could sit in a hospital room and display my terror only intermittently. On my first visit, Jeanne's boyfriend stood up from the bedside. A slim, dapper man about Jeanne's own age, his eyes were tired and wary in a soft, angular face the color of burnished walnut.

He asked Jeanne if she and I wanted to be left alone. I mouthed no, but Jeanne sent him away. When people accept that they are dying, they like to lock in for the intense eyeball-to-eyeball. She had an advantage in that she was hooked up to a morphine drip. I had an advantage in that I would be walking out of the room when we were done. One of Jeanne's feet was elevated in a sling, and the exposed toes were blackened. "I can't make it down to the smoking patio with my foot like this. That's what bothers me the most."

Ordinarily, I don't talk about myself in any way that means anything to me, but the situation inspired confidences. There was something about me nobody had ever heard, not Frankie, not any other girlfriend, not the wife-to-be, not my siblings, not my shrink, nobody. Jeanne wouldn't be around much longer. In retrospect, I imagine Jeanne's friends and acquaintances must have been unloading all sorts of misdeeds and failings onto her. Maybe mine weren't so bad. I told Jeanne about traveling to Canada three times in my mother's last year. I confessed that only hours before she died, after my brother and I had driven 21 hours straight to witness her passing, I had been unable to say the words, "I love you."

Jeanne pulled a pack of cigarettes out from under her covers. Her aspect was as if I had said nothing. "Let me tell you about the man I took care of as he died." She smiled. "The guy you thought I made up for my résumé."

The man's name was Bill, a runty Irish operator. He'd been multifaceted in his entrepreneurship, always returning to bank robbery, and successful more often than not. But the last prison stretch had broken his health. "Man, he could drink, and we laughed a lot when he did. We didn't talk much about love."

I stood sentry at the door and watched for doctors or nurses while Jeanne smoked half a cigarette and gazed at some happy juncture of past and future.

Over the weekend I attended a brunch at Duke's Coffee Shop up on Sunset Boulevard hosted by *Screw* magazine publisher Al Goldstein. Goldstein was a hairy, wheedling wheezer, grossly obese and lewdly garrulous. He fancied himself a bon vivant and insult king. These brunches were salons of sleaze. The guest list often included renowned penises such as Ron Jeremy and Tom Byron, sometimes both at once. Rodney Dangerfield might stop by the table, friendly in a Brooklyn way with New Yorkers Goldstein and Jeremy. Goldstein habitually accessorized himself with a female companion who posed as a friend who might or might not consent to relate to Al on a physical level. These escorts would be ex-porn stars or semi-legendary exotic dancers or quasi-innocents scheming to break into the business, whatever that business might be. The meals themselves could be gruesome, particularly if I'd caught a seat within the spray radius of Goldstein or Ron Jeremy, both of whom—for all their warmth and pleasant intentions—had trouble keeping their food in their mouths.

This Sunday forenoon, I slid in next to a quiet, sparkling, tiny old lady. We smiled and said hello, and Goldstein assumed his host aspect. "Allan MacDonell, you're sitting next to Sally Marr. You know who Sally Marr is, don't you?"

"Sure. You're one of the girls from the Profumo scandal."

She laughed, a sweet, polite snicker. She might have had something to say, but Al cut her short.

"This is Lenny Bruce's mother. A moron like you won't know who Lenny Bruce is. Was."

"No kidding? Jesus Christ." This was better than meeting Mickey Mantle's mother. Sally shrank back in the gust of my enthusiasm. "When I was a kid, I conned my mother into buying me a book called *The Essential Lenny Bruce*. It was basically transcripts of all your son's major bits. His way of looking at the world had a profound effect on who I am today ... which is not really much of an endorsement for the views of your son, I'm sorry to say."

"You should be sorry to say anything," wheezed Al, but I'd earned another sweet, polite snicker from Lenny Bruce's dear, slight mother. I'd made her laugh! How could I not marvel at life's rich tapestry? Imagine a world where Lenny Bruce's mother is laughing at jokes from a lump like me!

At the second hospital visit, on the next Saturday, I saw that doctors had chopped off a few of Jeanne's toes. What I'd taken for bruising had been gangrene.

"They say I'll never dance again!" She was giddy and defiant, though not to the point of hysterically denying the facts of life. "What do doctors know?"

Jeanne and I sat alone for a while. I wasn't the only person from the office who'd been to visit her. The snare of Jeanne's kooky web had crossed all company lines, and a trickle of LFP stalwarts had stopped in to say so long. Jeanne lifted out of a doze and pulled a pack of cigarettes from under her sheet. She turned the pack in her hands the way a religious person might finger beads. She recognized me and remembered she had something to tell me. "Allan, a lot of people are pulling for you," she said. "At your job. People care about you."

This was true. I haven't given this impression, but I admired almost everyone who worked for me, and most of the people I worked for as well. I was surrounded by decent, well-humored colleagues. My problem is that I fixate on the other type, the few, the foul. Jeanne unhanded the cigarettes to tap my forearm. "Don't let the assholes get you, babe. That's all I'm going to say."

"Sure, but what did you mean that time you said you saw me dying in a murder?"

This question pleased her. "Wait till those doctors see me spinning in my high heels!"

Jeanne lit a smoke. She could hardly suck the stuff in, but it seemed to give her a world of satisfaction. I put out the cigarette for her, she closed her eyes, and that's how we parted.

The memorial for Jeanne Diamond was at the rustic Little Country Chapel in North Hollywood. I drove out toward the Valley through the winding Laurel Canyon pass. Morbidly self-obsessive doubts wove in and out with the light Saturday-morning traffic. Did I belong out there at the funeral?

Jeanne's boyfriend gave the main eulogy. He spoke of her bravery, her honesty. He recalled his first vision of her, ascending a jazz club stairway, then he singled me out. "Jeanne said Allan was the easiest boss she ever worked for. Whenever she wanted things at the office to go her way, all she had to do was wear the extra-high heels."

The mourners, many of them co-workers, turned toward me and laughed. I felt no need to point out that I'd never really been under the thrall of Jeanne's legs. It was her mouth that had kept me on my toes. I was grateful to be the butt of her last little joke. No one in that quaint chapel wanted to murder me, and that was a good start.

Hustler Feedback

HUSTLER TAKES PRIDE in "keeping it real," a soufflé of a conceit that falls flat within the pages of the magazine. Flip through any issue: bogus sex confessions, spurious erotic dilemmas, fantastical articles and feigned female orgasm. But you can't fake everything. Up near the front of the book, the "Feedback" column presents a sampling of genuine communiqués from the actual folks who pay hard currency to own a copy of *Hustler*. Bent, hand-scrawled envelopes arrived daily, seven to 10 at a time. Aside from giving readers an opportunity to comment upon their favorite nude models, the "Feedback" forum also hosted an exchange of ideas among the *Hustler* community, something akin to the reasoned discourse essential to an informed democracy. The country is a more real place because the semi-literate and the fully deranged among the *Hustler* readership weighed in on matters of national debate. Often the month-to-month dialogue hinged on some basis of racial relations, commentary summed up by the arrival of a business card embossed with a line drawing of a hooded rider and the message, "The KKK is watching you, scum."

Shut-ins of several stripes reached out, desperate for basic human contact, sending self-portraits in photos and poems, proof positive of life's sorrowful limitations. I would open these envelopes and pause, mildly stunned. This bedridden flipper boy with his face painted in clown drag and his penis clasped between two fin-like hands? Am I this man's lifeline? And this feces-obsessed juicer and his geometrical drawings of grog-swilling buccaneers tormenting their shit-eating captives? This Second Amendment advocate grimly posing for Polaroids in the company of his armory? The prison inmates' artworks, their racist rants, their sad and homey real-world fantasies? All submitted with the confidence of receiving serious consideration from someone at *Hustler*. One subscriber wrote in to boast of achieving nirvana while sitting on the can, defecating, masturbating and peaking on LSD. At any other publication, you'd simply drop this brown-fingered crank's envelope into the trash bin and vigorously wash your hands. A *Hustler* editor is forced to wonder: *Are my brightest and sincerest efforts directed to a mass of toilet-fixated defectives?*

—————

CHAPTER 12

The Hollywood *Hustler*

I ALMOST ALWAYS answered my own phone. "Hello."

"Allan, why haven't you called me back?" Larry's voice. Impatient, verging on angry.

"I didn't know you'd called. I didn't get a message."

"Are you saying I'm a liar?" The voice had crossed from impatience to irritation.

"No, I'm saying I never received the message. I always call you back."

"You too much of a big shot now to check your own messages?" A scornful tone, but with a gruff pinch of self-parody.

"I check my messages every chance I get."

"You must be working for somebody else then, and they're eating up all your time."

"Who's going to hire me after working here? Look, Larry, I know there's a reason for your call."

"I'll tell you, Allan. You come up here and fuck Liz for me. If I have to put it to that monkey one more time, I'm going to find a steep hill and kill myself." Cackling laughter. I'd been had.

"Fuck you," I said, "whichever one of you ..."

Anyone who worked six months for Flynt developed an imitation of the boss' distinctive bullying twang. It wasn't unusual to hear a pair of editors conduct an entire conversation in Flynt character, admonishing one another to "keep it real."

If I suspected an underling of untoward ambition, I might appropriate Larry's phone persona myself, saying: "This is Larry. I want to know what you think. Who's smarter than Allan MacDonell down there? I'm tired of that guy. Who have we got down there smarter than him?"

"Shit, Larry. I really don't know. He's pretty smart, not as smart as he pretends he is, but pretty smart."

"I suspect you have an idea of who might be smarter."

"Well, I don't want to say just off the top of my head."

"You think about it. I'll be expecting you to let me know."

"Will do, Mr. Flynt."

"When you're ready, call my secretary and tell her you want to speak to me about brainpower."

An hour later, or maybe in the next day or two, I'd pick up the phone and hear the hotline voice. "Larry here. Allan, you need to bring in some gay editors. Who you got down there that's on the fence? I want one of you fellas to suck some cock."

Line B would flash. The assistant was never around when I needed her to pick up.

"Larry, can you hold? I have someone on the other line."

"Make it quick."

I'd switch over to B.

"It's me, Larry. You know my cameras are watching you, Allan, wherever you go on my premises. I see you stealing my paper and pens, and I'm sick and tired of you banging my fiancée."

Probably both these Larrys were fakes, but who could be sure? The temptation was to tell every seemingly bogus Larry to fuck himself, a dangerous course of action. Any presumed imposter might be the real Flynt. Then again, according full obeisance to some interoffice wiseacre's spurious cracker twang chumped my authority. So, if Larry's secretary hadn't announced him first, I was leery of incoming Flynt voices and dampened my affect, suspecting an attempt to fuck with me. All this caution and counter-caution might seem paranoid, except that rivals were attempting to fuck with me. Proof of duplicity was never more than a phone call away.

"Hold for Mr. Flynt."

"Allan? Larry. Who's this Thad Simpson, and why is he bugging my secretary about increasing brainpower?"

"I'll call and straighten him out as soon as we hang up."

"Do I know what this Thad looks like?"

"He's nobody you'll remember."

Larry had eyes everywhere, and not just the suspected fiber optics installed in air-conditioning vents and light fixtures. The boss' brother, a daughter, a pair of nephews, his former nurse (fiancée), the fiancée's brother, that brother's best friend, the fiancée's sister, that sister's daughter and the fiancée's best girlfriend were all installed in crucial vantage points throughout the company. Furthermore, Larry had bestowed charity jobs upon shambling relics from bygone *Hustler* eras, editorial liabilities whose last brush with relevance had come shortly after Ford pardoned Nixon.

Larry was vulnerable to any toady who ever sucked up to him back when he could still walk. Old-time freeloaders roamed throughout the photo department, the art stations and the editorial domain. In common, they were 10 to 20 years older than me, unhireable outside of Larry's largesse, ambitious without being industrious, and they all professed—not where they thought I would hear it—to know better than I did how to run *Hustler*. For fun, let's create a composite out of three or four of these nicotine-stained, dandruff-flecked, belly-stretched, borderline bewildered, semi-kempt, raging bullshitters. For starters, we'll name him Narcisco Smelt.

Narcisco had left his original position as Larry's left-hand man under an acid cloud of suspicion and recrimination. Diverted freelance funds, expense exaggerations, misapplication of Flynt resources—the small details are hazy, but the big picture is clear. In his years outside the LFP fold, Smelt had illustrated a compromised aptitude at a succession of down-market magazines and adult outlets, each markedly shabbier than the previous. On why he'd left LFP in the first place, Narcisco was vague, but he loved to reenact a scene in which Larry begged him to stay.

Smelt's token return employment at *Hustler* was to accompany staff photographers on photo shoots and promote some vague aesthetic imperative. Smelt liked the photo position because it put him in contact with Liz Berrios, who was closer to Larry Flynt than even Narcisco wanted to be. When Smelt sat down confidentially with Liz, he failed to anticipate that Liz's assistant would report their conversation directly to me.

"You know, Liz, the photographers all say that Allan never picks their best shots. He deliberately uses photos that he should reject. By the way, why is there no sexual horoscope in *Hustler?* Trust me, people love sexual horoscopes."

A few days later, Liz might corner me in an elevator and inquire: "Allan, why is there no sexual horoscope in *Hustler?* People love sexual horoscopes."

"That's true," I would acknowledge. "Women people do, and gay people do."

"What do you mean?" She would have become defensive, one stop short of flustered, which is only a step away from angered.

"Liz, I've given the question of horoscopes in *Hustler* some thought. Generally, magazine horoscopes are confined to titles that cater to women, such as the fashion magazines, or magazines that appeal to a combination of women and gays, like *Vanity Fair.* Men's magazines—*Playboy, Esquire, Hustler*—rarely if ever feature astrology except to make fun of it, and I don't think that's an accident or coincidence."

"Oh. Okay. I'm just saying that I think you should consider it."

"I will, Liz. I'll discuss it at our next editorial meeting, and then I'll see what Larry thinks."

"You do that."

While I'd been fending off Liz, Narcisco would have been putting the twist on Jimmy Flynt. Smelt and Jimmy had shared a hooker 12 years earlier at a distribution conference, to hear Smelt tell it. Jimmy was tougher than Liz to suck up to because he had been spending a lot of time working in the field since Liz had appropriated his office furniture. Still, Narcisco was prepared to pounce when Jimmy ventured onsite.

"Jimmy, I just don't know what Larry sees in Allan."

No dope, Jimmy was slow to be drawn into partisan discussions, unless he was instigating.

"Well, Narcisco, maybe Larry sees Allan as hard-working and a pretty smart guy."

"Geez, remember that big blonde we did back in '81? Where was it, Cleveland? Those were good days, weren't they, Jimmy?"

"What was I doing in Cleveland?"

"You know what Allan wants to do, he's so smart? He's pushing for a horoscope column in *Hustler.*"

"A what?"

"Astrology. Three pages every month. What's he trying to do? Cross-over appeal to women and fags? What's Larry think is so smart about that?"

Jimmy might have felt the need to visit me in my office. "Allan, do you ever get the feeling that *Hustler* might be veering in a direction that's just a little too … arty? I mean, keep in mind the readers aren't all so sophisticated as you and I."

I might scan my desk and hold up an attraction from the current issue, a four-page spread of fine-art renderings depicting 16 vaginal varieties, four to a page. Under each orifice, a concise text claimed to interpret a female's personality traits as revealed in her labial disposition.

"Jimmy, are you afraid we've gone sissified? No one here is losing sight of what we're all about."

The vaginas pleased Jimmy, as they were intended to.

"Maybe you got a point there, Allan. Maybe you do."

On average, I spent a quarter-hour a day in the office of Larry's secretary—waiting to be shown in for scheduled conferences, setting up appointments for face-to-face strategizing, stopping in after being summoned for a quick consultation.

"What's with Smelt?" Larry's secretary might ask. "Larry blows him off three days in a row, and he still keeps bounding in."

"What's he sucking Larry for this time?"

"He wants to start a magazine that's all vagina comics. Larry can't stand him these days."

"Then fire him."

Larry rarely fired a Narcisco Smelt. Aside from nostalgic affection for those who had known him as an ambulatory being, strife and sparring in the lower echelons entertained Larry. I assumed that Smelt was still slipping in his shots. He had the interoffice memo at his disposal, plus that tremendously convenient innovation for undermining and backstabbing—the e-mail. Prior to rehiring him, Larry had forwarded a letter from Narcisco: "Larry, I don't know why I am writing this. I have nothing to gain. My wife says I am crazy to get involved where I am not involved. I suppose that I simply cannot outgrow the loyalty grown during all those years we worked together.

I try to look at the magazine and let what I see slide off my back. But I cannot. I'm afraid, Larry. For you and for the future of *Hustler*. I say this with no thought toward job or reward. The magazine has gone stale. Where is the wild sense of adventure that we trailblazed? Call me any time. I'm at home these days, and could devote as much time as you see fit."

Smelt's antics delighted me less than they did Larry. I had work to do: a pile of manuscripts to be marked up, test shots to be evaluated, time sheets and photo expenses to be reviewed and signed. I wondered with a weighty sigh: *What can I do to shake the Narcisco Smelts of this small, imperfect universe off my back?*

The answer and my deliverance came in a Hollywood love letter. Columbia Pictures in conjunction with producer/director/gadfly Oliver Stone published their intentions of filming a biographical feature based upon the life of Larry Flynt. This was a major production, with real money and Academy Award-winning director Milos Forman. I scanned the next memo I saw from Smelt to Flynt with greater amusement than apprehension. "Larry, I read about the film being made and immediately my concern for your best interests sprang to the fore. I attempted to contact Oliver Stone directly, but he has forgotten our connection. I'm sure that you are committed as I would be to an authentic portrayal of the golden days of *Hustler* glory. I seek nothing for myself. Certainly we can all benefit mutually from sitting down to break bread with Mr. Stone, yourself and my current agent."

In the blinking glare of Hollywood tinsel, the printed word lost its luster for Smelt. He, and all of Larry's other ambitious deadbeats, shifted their focus to milking the Flynt movie. Being only in charge of hidebound magazines, I was freed up from intrusive climbers and their opportunistic forays, which allowed me to juggle workflow disruptions caused by the movie.

The trade-paper hype on Larry Flynt's bio-pic attracted swarms of nosy TV crews. Our gold-plated chairman invited major networks and local anchors to accompany him on his daily rounds. Young art director Bill and I set up a dozen real and feigned consultations in the photo-edit room. Under the heat of portable lamps, Larry picked through slides of nubile females. Young Bill and I sat to either side of our star-quality leader, dropping cryptic but prurient comments, such as: "They're fakes, but very good fakes—preferable to real ones that droop." "The look on her face says as much as the space between her legs." "You don't usually see a girl this beautiful twisted up in a pose like that."

As filming of the Flynt epic grew closer, scruffy European documentarians washed ashore with requests to gather footage. Larry delegated the bulk of those interviews to me. Overseas crews generally traveled in sponge-bathed packs of four. Uncomfortable with California's tobacco regulations, our Old World guests invariably would position their lamps, place a light meter to my face, consult clipboard and notebook, pin on my microphone, and halt all activity.

"Do you mind, Mr. MacDo-all? We must conference, one to another. For a moment, we will step away?"

The group would shuffle outdoors. Taken as a whole, from my window 50 feet above, these stooped circles of cigarette-sucking intercontinental media seemed insignificant and insular, but their finished products might spread to a consequential audience. Standing to address their tripod-mounted cameras, as serious and dedicated as if I were a Presidential spokesman, in my mind I was presenting Larry to the world press. I exuded a quality that money can't buy, a core belief that I spoke God's honest truth: "The fact that Larry Flynt's life was chosen as the subject of a major studio film, and not Bob Guccione's or Hugh Hefner's, tells you something about Larry Flynt. Larry Flynt is one of the country's most enduring and most endearing outsider rebels." My mind wandered, always the inquisitive organ, if only within a limited sphere. I wondered how these European gypsies split up for bunking. Often the crews would have one girl, usually attractive in a quirky, slightly unwashed way. Did she room alone? Was she sharing mattress space with one of these hairy, foreign-inflected fellows? Were all three males benefactors of a free-love fringe benefit?

Although I'm loath to generalize, German and French males seemed to expect their women to function in a role of servitude. With crews from England, mainly the girl would be in charge. British men must have grown accustomed to being bullied by nanny goats gruff during the Thatcher reign. If my observation means anything, U.K. women, given a small amount of authority, tend to adopt the attitude that they are smarter than everyone they meet in America, especially brighter than bespectacled men who administrate crass magazines for the enrichment of bloated smut tycoons. My main objection to the behavior of French and German women during these interviews was that, while stooping to the chores of their Bavarian and Gaulish over-lords, the slavish lasses wasted attention that might better have been applied to me.

To the Germans and the French, once I'd finished speaking, I simply ceased to exist. The women would efficiently pack up their gear, and everybody would go. The British seemed intent on not leaving until they'd made a point of personal perspective.

"Thank you, Mr. MacDonell." The arch British alpha female would pronounce my name with an enunciation more precise than I could ever hope to give it. "You were so thoughtful and generous to share with us this rich portion of your time and insight, which are obviously of the highest value and rarity."

These scornful falsities were not lost on me. Despite the posh accent and supercilious attitude, there was always a bit of the Spice Girl about these women. I had only to wait a moment, and she would be back, tapping at my office door.

"Frightfully sorry, Mr. MacDonell. But have I left my bag on your premises? Ah, yes. Here 'tis. Frightfully sorry."

Backing out, mildly abashed, Posh's ingratiation would give way to sullen chagrin when I would point out a neglected carrying case. "And that lens," I would say. "I'll bet it's an expensive one and that you will be needing it somewhere down the road."

"Surely."

"And do you require directions to find the elevators?"

"I'm quite all right on that account."

Five minutes later, I'd step out for the men's room and find her leading her countrymen in circles, begging a way out from a passing copy editor.

Margo, a bitter ex-assistant who had evacuated under the wrath of Liz Berrios, landed a spot with an entertainment firm and mes-sengered over a copy of the working script to what we at LFP referred to as Larry's movie. The screenplay was goofy, slight and unbeliev-able, featuring a madcap porno cripple who zipped through the flowered lanes of American complacency in a super-powered motor-ized wheelchair. The story struck me as a stinker. At least two of my fictive exposés, "Interview With a Lesbian: Straight Talk With a Bent Woman" (November, 1994) and "Diary of a Child Molester: A Short-Eyed Journal Into Hell" (September, 1995), struck me as more complex, convincing and illuminating of realities than the one estab-lished by this so-called true life tale. But there was no denying that the scriptwriters were making two tons more dollars than I was, so I had to concede that their work had much greater value than mine.

Several copies of the same script I had privately disparaged became public property around the LFP offices. My co-workers formed chat cir-cles to lament the script's perceived dearth of merit. I resisted the temptation to toss in my trashy complaints, a rare prudent discretion to keep my trap shut. Larry circulated a memo expressing unhappiness that people whose livelihoods depended upon him were mocking the story of his life. I reproduce this memo, errors included for flavor.

December 13, 1995
To: All Employees
From: Larry Flynt

It has been brought to my attention, that a copy of the movie script based on my life to be produced by Columbia pictures, is being passed around the company and read by employee's.

I am appalled about hearing this;

1) The script is not a final draft.

2) It is none of your business in the first place.

3) It is inappropriate.

4) I don't view any employee playing any part in this as being loyal in my sense of the word.

If I find how and who made the script available, they will be terminated without hesitation.

The phone rang, and I picked up to the voice of Flynt. "I hope you got my memo, MacDonell."

The speaker might really be him. He was fond of making ambush calls. "Yeah, Larry. I've just finished reading it."

"Well, you fucking better not be how and who made the script available."

At this point, I was reasonably sure I was being addressed by an imitator. "By terminated, Larry, do you mean fired, because I would recommend something more lasting."

Eventually, filming started on *The People vs. Larry Flynt*. Since late adolescence, I'd been living in neighborhoods where at least one street every day was shut down for location shooting. The sight of gray, burly policemen lounging on their motorcycles, long tractor trailers full of wardrobe, folding tables stacked with steam-tray cuisine, clipboard-waving twerps gibbering into headsets with the urgency of NASA commanders and onscreen meat being escorted to and from the cameras with all the solemnity of heads of state being positioned at a royal funeral—all this was old news to me. I calmly went about my business, until casting maven Deirdre Cochrane blew through the workspace, Polaroid camera in hand, assistant with clipboard at her side. Tall as a fashion model, Deirdre had a mannish figure matched with a square-jawed, hawknosed face. I regarded her with patient doubt.

"Hold that," said Deirdre. The camera flashed. The film slid out. Deirdre shook the film. While waiting for the picture to develop, she looked around for something to talk about. My plain beige walls supported two large, framed art-deco prints that I suppose were marketed as having been all the rage in 1920s Paris. The entire editorial suite was littered with these glitzy old things.

"What's with the gay decor?" Deirdre said.

"Larry wants the office to look professional for filming. You will notice that no wires are showing from our computers. That is part of the Flynt dictate for a clean, streamlined aesthetic. Fittingly, we have no bulletin boards or personal items hanging on the walls."

Deirdre paid no attention to anything I said. Her assistant—a tightly bundled peroxide blonde whose black eyes were pinpointed by the thick, dime-size lenses of her tortoiseshell glasses—peered at my shoulders, neck and arms and made notations on a clipboard. She stared at my waist and ran her eyes up and down my legs and jotted something else on the clipboard. She took stock of my feet. "Shoe size 11?" she said.

I agreed. Deirdre flexed her biceps as if she might want to put someone in a headlock. She flipped the picture impatiently. It was almost done.

"Have you been upstairs?" she asked. "We've recreated the entire *Hustler* creative area, the art room and where the editors would be, from the early 1980s. We did an awesome job."

I had been up there. Larry had set aside an entire floor of the building for construction of a publishing set. It didn't look like any *Hustler* offices I could remember. I saw no point in saying so. Deirdre and her assistant bustled out, taking with them their collection of employee Polaroids, all of us males smiling lamely in our dour Fuller Brush Man ties and shirts.

A few nights later Deirdre called me at home. She'd been ringing my office, and I'd been ducking the calls. The wife-to-be and I had recently combined our resources and bought a house in the Hollywood Hills. We were positioned between the world-famous Hollywood sign and the equally notorious Griffith Park Observatory, location of James Dean's climactic crying jag in *Rebel Without a Cause*. I felt perfectly situated to take a call from the movie industry.

"Milos loves you," she said.

"You mean the director? He's never met me."

"He's seen your picture and your information, and he wants you on the set. He has a special idea for you. I've been trying to tell you about this all day."

"I really can't afford to be taking time out to play movie extra."

Larry's office had been encouraging his peons to function as background props in the movie. Several employees had excitedly agreed to participate in the filming, and were then told that LFP would not pay them for those days that they spent on the set rather than at their desks. The production company would provide a day rate for standing around waiting to be part of a crowd, plus lunch of some sort. The experience promised to be a profitable one, along the lines of jury duty.

"Look, Al," insisted Deirdre, "I'm calling you from my house on my own time. That's how important this is. I believe in Milos, and I'm willing to take this extra step for him. Perhaps you are unaware of what's at stake here, but I would firmly suggest that you believe in

Milos as well. If Milos says you are essential to the scene, then, Al, you are essential."

Go ahead, call me sucker. I agreed to report for duty at eight the next morning.

"Maybe this will be your big break," said the wife-to-be. "It might lead to something. Stranger things have happened."

She pissed me off. I'd been thinking the exact same thing.

In the morning, I drove in earlier than usual. Support staff from all of Larry's various magazines and clerical departments crowded the area where Deirdre had told me to report. I sidled up to a *Film Threat* intern.

"Hey, Gabe, did Deirdre call you at home last night?"

"No, she caught me yesterday at work. But Lois and Jim and Peter all heard from her last night."

"And the shtick that Milos insists you're perfect for the scene?"

"We all got that."

A gum chewer equipped with headset and clipboard ordered the office drudges to listen up. Then we were put in a van and shuttled to a double-wide trailer parked two blocks from Flynt's building. One by one, we would-be movie stars stood in front of a gray-haired guy and his nymphet apprentice. Both wore down vests to fend off the early morning chill. This wardrobe duo would toss a wig or coat down to the newly-minted "extra." Eventually, the line dwindled to me. The duo glanced toward each other, shook their heads slightly and told me, "sorry."

Film Threat Gabe pushed up behind me. "Are you kidding? You don't know who this guy is."

The wardrobe duo tensed. Gabe sensed victory: "This is the editor of *Hustler* magazine. You can't reject the editor of *Hustler* magazine for Larry Flynt's movie."

The wardrobe duo relaxed. For a moment, Gabe had had them running. They'd almost mistaken me for a person who mattered. I plodded off to go about my regular day.

"I thought you were in the movie," said my assistant, who refused to be baited into such foolishness.

"Been rejected as an extra," I said. "Feels bad."

My to-be and I became man and wife on September 14, 1996. The marriage ceremony, a traditional Catholic rite, was performed at Sacred Heart, a church in the strained heart of Hollywood's Sunset Boulevard. Principled atheist Larry Flynt, in the company of Liz Berrios and a bodyguard to handle the golden chair, attended the reception on the grounds of Wattles Mansion, a Los Angeles landmark giving southerly views of the vast L.A. basin, a vista that the original Mr. Wattles had carpeted with citrus trees. We seated Larry and Liz at a table with young art director Bill and atrocity director Greg Dark. Greg brought along a famed dominatrix as his date. I caught myself worrying about Larry. Was he bored? Were my new wife's gauche family and friends gawking at him? Had the priest attempted a conversion? But Larry seemed pleased as a toad. Soon to be a major motion picture, my boss surveyed me in my electric-blue Gucci silk suit and proclaimed: "Finally you look like a *Hustler* editor."

The wife and I had planned our honeymoon, scheduling around the multiple deadlines of her job and mine. Before leaving on the trip, I faced Larry across his massive desk. A petite, shapely hairdresser stood behind Larry's chair, tinting his hair its trademark red.

"You cain't just get up and leave your job for 16 days," Larry said. "A person in your position gives up the idea of taking vacations."

"If I give up this vacation, I can give up the idea of keeping the wife."

"That might not be a bad idea." His emerald green eyes shifted under their hoods toward a portrait of Liz Berrios. I don't know if this shift had been for my amusement or if it were an unintended tell. "Where you two going?" Larry asked.

"Italy."

"I hope I'm not paying you enough to afford Italy. Are you going to Naples?"

"We'll pass through."

"You'll have a wonderful time in Naples. Check for a whorehouse there, right down by the waterfront. Back when I was in the Navy, some of the best pussy I ever had was in Naples." He looked at me with a mixture of nostalgia and envy. "Your wife is a plum," he said. "I don't know what you ever did to get so lucky."

Coming back from my honeymoon, I sensed that interlopers had been prowling about the *Hustler* offices. Now that Narcisco Smelt's movie ambitions had failed him, he turned his genius back upon the magazine world.

"Allan, Larry. I want you to sit down and talk with Narcisco. He has some plans for reorganizing the editorial structure down there. I don't know why you didn't think of these ideas first. Make sure you talk to him today, before you move along too far."

I slammed down the phone and bolted for Narcisco's office. Every couple of steps, I'd pass one of my staff. "Hey, you're back," they'd say. "How was the honeymoon?" "Jesus, you've put on some weight." "Hey, what's the matter?" A sizable audience formed in my wake and witnessed me pushing open Narcisco's door. I caught him napping.

"Smelt," I said, "I don't know what kind of fake ideas infiltrate your feeble brain, but I'll put one fact in for you right now: me or nobody who works for me will ever report to you. Is that plain English? You will never be in any kind of supervisory position over me or anyone who is on my staff. Is that plain enough for you?"

Narcisco came awake quicker than I would have given him credit for. He rose to his full bulk and expanded toward where I stood rooted.

"I don't know what the fuck you're talking about," he said, "and I'm fucking offended."

I've often found the appearance of retreat to be a slick mode of attack. "In that case, let me apologize," I said. "If, in fact, you are not designing a plan to put yourself in some decision-making capacity regarding *Hustler* or any of the other magazines I oversee, then I am sorry to have considered you a sneaking cur. That is, if in fact you are not attempting to insert yourself in some decision-making position that in any way effects me or anyone who works for me. If that is in fact true, then I apologize."

Narcisco loomed bigger than me, and just as angry, but he was old and out of shape. He also was not accustomed to the subtleties of direct confrontation.

"I could throw you out this fucking window," he said.

"You can do that, but you still won't boss me or anybody I work with."

"Who in the fuck are you to be making Larry's decisions for him?"

"It's not Larry's decision. It's my decision. You will never work with me."

"We'll have to see what Larry says when he hears this."

"Run along, Smelt. Have your say."

I walked the gauntlet of my grinning staff, returning to my office to sort the piled-up honeymoon mail. Hand tremors betrayed my pretense of calm. The research director stuck his head in. "Smelt took the elevator upstairs. He's in talking to Larry right now."

The research director was happier at this development than an uninvolved observer would be. I clasped him by the arm, and his smirk vanished.

"It wasn't Larry who called me. It was you."

"Dude," he said, "paranoia is not attractive on you. But the information you received in that phone call, was it timely and correct, or what?"

My phone rang and I unhanded the research guy. It was Larry's secretary. Larry wanted me upstairs, right away. I reached the 10th floor, Larry's floor, determined to tell him exactly how I felt about what had happened between Smelt and me. I walked across the thickly carpeted no-man's land between the door to Flynt's office and his desk. Larry shifted his eyes to the chair opposite him, and I sank into it wordlessly. We were alone. He adjusted his glasses and looked me over. His expression was searching, as if he'd missed some telling aspect of my appearance that should have been obvious to him. After a moment, he was satisfied. He had reconciled what he had learned of me with what he saw in me. "All right," he drawled, "I'll see you later."

The phone was ringing as I slid behind my desk. Surely the fireworks were over for the day. It was Larry's secretary. Mr. Flynt wanted the wife and me to join him that night for dinner at Spago. In those days, Spago was located on a hillock overlooking the Sunset Strip, across the street from Tower Records. You seldom saw anyone in there with less than a seven-figure net worth.

The wife, as usual, was unable to arrive on time. Fifteen minutes late, she screeched to a halt in the queue for parking and promptly locked her keys in the running car, stumping the valets. After a scrambled negotiation and handing over her Auto Club service card, the wife submitted to my stranglehold, and we scurried in tardy for a glare of irritation from Flynt. Lording in his golden chair, Larry's displeasure lasted only a moment, thanks to Tony Curtis. The film legend and his young, tall blonde beauty of a spouse, Jill Vandenberg, stopped by the table. Tony and Larry had owned the same piece of Bel-Air real estate. Larry introduced the wife and me, and suddenly it was as if we were hobnobbing with the immortal star of *Sweet Smell of Success* and his wife. Curtis blushed and grinned as if he were the one charmed to his toes to be meeting the wife and me! Where does any mere human learn to be such a gracious bastard?

Tony wished he was available to sit and dine with us, but split for his own table. Larry leaned in and whispered confidentially. "Curtis tells me that Marilyn Monroe was a better lay than her reputation might lead you to believe." Larry sipped a drink, and irritation came back to his face, although not with me. "I'm still pissed off at that fucking Tom Hanks. He's a personal friend, and he had a chance to play me in the movie, and he turned it down. Thought it would be bad for his long-term image to play Larry Flynt. What kind of logic is that? He'll play a fucking retard, but he won't play me?"

The wife and Liz Berrios hunkered in for a private chat, but Liz remained fully vigilant of Larry's needs, napkin at the ready.

"Hey, Allan," said Larry. "Make sure you notice the ass on that broad over to your left at the bar."

The woman stood unsteadily, half-on, half-off her stool. Other than being fully unaccustomed to the height and pitch of her heels, she had the appearance of a mid-range prostitute.

I mentioned that a faction among Kennedy assassination theorists held that Woody Harrelson's father, currently imprisoned for the murder of a federal judge, had been a Grassy Knoll bum, and the actual shooter who killed the President. Larry had heard this theory previously and did not reject it outright. He wanted to talk about Courtney Love. Apparently, Courtney believed that playing Althea Flynt in Larry's movie gave her the right to mouth off. During an interview in *Rip*, a magazine Larry owned, Lady Love explained: "[Althea's] story is that she took your publisher's empire and made it 375 percent more profitable. Larry was dumb, and Althea was incredibly intelligent. She was a bit of a sociopath, but I think if she was around, your magazine would be better."

Larry twisted his mouth as if he had just bitten into a canker sore. "Who is that slut to say Althea was crazy?"

My wife's former boyfriend had been the manager of Jumbo's Clown Room when Courtney Love had peeled at that down-market strip bar. Having claimed Larry's full attention, I delivered the payoff: "Of all the strippers and hookers at Jumbo's, Courtney Love was the one they named the Pig."

Larry took in this information, and it seemed to lessen the bite of Love's on-the-record insensitivity.

On a rainy December night in 1996, I loitered on the red carpet at the West Coast premiere of *The People vs. Larry Flynt*. The wife skidded in as the opening credits rolled, and we didn't miss much. I knew the story by heart, so suspense and dramatic tension were virtually nonexistent. Larry was presented as a basically harmless and principled eccentric. Familiar workaday faces drifted across the screen, bloated to the size of gods. Doug the bodyguard, bear-like in real life, stood 50 feet tall and half as wide. He spun and pulled a gun out from a holster beneath his jacket. I applauded, ever conscious of an opportunity to suck up to a bodyguard.

In the afterglow of the screening, Flynt commandeered a Westwood pasta house. Jimmy invited the wife and me to join the family. We ordered food and were presented with separate checks. Woody Harrelson and Courtney Love looked in through separate windows. I won't be revealing any national secrets to say that Woody lurked outside in the drizzle smoking a reefer. Larry sat in a corner of the dining room, enthroned, his eyes blazing with gratitude and nostalgia, humbled and in awe of his own story. The man was sharing one of the happiest nights of his life with us. The wife and I wove our way through the supplicants and congratulated him.

"That means a lot coming from you two," Larry said. "I know how fucking critical you are."

The film won a few Golden Globe prizes and was nominated for a couple of Oscars, but nothing recaptured the blissful pitch of that opening night. On the morning after the Golden Globes were awarded, seasoned insider Larry dissected the politics of the previous evening: "How do we win for best script and best director, and not take best picture?"

The movie brought along a backlash, largely whipped up by professional feminist and trophy wife Gloria Steinem. Simpletons may say that all publicity is good publicity, but negative press has a chilling effect in an image-conscious industry such as the movies. On the eve of the 69th Annual Academy Awards, Larry was disinvited by Columbia Pictures from attending the tribute as their guest. Larry hired a plane to sky-write COLUMBIA SUCKS above the Shrine Auditorium, finagled a pair of tickets to the ceremony (rumor had Jack Nicholson donating his) and sat in a prominent aisle seat, victorious and resplendent, insensitive to whether or not the exalted purveyors of the storyteller's art wanted him in their daisy chain. *The People vs. Larry Flynt* lost in all categories.

I sat in the boss' office, inducing him to elect one of my candidates for "Asshole of the Month." The boss and his secretary riffled through his mail. He'd apparently had drinks with lunch and was playing helpless. The secretary took an envelope from his hands and slit it open.

"This letter is from a wheelchair racer who wants sponsorship. See, here's his picture. He races wheelchairs in marathons."

Larry handed the photo back to her. "Fuck that guy," he said. "I fucking hate cripples. And old people, and sick people."

His eyes cleared, and all traces of inebriation vanished. "I'll tell you who the Asshole is. Make it the Oscars. Don't hold back."

By coincidence, the Academy Awards "Asshole" fell in with our July 1997 Anniversary Issue, so the Oscars were elevated to "Asshole of the Year." I waxed anti-poetical, starting with "Hollywood is a make-believe kingdom of pretend reality, a mythical realm where the hopes and passions that unite all humanity are turned, as if by magic, into shit." I defined Oscar as "a shiny, stunted eunuch, plated the color of money," who "although driven by vanity, is loath to look in the mirror, unless the reflective surface is lit of special effects." After several paragraphs deriding "a rotting medium, a commercial fakery," the rant concluded: "Ever since *The People vs. Larry Flynt* premiered, Hollywood's shitheels have honored themselves for making a movie about a 'scumbag.' Let the prick who is without sleaze be the first to call scumbag."

Larry phoned to tell me the column was "too soft." It was the only time he ever called to complain about an "Asshole of the Month," assuming the caller was not an imposter.

Hustler Beaver Hunt

"BEAVER HUNT"—a six-page spread of snapshots mailed in by *Hustler* readers of their nude, spread-legged girlfriends and wives, 17 per issue—is another brilliant and lasting concept, this one lifted from a magazine called *Gallery*. The "Beaver Hunt" ladies are exotic dancers, waitresses, truck drivers, "bored housewives" and retail clerks, ranging in age from late teens to 40s and beyond. Their Polaroids capture the great American Beaver out in its natural habitat—fake wood paneling, picnic tables, kitchen counters and wheat fields. Confederate flags and infants' toys are littered throughout. Beauty is not the only criterion for selection. An older woman with sagging breasts posing in a snowbank is rewarded for her courage and forgiven her surrender to gravity. A holiday-season supplicant's meaty bits may be muddied by shadow, but who can reject a plucky gal splayed beneath a Christmas tree, nude except for a Santa hat and a shotgun?

Appearing in *Hustler* means a lot to these women, much more than the $250 they are paid if their image is selected. Many of the women claim to have harbored lifelong ambitions to be nude models. "Beaver Hunt"—anyone with desire and a derrière can be a star! "Beaver Hunt"—democracy in action!

CHAPTER 13

Disturbing Fornicators I Have Seen—Famous and Infamous

WORD CAME TO me that Bernadette was in crisis at the "Beaver" box. Bernadette was the editor in charge of "Beaver Hunt." She was also responsible for writing girl copy in *Barely Legal* magazine, and she assembled the *Hustler* joke page and provided one or two "Hot Letters" every month. A sensitive, lanky and intense brunette who recently pushed 30, Bernadette had grown up a Rhode Island redneck and then polished her rough edges at one of the Seven Sisters colleges. Along with a fine ear for turning a vile phrase, she exhibited a winning blend of Atlantic Seaboard stoicism and Irish Catholic emotionalism. Crafting the smarmy come-ons of *Barely Legal*, sifting through the jailyard jokes, concocting ludicrous, lascivious confessions—none of this fazed Bernadette's cocked-hip sang-froid. But the "Beavers"? Almost every month these far-flung, wide-eyed, lewd innocents precipitated a breakdown.

The "Beaver" box was situated in the Research Department. Bernadette slumped over the box, head in hand, waving a completed "Beaver Hunt" application in front of her face as if to fan away a hot flash. A corporate-strength paper shredder purred at her side. Tears brimmed in Bernadette's fierce hazel eyes, and she abruptly thrust the "Beaver" application, photos and all, into the whirring blades of the paper shredder. A backlog of utterly mundane "amateur nudists" had amassed. Their drab portraits would never brighten the pages of *Hustler*, or any other magazine. Bernadette sighed, rolled her neck and noticed my look of forbearance.

"These cover letters are heartbreaking," she said. " 'All my friends in Little Rock swear they will buy your magazine if you put my picture in.' Her desire is so basic and touching, and we're denying it. Can't I at least send the pictures back with a conciliatory note?"

"You're killing me. Putting these pictures in the mail, you're asking for trouble. What if her mom opens the envelope? Or her brother?"

I generally indulged Bernadette. The many great women who worked for me at *Hustler* tended to be chipper, intelligent and naturally independent. Bernadette knew I was fond of her, and she decided to push her luck.

"Listen to this one, Allan. Have a heart." She directed my attention to a muscular, heavily tattooed peroxide enthusiast whose abdomen distended as if in advanced cirrhosis. A boa constrictor was draped listlessly over her pierced, granite breasts. "Her name is Gwendolyne. She enjoys poetry and collecting unicorn memorabilia. Sexual fantasies? 'To be made love to on a bed of rose petals, or on a Harley under a waterfall, anything involving vampires.' I feel like I know her."

"You don't know her, and thank Christ you don't know her. It's weirder when you do."

The video age had ushered in the celebrity sex tape. Familiar faces were forever showing up, naughty home movies shot by famous couples, intended for their private diversion, brought into the office by unsavory capitalists. Every one of them arrived with the same asking price: one million bucks.

These adventures in A-list lust usually began with a phone call.

"This is Judge Burt Baker. I'm calling from Amsterdam." The cigarette-parched whiskey voice had interrupted my afternoon reverie. I forgot the caller's name as soon as he said it, and I've presented only an approximation here. Judge Baker coughed at length, and the wracking hack of his phlegmy wheeze came out in a Southern drawl.

"Congratulations," I said. "I've often dreamed of going to Amsterdam."

The Judge was paying for this call, and he had no time for small talk. "I am in position to provide you a videotape of one of the most famous celebrities in the entire world, engaged in sexual activity that is, let me put it this way, execrable in the eyes of many. This is a million-dollar investment."

"Who is this famous, execrable celebrity?"

The Judge coughed delicately. "I'd rather not say until we are face to face."

"But you're in Amsterdam."

"My feeling is that you can send your Amsterdam desk over to our hotel, and that should be all you need to see that a million dollars is a bargain."

"I don't have an Amsterdam desk. We don't even have a San Diego desk."

This threw him for a second, but the Judge was a solutions person. "Then I suggest you book the first intercontinental flight at your disposal. You do not want to miss this."

"You're still not telling me who it is or what that person is doing."

"The name and the actions are too volatile."

"What have you got against Beverly Hills? Our offices are situated in a nice, cozy community here in Southern California. You can bring the tapes over, we'll see what we have to discuss, and you don't even have to tell me who it is."

"Ah, that won't work. My client, and I concur, my client feels that his safety is at risk in the United States, and that's why we picked our bargaining position from the European continent."

This Judge Burt Baker was evidently the brains of the operation, whatever the operation was.

"Look at it my way, Judge. You're asking me to tell my boss that I need to fly to Amsterdam to view a tape of a person I don't know who it is doing something I don't know what it is, with a price tag of a million dollars."

"You're making it sound more difficult than it is."

"Call me when you're in L.A."

That would seem to be the end of that, I thought, but a couple of weeks down the line a whiskey rasp interrupted my afternoon reverie.

"Mr. MacDonell, it's Judge Burt Baker. I've taken your advice."

"You're in L.A.?"

"Only for a limited time."

"Are you really a judge, Burt?"

"Let's just say I've labored extensively within the court system."

"Let's just also say that you tell me who is in this tape and what she's doing so I'll be prepared for what I see."

"We're willing to bring down the price to one half-million dollars for expediency's sake."

"The name of the celebrity?"

"This material is gonna knock the socks off the world. He's someone known and revered the world over."

"I was hoping he would be a she."

"I will tell you that this luminary is a guiding light within the world of rock 'n' roll. You will not be disappointed."

I liked the Judge. I sensed that he was a man of convictions, probably in more ways than one. What did I have to lose? He promised to produce his client and the scandalous video on the very next day.

"I can't rightly advise you as to whether it would be better to see this before you eat or after you eat," he said in closing.

I set up a morning time slot with the editor of *Rip*, and the next day we, along with a young LFP lawyer, hosted the Judge and his two clients. All three of these guys had the range-riding slouch and measuring squint of long-term shitkickers. They wore cowboy boots, denim pants, flannel and denim shirts. The Judge carried himself with the plump aplomb of an educated hellion. The *Rip* editor took a hard-to-impress pose.

"I hope this is good," he said.

The hicks sneered and groveled simultaneously. A neat trick. They handed over the tape, reluctantly, and the *Rip* man slid it into his VCR.

"This here's just a selection," said the primary client. He identified himself as Vince Huck. "We come into a ton more of these tapes. We put these ones together so you all could see there's no bullshit."

"This is an edited version of a shocking whole," clarified the Judge.

A familiar lantern jaw line and nut-brown complexion appeared on the television.

"Jesus. That guy looks just like Chuck Berry."

"Good call," pronounced the Judge.

A slinky, pants-free female wriggled her bare bottom mere inches from the face of the man we took to be archetypal rock 'n' roll guitarist Chuck Berry.

"And these materials came into your possession how?" asked LFP's lawyer.

"We found these tapes out in the trash bin behind Chuck Berry's restaurant in Wentzville, Missouri." According to the man who presented himself as Vince Huck, his wife, Hosana A. Huck, had been employed as a cook at Chuck Berry's eatery, a joint called the Southern Air Restaurant. The names of Vince Huck and his wife Hosana are well-documented in conjunction with Chuck Berry and legal squabbles centering around supposed surreptitious sex tapes. On the TV, we followed Chuck's face as his tongue progressed high up the rear thighs of a trashy-looking brunette. The woman leered over her shoulder and squeezed her ass closer to Chuck's nose.

"You heard about what's going on down there where we come from, in Wentzville, Missouri?" asked Vince Huck. He evinced surprise that we were unaware of any Wentzville situation. "Berry been taping women in the restroom when they go to pee, and doing other stuff too." Apparently, cameras had been discovered, and several of these women stood prepared to file criminal complaints and civil suits. Hosana Huck, if these fellas who were attempting to sell sex tapes of a celebrity without that celebrity's consent were to be believed, had been one of the women who'd undergone intrusive restroom surveillance. If our eyes could be believed, what I had taken to be a large mole high on the back of the videotaped woman's thigh was whisked away by a pass of Chuck's tongue. I refused to believe that the woman had been defecating. We rewound the tape to be sure. It was like log-size Tootsie Rolls were being dispensed from an elastic purse. Chuck lapped them up as quickly as they popped out.

"Straight from the oven," said the Judge.

This could not be Vince Huck's first viewing of Berry's feces feast. Huck was disgusted, his outrage partly physical, partly moral. "Every time he has sex with a woman, Chuck pays her extra to leave him a dropping. He puts them in the Tupperware and keeps his freezer stocked. That boy's out on the road most of the year. When he comes home, he likes to pick a favorite and pop it in the microwave."

The Judge concurred. "Our sources report that Mr. Berry keeps fecal nuggets from his fondest dates in his icebox, labeled with name, date and location." For having found these tapes in a trash bin, the

Judge and Huck certainly had uncovered a wealth of biographical data. Vince Huck's companion, a man who was never introduced and said next to nothing, pulled out a copy of Chuck Berry's autobiography and opened it to an earmarked page.

"He talks about how much he loves fartin' right here," said the quiet man. He pointed to a highlighted paragraph as if the passage proved some grave culpability. The topic segued to drug smuggling, with allegations of Berry's involvement in cocaine importation that were outlandishly grand. Chuck was famous for traveling with one guitar case and a change of clothes. Where would he stash 100 pounds of uncut dope? Onscreen, Chuck had finished his chunky snack. The lady dispenser turned her front to him and released a full stream of urine. It was hard to pay attention to what these Missouri entrepreneurs were saying. The composer of "Sweet Little Sixteen," "Maybelline," "Roll Over Beethoven" and "Too Much Monkey Business" washed down his double helping of crap with gulp after gulp of gushing piss. Chuck's Adam's apple bobbed with frantic urgency. Berry flashed a sheepish smirk.

The Judge winked. "I believe we are all familiar with the expression 'shit-eating grin.'"

"This is all very compelling television," I explained to the Judge, and also to his constituents. "But I don't know how much value it has, dollar-wise. I'm not sure we can legally print any of this stuff."

"There are several points of discussion," agreed the LFP lawyer.

The quietest Missourian wrapped the tape in a paper bag and zipped it into a backpack, which he slung over an insolent shoulder. *This is the one who carries the gun,* I thought.

The Judge smiled in a kindly way. "That half-million, it's a firm number, but not rock-solid," he said. "We've had our expenses, over there in Europe, our other travel and lodgings. We're just looking to recoup and profit."

He declined to give us a contact phone number, preferring to leave the name of their current hotel a mystery. For the next two days, I held discussions with various Flynt executives about the feasibility of exploiting the Chuck Berry tapes. The Judge called approximately twice an hour. I did not shut the door on hope, but each conversation slid the window of chance slightly more closed. On the second day, the Missouri trio came to visit, unannounced, unasked for. I still had no dollar number to offer.

"We'll go back to the hotel and wait poolside," said the Judge. "Bear in mind: our deadline is not open-ended." When he, Huck and the bag man had sauntered out, I noticed they'd left behind a satchel, a backpack much like the one that had contained the tape. Certainly they would not have deliberately left their cash cow unguarded. Naturally, I suspected a bomb. I ordered a copy editor to wait five minutes and then go through the pack. Needing to think the situation over, I went outside to walk around the block. Strolling up Wilshire Boulevard, I saw one parked car that stuck out from the uniform Beverly Hills lineup of European coupes. It was a large American sedan, tilting curbside, in need of shocks. A clothing rack stretched across the backseat, bent under its burden of flannel and denim. Missouri plates. I passed on the sidewalk within feet of the passenger window. The Judge, Huck and their mule were snuggled in there, cozy as dogs. I pretended not to see them and hoped they hadn't seen me. The mystery of their hotel had been cleared up.

Having heard no bomb blast, I hurried back to my desk. The satchel had contained two gas-station sandwiches and what were presumed to be clean changes of underwear. Eventually, the finance department passed the word: Offer $7,500, for all rights indemnified. Feeling pretty good about my part in negotiating the Missourians down to less than 10 grand from a million, I was prepared for the Judge's next call.

"We may have a deal," I said. "Tear yourselves away from that swimming pool and come on down."

The three tape merchants arrived at my office in under 10 minutes. They accepted my offer to be seated. "We can go 75 hundred," I said.

The Judge and Huck looked at one another, their silent exchange plainly saying that 75 hundreds were better than 75 nothings. My phone rang.

"One second." It was an LFP lawyer. He informed me that Chuck Berry had declared a public notice that personal video tapes had been stolen from his home. I passed the bad news to the Judge and his clients.

"We've just discovered that these materials have been reported stolen. If we were to purchase them, it would be like we were fences."

The million-dollar dream had dropped from the Missourians' eyes, 50 thousand, 10 thousand, 25 hundred dollars at a time. These three souls had plummeted to the penurious depths. Silently, without visible rancor, they split.

Within weeks I read a news item in *Rolling Stone* that the Drug Enforcement Administration, acting on information supplied by a man named Vincent J. Huck, had orchestrated a raid on Chuck Berry's Missouri compound, Berry Park. Minimal quantities of hashish and marijuana were found, along with 120 grand in cash, plus sexually explicit videos, slides and books. No mention was made of Tupperware turds in the icebox.

LFP published an affiliated magazine, *Hustler Erotic Video Guide*. A new editor had been hired, a former junior-college wrestler from California's agricultural midlands. Though gentle by nature, he had the bulk and bearing of an enforcer on a crew of unruly longshoremen. He fancied himself an idea man and came up with a fresh screwy notion every time he went to the can. One of his ideas was that *Hustler Erotic Video Guide* needed to buy no more reviews from me.

Confrontation, I'd recently been warned, was not my best suit. So I did not threaten the new *Video Guide* editor who called himself a name not unlike Moose-O Kist. How he ran his magazine was his business. I had no right to interfere. Still, losing that income galled me. Then Moose started spouting ideas how to improve *Hustler*. Rather than discuss these concepts with me, he floated them over my head. A personal visit would come to me from someone high up in distribution.

"Allan, I've been talking to Moose. Interesting perspective. What do you think about a 'Hole of the Month'? You have 'Asshole' already. This would be a sexual thing. No? Here's another one. Listen to this: A photo set with mannequins instead of real humans. That way you could print totally hardcore action, and no one could stop you."

The answer of what to do to neutralize Moose arrived in the form of a niche pornographic tape mailed in for review. The tape's star was an aged, gothic-inspired dominatrix named Mistress Tantala who taught her graying vagina to fart on command.

The video clearly showed co-star Moose-O Kist placing his face adjacent to the bum of Tantala. The camera pulled away slightly, and so did Moose-O Kist. His pursed lips quivered in anticipation. Tantala's vagina fluttered, made a popping sound, and a quantity of something like hand lotion spewed out and splattered across the rapturous mug of Moose-O Kist. If the Chuck Berry tapes had not inured me to such activity, I might have been aghast. I thought, *here's my ammo.* If this sucker pushed me to confrontation, I'd threaten to play these damning minutes of scum-licking depravity for the higher LFP powers.

Secure in having Moose-O Kist at my mercy, I condescended to attend a party at his home. Moose lived in a walk-up over an instant-printing store in Culver City. Country rock came loud and distorted onto the landing from the party inside. The door opened, and O Kist greeted me dressed in a pink, frilled apron, such as a Beverly Hills matron might affect in the spirit of Halloween irony. Aside from the apron, O Kist wore nothing, not even shoes. I'd been unprepared for the vision of a 230-pound man posing in a wisp of skimpy lace. Behind Moose, a few familiars from the office were all avoiding eye contact with the rear of his costume.

A statuesque blonde propped upon six-inch platform soles and nine-inch heels ordered, suitably whip-like: "Don't be an ass, worm. Ask the man if he would like a drink."

"Would you like a drink?" said Moose-O Kist.

"That's no way to address a guest. Where are your manners?" The grand dame produced a leather strip and lashed Moose's backside. I saw Moose's pleased reaction. He had muffed his etiquette on purpose.

"Your humble worm requests the pleasure of serving you the beverage of your choice, sir."

"That's okay, Kist, I'll be helping myself." I drifted to the safety zone of my current assistant and her incredulous boyfriend. Moose knew I shunned alcohol, and he stocked his refrigerator with canned iced tea, which I drained compulsively. Our host was a considerate person, thoughtful and kind despite the dopey ideas he dropped at work all day. Plenty of chairs and a low sofa serviced his living room, but none of the partygoers were eager to sit. The idea was to stay on your feet, maintain your mobility and not be at eye level with Moose's massive, whiskered ass. The party disintegrated early, and I wanted to leave before I became conspicuous in the thinning crowd. First, I needed to dispense with all that iced tea.

The bathroom door was ajar, so I walked in.

"You call that clean, you wretched worm? You expose your guests to the filth of your toilet? You should be shamed."

Moose was crouched on his knees, apron-clad, hunkered over the commode. His broad shoulders and powerful arms were left fully exposed by the pink chiffon. The overbearing broad stood above him, then swung a riding crop that struck with a wet slap. "Here, worm. You missed a spot."

Following the blonde's direction, Moose licked the rim of his toilet, attempting to put a spit-shine to the aged and yellowed porcelain.

I wouldn't die from holding in all that iced tea until I reached home. My car started right off, but my thoughts were overcast. There is no blackmailing a man who so extravagantly revels in shame.

Back at work, my assistant stewed over the vision of lace-trimmed Moose. "I can't stay on this job much longer. Do you think something like this would happen at a real news magazine?"

I doubted it, but I reserved opinion, and rightly so. In time, a phone call came in from an opportunist claiming to offer video of Donald Trump sexing his mistress, Marla Maples. The caller was businesslike and efficient. We set a meeting for the next day, and at the appointed time a white male in his late 20s, displaying a close-cropped military bearing, marched into the offices of my associate editors and produced an unmarked videocassette. Three editors and I watched as the television screen came to life with three-way sex action.

"Hey, you say that's Donald Trump, but it looks a lot more like Ted Turner and Jane Fonda doing some other broad."

"Correct," said our visitor.

"Don't you have anything on Donald Trump?"

"I think this will suffice."

He was right. My editors and I were convinced we were seeing Atlanta's most famous couple and not parallel universe doppelgangers. Even if Turner were to insist that the performers on this tape were in actuality incredible simulations, my fellows and I will believe unto death that the media mogul and his icon bride had been documented in a manic kink indulgence.

Ted and Jane's play friend, a tanned brunette, had plush breasts and a pleasant, oval face. Ted was obviously in command. At his direction, the brunette reclined on a sofa and opened her legs. Ted positioned himself between her thighs and inserted his penis. He looked over his shoulder and waved a hand toward the camera. The focus zoomed in. The lighting and resolution were professional quality.

"Holy shit! Ted has a fucking cameraman in there with him."

In the course of our duties as *Hustler* editors, my three cohorts and I thought we'd seen almost everything. This was the first time we'd ever watched what we believed to be two-time Oscar-winning actress Jane Fonda naked and harnessed into a strap-on dildo. Jane's body looked great. She must have been 50 at the time. Perhaps the tits had benefited from cosmetic tweaks, but the abs and ass were exclusively her own. Also seemingly genuine was the penetration of Ted Turner's anus by Jane's strap-on while Ted was linked inside the brunette. Turner broke the cardinal rule of theater and addressed the camera:

"Are you getting this?"

The lens moved in to capture the dildo's point of entrance. Turner's buttocks heaved as he pumped into the supine brunette beneath him. Pushing up the rear guard, Jane Fonda adjusted her thrusting to the rhythm of Ted. Turner shivered in grim ecstasy.

"My dick feels as big as a house," he exclaimed, picking up the tempo.

Jane lagged slightly behind the pitch of Ted's humping. After several awkward plunges, the dildo accidentally sprang free from Turner's ass.

"Damn it, Jane," he shouted.

Hurried and dutiful, the wife reinserted her phony plunger, and the threesome roiled to a crashing, groaning orgasm. Turner at least seemed to have a crashing, groaning orgasm. The two women may have been faking.

Four *Hustler* editors in one room, and none of us had a thing to say. We shared a single thought: *Someone could get killed over this.* We stared at the guy who'd brought in the tape.

"I'll bet you want a million dollars for this," I said.

"That's the number that came to mind."

The seller was reasonable. He realized that Flynt would require a firsthand viewing of the tape and that legal issues demanded a thorough discussion. He offered to call back in two weeks and suggested that we prime Larry so that he would be available for viewing. Larry's availability was tricky. The boss had kicked dope, and his involvement with the magazine was steadily escalating, but no one could predict which days he would be in the office.

I asked for at least 24 hours advance notice. "And I'll tell you right off. There's no way he'll go a million." The seller sized me up, calculating the odds that I was setting a trap, and agreed to give a one-day heads-up.

I described the contents of the video and reenacted some of the stronger segments for Larry, who beamed. During his actual viewing, he dampened his delight, an old poker tactic. The seller remained in the room while Flynt and a trusted lawyer examined the tape, searching out any remote justification for airing it. Larry's feigned disinterest only aroused the seller's disdain. They parted with a huge disparity between the asking price and Larry's counter.

"Don't worry," said Larry. "Where else can he go?"

The seller did return contrary to my expectations. He reached me while I was in the photo edit bay, coincidentally with Flynt present.

"Larry, it's him. With the Ted Turner stuff. He wants to know if you want another shot at buying it."

Larry quoted a dollar value that wouldn't purchase a basic new car outright. "Tell him that."

The guy hung up without replying.

"Trust me," said Larry. "He'll call back."

He never did. I imagine that low-balling this deal haunted Larry in the same way that the unsettling specter of the tape disrupted my inner calm. I tried to explain to my therapist, Joan, that seeing video footage showing one of the earth's most powerful media manipulators being anally penetrated by his movie-star wife's strap-on dildo had discolored my worldview. I mentioned them by name, just in case some random mishap were to befall me.

"I was not meant to see this."

"Yes. And how is this different from the other things you've seen at your job that you were not meant to see?"

Joan was uncanny. I'd never told her about the original rocker chewing chunks of organic chocolate. Or about Moose-O Kist and his pink apron.

232

"Allan, I'm confident we'll work through this confusion. You're innovative. You'll find a way to process it."

After these videos, I would catch myself recoiling from my own voyeurism, even while viewing real porn created for public consumption. My colleagues who had shared witness of the Turners' romp also reported disruptions in their ability to digest hardcore fare. Recovery would only come through action, and the first step was to unburden ourselves of this toxic secret knowledge.

Our therapy consisted of taunting the Turners in "Lovestyles of the Rich and Famous" (February, 1995), a narrow joke that pivoted upon a large composite shot that faked Ted Turner rammed up the behind by a dildo-wearing Jane Fonda, just like in the video.

I still couldn't see a cumshot without cringing. This mild stomach-curdling might have cautioned a more evolved soul to reevaluate his relationship to XXX entertainments. I dived in deeper. Franck Vardon and *Hot Video* extended a return invitation to once again document their annual *festival du fuck*. Off I flew to the south of France, trepidation-free, blithely anticipating a working vacation in a region of mellow sun, airy pastries and savory sauces.

The *Hot Video* crew scooped me and a smattering of American flesh sirens up at the Nice airport, and shuttled us to the Royal Hotel Casino in the village of Mandelieu, a few klicks up the Côte d'Azur from the port of Cannes. Year by year, each *Hot Video* awards extravaganza was more lavish than the preceding one, drawing increasingly large and unruly crowds of XXX hucksters from around the globe. The *Hot Video* brain trust had opted to self-contain their event. Everything would take place at the Royal Hotel Casino.

That year's breakout star was a glory-entitled newcomer named Jenna Jameson. Blonde, young, a typical middle-American of the uprooted and migratory type, Jenna exulted at a table of XXX cognoscenti in the lobby bar of the Royal Hotel Casino. Jameson's body oozed out of a black second-skin jumpsuit that revealed 80 percent of her pneumatic breasts. Male admirers clanked beer bottles and clinked wine glasses, toasting this desert nymph who had risen from nothing to become a world-famous exaltation of temptation and sin, just like the miraculous apparition of her native Las Vegas. In French and English, Jenna's lavish praises were sung to the brink of idolatry. Behind her, a

raised TV played tape of American daredevils stunt-jumping motorcycles. A lesser exhibitionist than Jenna might settle for being the center
of attention. She naturally aspired to be a crowning glory. On the TV,
some highflying biker ate dirt, and Jenna yodeled like a drunken rodeo
clown. Scrape away all the glitz and glam, and she was basically a
tomboy. That's how she knew so much about what guys liked. She practically was one. Except, of course, for the obvious and stunning visuals.

The next day's press luncheon, held outdoors under the high
midday sun, attracted far more interest than the space was able to
accommodate. Gangs of excluded reporters smashed against the
glass double doors that separated the hotel lobby from the buffet
steamers on the patio. *Hot Video* veterans recognized me at the rear
of this melee and motioned me forward. The crowd refused to part,
closing ranks with sharpened elbows and lit cigarettes. My hosts
caught hold of my arms and pulled me deeper into this garlic-mari-
nated, Gitanes-cured mob.

"Excuse *moi*. Beg your *pardon. Merci. Sacre* shit."

I popped through on the outdoors side of the double doors, under
the blazing, clear sky, and I was amazed. The Royal's shimmering
swimming pool is set seaside along the deep azure of the softly lap-
ping Mediterranean. A low cinder-brick wall separated the cement
deck from the warm, sanded shore. Several hundred photographers
and video crews hungered for something nubile and bare to shoot.

A seven-foot-high reproduction of the Hot d'Or trophy—an
ascending, streamlined, female figurine—stood poolside. Blue
screen starlets took turns posing in embrace with the wobbly stat-
ue. The mildest breeze came in off the Mediterranean. Surfing
ditties blared across the sunny beach. "Two girls for every boy,"
sang some long-gone California dreamer. The extreme gender disparity, about 10-to-1 male, made it ugly being a man. I hoped for
the best from my antiperspirant.

Uncannily fresh Jenna Jameson snapped her bubblegum-pink
lipstick and moved easily within a phalanx of news crews. Jenna wore
a miniskirt suit of electric-blue silk. She licked her candy lips in the
company of a lady reporter from England, the most influential writer
on hand. "It's a very small world," observed Jenna to the English
writer. "We're all the best of friends or else deadly enemies."

Jenna was somebody to fixate on, but the strut of Italian stud Rocco Siffredi overshadowed her cheeky star. Impeccably tailored, accentuated by his stately wife and plump, pink baby, Siffredi was at the peak of his decade-long reign as the king of king snakes. The royal couple coiled with serpentine ease through the crowd, pushing a navy-blue baby carriage to clear out the flotsam. Greetings of *ciao, ciao*, fired off like strings of flashbulbs. A slithering dude with dripping long hair fussed over Rocco's offspring while his own child squealed ignored in a stroller behind him.

An Asian sylph in shiny gold leaf posed at the shoreline. She lowered her top to her waist and held her leg out in a martial arts kick, stiff-nippled. Her white panty strip quavered in the breeze. A crazy-eyed girl wearing silken fishnet above her waist profiled the forms of her excellent breasts. A streety black fertility goddess showed hyper-inflated tits to a closing mob of camera fiends. Fat lips snarling, she seemed addicted to the attention. A bargain-minded Spanish temptress made the most of a simple white slip, lifting the silken hem to reveal her clenched cheeks. A floss of lace was all that protected her modesty.

Paparazzi literally crawled atop one another, like crabs in a tank. A disproportionate number of French journalists evidenced some form of physical deformity: skulls flat in back, foreheads sloping to severe recession, chins evolutionarily lost.

Two old-time mensches from Porn Valley, U.S.A., sipped mixed drinks on the sidelines, sunglasses in place to deflect the glare off their gold bracelets and neck chains.

"Jenna Jameson. The next big shit?"

"She knows how to spend money."

"She knows the paper's green and it's got presidents on it, and different numbers have different presidents."

The cement around the pool was precariously crowded. Roving packs of documentarians hounded flashing talent up and down the beach.

Dueling porn Fabio clones glared at one another from five paces, a standoff of tossing shoulder-length manes and locking biceps. In the lunge for news coverage of this preening confrontation, a suit-wearing Italian moneyman was bashed under the chin by a lurching video camera. Blood streaming down his open-neck dress shirt, the

XXX financier charged after the paparazzo who clocked him. Shutterbuggers flocked to snap the attack. A dwarf crouched to shoot his camera from between the legs of his cohorts.

I headed for the hotel lobby, passed the bar with a wistful glance, and retreated toward my room. The sun had worn me down. I dragged into the elevator. As the doors slid shut, a burst of blonde eroticism slipped in and stood at the panel of floor indicators. There I was, alone with Jenna Jameson. She was so new to illicit celebrity that she would venture into an elevator without a bodyguard or escort. She looked pleased with the way lunch had turned out.

"If you don't win that best newcomer award, the whole place should riot," I said.

She turned to me, sniffed the air. Her pert nostrils recoiled.

"What's that smell?" she said. The elevator stopped, opened, and off she traipsed. The doors closed, and the acrid scent she had pointed out remained. What was the stink? It was me. Within the hour, I sold the remaining nights on my room to a man-and-wife XXX team I knew from Los Angeles, and financed an early flight back to Paris. I made the Left Bank in time for a dinner of steak and *pommes frites*.

Over the next five days, I experienced what was either a nervous breakdown or a spiritual awakening—conceivably both at once—along the banks of the Seine. Holed up in a garret off the Rue St. Germaine, I contemplated that rank ooze that stunk up the elevator with Jenna Jameson.

The morning of my flight home, after breakfast croissants and chocolate, bolstered by 1,000 cups of jolting espresso, I made a pilgrimage to the Luxembourg Gardens and sat with 20 other restive souls in chairs lining a meditation pool. Gathered strangers, we granted one another the dignity of being acknowledged and left alone. This struck me as a height of civilized behavior. I derived a simple, great comfort from being included in these ordinary courtesies, and I headed back to the job refreshed and renewed, as if I'd been on a free vacation, and not one where I'd been forced to reevaluate, confront and accept myself all over again.

Soon after my Parisian expense check had cleared, I fielded a call from the Cayman Islands. Larry. I girded to defend my French disappearance, but my absence seemed to have gone unnoticed. "Allan, you remember that guy who brought in the video of Ted Turner and Jane Fonda?"

"Sure. We're still waiting for him to come back on your counteroffer."

Larry laughed. "Fuck you," he said. "Listen. Ted Turner just called me about that whole business. You wouldn't have a contact number for the guy who brought in the tape?"

"I wish I did, but he was too careful for that."

"Ted would really like to get a-hold of that guy."

"I bet he would," I said.

A second batch of Ted Turner tapes popped up. These vignettes predated Ted's marriage to Jane Fonda and presented the CNN founder putting the screws to a procession of mutely indulgent participants. Larry purchased this potentially explosive entertainment with the express intent of currying Ted's favor. Naturally, before handing over the tape to its world-changing star, Larry wanted a copy. A video duplication studio down the street from LFP provided a closed room and secured equipment. I assigned supervision of the copy process to sensitive, intense Bernadette. It was her birthday. I thought she might appreciate the chance to get out from in front of her computer screen. She'd called in and complained to my assistant about this extra duty, so I drove over to spell her.

Slumped at a video console, Bernadette pulled her hair back from hooding her face and rolled her fierce, hazel eyes. "Ted's humping in his office. Ted's humping outdoors in sagebrush. Here he is taking hits off what my high-school experience tells me is a hash pipe. How did he persuade these sorority girls to go with him, with their '70s hairdos?"

"Don't let the hair confuse you. He's in Georgia, where the stewardess look was fashion-forward well into the '80s."

"What you subject me to is so gross," said Bernadette. Within three weeks, she was gone, taking a job with more drudgery and less pay at an internet encyclopedia site. Writing sleazy *Barely Legal* asides, rooting through the racist misogyny of the penitentiary-bred joke page, parsing the lewd absurdities of her "Hot Letters," even the sorrowful yearning of rejected "Beaver Hunt" applicants, all of this Bernadette might weather. But one afternoon of Ted Turner in the wild was all it took to blow her away.

Hustler's Photo Layouts

LET'S DEFINE YOU as a male, heterosexual, vision 20/20, service-able blood flow. You inadvertently inherit a stack of *Hustler* magazines, all in unmolested condition. No one is present to observe you, not even a dog. You sit, warm and alone, with a pile of *Hustler*s. You have no pressing engagements, so you pull a maga-zine from the stack, flip it open and browse at random. Chances are the pages will fall open to artfully cropped visuals of a naked girl, perhaps two naked girls. Their thighs will be taut and spread. Their vaginas will be open and pink, like slices of dripping tropical fruit. Their feculence-free anuses will wink knowingly. Your eyes gorge on the four-color stimulation. Sweat glistens on skin tones so warm and fleshy that they seem to flush at the touch of your fingers. Is it possible to suppress a physical reaction?

Saucy, pouting nymphs; knowing, leering seductresses; wickedly smirking playthings, their mouths and eyes conspire to drain a man of his reluctance. These girls, so young and so unblemished, stare out with a natural insouciance that is inviting and ubiquitous. You gaze back upon this insistence of activated libido, and an epiphany bursts within you. You think back upon your day-to-day interactions with women, both those you know and strangers you encounter, and you have a notion: this same omnipresent come-on that you see in the magazine is on the street all around you, every day. When next you venture into polite society, you will be attuned to the signals, the subdued semaphore of the fair sex, and you'll take advantage of this knowledge.

The process of executing a photo shoot taught me one lesson: pictures lie and photographers lie, too. On many occasions, photographers brought in prospective models and sat them on the other side of my desk, seeking the go-ahead to photograph the girl for *Hustler* or one of the other LFP titles at my command. Often, the young lady sat like a lump of meat. Somewhere along the line, she had been offered the fallacy that she wasn't worth shit, so why try? And she'd swallowed that bitter lie, which accounted for her sour pout, the cheated distaste in her eyes, the quivering lump in her throat.

Other times, the would-be photo star believed herself to be extra-hot, beyond the hotness that she actually possessed. She had been led to believe she was hot beyond compare. I, dispassionate observer, would see her window of hot opportunity sliding shut. This information had been withheld from her, a lie of omission.

All the skin photographers I met reinforced the prejudice that theirs, more than any other, is a craft of deception. The girls are fooled into believing they are receiving free money. The viewer is duped into believing the photographer has captured the girl in a moment of ecstasy. One photo shoot visit too many ruins the illusions. Afterward, you look at a "nude glamour" shot, and you see a strained expression held for the duration of a camera click. If you are not careful, your cynicism penetrates beyond the illusions of the photo layouts, and nothing in real life seems authentic anymore.

CHAPTER 14

▬▬▬

More Naked Truth

VISIONS OF ANUS were plaguing me. Piles of fat manila envelopes, 30 and 40 high, tilted and tottered all about me. These were freelance photo submissions. They arrived almost as fast as I could review and dismiss them. We needed fresh faces, fresh breasts and all the fresh rest for *Barely Legal, Chic, Asian Fever, Honey Buns, Leg World* and *Taboo*, at least seven sets for each issue of each magazine. LFP, through me, bought more skin shots than any other magazine company. Some photographers would send two dozen sets in a single package, without repeating a single model. Other cameramen would mail in eight packets, all crammed with photos of the same winsome lass. The one constant was the anus. Every girl, no matter if I saw her once or a dozen times, turned her nether checks, and her private brown eye peeked out at me. My nostrils pinched in contemplation of too many greased sphincters; it was as if during my wastrel student years I'd applied myself to my studies, excelled beyond all expectations and become a proctologist.

What did I hope to find up there? I remember particular girls with pointed affection; from their pictures a lasting fondness has sprung. I recall the tilt of a chin, the delicate nobility of a narrow brow, the interrupted fall of hair clipped behind a pink and precious ear. But when I was in the trenches, receiving eight or 10 packages of freelance photographs a day and squinting into thousands of slides shot by staff photographers every week, my vision tunneled into the browned vent.

Let's say I just concluded a two-hour stretch of midmorning anal immersion. I would straighten my back and rise from the viewing table, and stand eye-to-eye with staff and visitors. Perhaps I would head out to lunch with a colleague. Our favorite waitress might approach the table with a welcoming smile, and I would be acutely aware of an anus just under the skin in the center of her forehead, like a portal to the lower realms lurking beneath the limits of perception. This not-quite-seen but all-seeing sphincter leered over my shoulder as I forked in lunch. How many anuses had I seen? Five thousand? Ten thousand? Eighty thousand? More? Surely the number was calculable.

Sometimes, when the wife was talking at me in the car or in a furniture showroom, her mouth would morph into the backdoor orifice. What was that thing saying? How did it ever start talking in the first place? My sense that her sentiments were emerging from the same hole that discharged her solid bodily wastes prejudiced me against her message.

"You're talking a lot of shit," I would say.

This floating asshole syndrome was sporadic and passing, but its spell made for tough going on the job. Aside from pop-up anal intrusions, the fake cumshots were a headache. One of Larry Flynt's clever breakthroughs was the application of bogus semen at the climax of Hustler's feigned depictions of heterosexual copulation. Larry directed the photographers to concoct some kind of viscous, translucent liquid that would approximate the look of ejaculate. This potion was to be smeared on the female model as the male's erect penis waved nearby, simulating orgasm. Hustler's first fake cumshot appeared in the March 1995 issue, in a beachside boy-girl set titled "Jessie & Randy: Sea Man." A puddle of paste-like fluid pooled on the face and the neck of the female model at the conclusive spread. It looked like a poster hanger had accidentally upended his entire glue bucket upon her.

The fabrication of a convincing genetic splash should have been a simple enough task. Years slipped by with no great improvement. I was no help. One windy autumn evening, young Bill the art director and I drove north on Doheny. Commuter traffic closed us in, and droves of workers inched toward warm hearts and homes. I waved a hand at the idling mass that contained us.

"Every one of these cars has an anus inside," I said. "At least one anus."

Young Bill was ambitious and practical. He raised his eyebrows, indicating interest. Darkness of night had come to stay, but our day job was not done. The boss had been in compromised health lately. He'd been released from hospital to home care with strict instructions to maintain bed rest. While he healed, deadlines pressed.

Young Bill and I turned onto Larry's bird street. Parked cars lined both curbs for 30 yards from Flynt's house—primarily black vehicles with shaded windows, Mercedes, Cadillac—big sedans like crooks drive on TV. We parked my black-on-black Impala Super Sport and walked to the house. Extra security stood at the front door. A sentinel surveyed the street from a rooftop turret. A familiar bodyguard met us at the service gate and herded us up the driveway, past Larry's Bentley, and into the kitchen.

"Wait here. I'll see if he's in shape to take you guys."

The bodyguard marched from the kitchen into a hall that branched toward the bedrooms. I heard a quiet commotion. The crowd that gathered kept their volume muted, no doubt in consideration of the invalid snoozing in his bedroom. The bodyguard returned.

"Come on."

Young Bill and I gathered our stack of production flats. We also carried a miniature light box, its surface about the size of a three-ring notebook, and a jeweler's loupe for Larry to glare through. We were ushered toward the bedroom, and directed to make a hard left, into the living room. Space had been cleared to accommodate a poker table. Ten or so gravely occupied men sat around the deep green felt, under the soft, yellow light of an overhead lamp. Piles of poker chips were stacked in front of each formidable opponent. The only woman present, a nonpartisan professional, dealt the cards. Young Bill and I hesitated.

At the head of the poker table, Larry was lying on his side, stretched out on a gurney. Propped on an elbow and a cascade of pillows a foot and a half above the level of the table he looked like some great sybaritic Roman emperor lounging in state. Cards whisked across the green felt. Larry motioned Bill and me forward. Respectfully keeping my eyes off of the players' cards, I made my way to the side of the gurney. Larry called for two more cards and added the new draws to his hand. We wedged the light box under his arm on the stretcher, and he took the loupe in one hand. Young Bill held up enlarged printouts for easy viewing. Larry consulted the printout for the disposition of each shot, then checked the individual slides to ensure the particulars passed muster. No actual cash was anywhere to be seen on the poker table; precious metals and gems shone in abundance at wrists and necklines. The game seemed friendly enough. Larry took the loupe from his eye.

"That cumshot don't look real," he said.

"Clive insists it is real."

Normally, in a group of 10 guys, at least one wiseacre would have offered to supply a real cumshot, but these dudes were too removed and calculating for that. In a few years, Larry would open a poker club across town. Until then, this nightly match would do. Thousands of dollars were pitched back and forth with every hand. I tried not to look too interested in anyone. Larry tossed a few chips to stay in the action and put the magnifying lens back to his eye. Somebody called, bringing the betting to an end. Larry threw in his cards, face down. I must have witnessed Larry playing poker at least 100 times. I can't remember ever seeing him win a hand. He pushed the slides back at me.

"These are okay, but if those cumshots don't start looking real, somebody could end up fired."

Hustler's next photographic innovation came in a fit of pique in the summer of 1997. A biker fan of *Hustler* had pressed me to place his car in the magazine. Showcase autos were a common *Hustler* photo prop, second only to sandy beaches. The biker's car, a hot-rodded '40s Chevrolet sedan-delivery panel wagon, paint job tricked out a bright yellow, was an easy sell. Clive "Iago" McLean claimed shooting rights on the panel wagon. *Hustler*'s senior photographer was a lively hybrid of ferret and hamster. Grabby eyes darted behind wire-rimmed spectacles that reflected the gleam of his silvered pompadour. Clive's phony semen shots had continued to disappoint. I found him in the talent office, riffling through Liz Berrios' file cabinet while she was away from her desk.

"Larry's never liked my cum," responded Clive. "What do you suggest I do different this time?"

"I'll tell you what to do, Clive. Shoot the couple like they're driving out to Las Vegas. They want to get married real quick, but the car overheats on the highway in the middle of the desert; so they climb in the back and drink beer to cool down, and then the chick has to piss with nowhere to go, so she climbs out on the side of the road and lets the whizz flow. That's where you come in with your camera."

"You can't be serious," he said. "Shoot piss?"

"I am serious," I said. "Bring back those piss shots." I didn't imagine our legal team would ever allow urine photographs to be published. The point was to compel Clive to shoot them.

A couple of weeks passed, and the film came in. A stringy, speed-freakish blonde stood next to the highway, stick-figure legs akimbo. A bright yellow stream—uncannily matching the paint on the Chevrolet panel sedan—flowed from the model's crotch and soaked into the embankment sand. Young Bill enlarged the pee view into a two-page opener, and he and I trekked back up Doheny to present the results to Larry. The same poker game seemed to be in play, although Flynt was off the gurney and back upright in his golden chair.

"Okay," Larry said.

"Are you sure? I mean, check out the piss."

There was not an iota of change in any of the expressions around the table.

Larry tossed in a few chips. "That's okay."

The resultant photo feature, "Dave and Rose: Pit Stop" (October, 1997), set off a pissing contest with *Penthouse*. Their first photos of girl urine appeared on the newsstands almost exactly to the day that ours did. I marveled. Here were two rival publishers, Flynt and Guccione, who never communicated in any way. Baffling but true—both were inspired to start printing pee visuals at the same moment.

Once the pee gates had been opened, there was no shutting them. Any girl who consented was shot while she squatted. Some rules applied. The model was confined to urinating in a natural way—meaning on a floor or on an outdoor surface—and the gush was forbidden to splash onto any human being. The magazine's fans appreciated this glimpse at the intimate realities of actual women. Orgasms, sexual arousal, sentience itself could be faked, but flowing pee was a stream of authenticity. We created a win-whiz situation. But not every publishing genius appreciated the piss revolution.

The wife and I arrived late to the LFP Christmas party, held at the Beverly Regent, the hotel featured in the Julia Roberts movie *Pretty Woman*. We had missed the salad course. The fowl was being served. A couple of temporary employees were sitting at a table on the far outskirts. The wife and I joined them. Our plan was to put protein in our stomachs, then move around and salvage the evening.

I let the fork drop from my mouth. Danger approached from the flank. Dwaine Tinsley and his new soul mate Ellen sleazed into two empty seats at my left. Tinsley had been reinstated as cartoon editor, but worked primarily at home in the central coast town of Cambria, a four-hour drive from *Hustler* headquarters. Dwaine generally tied his grayed long hair in an artisan's ponytail. He'd let the locks loose for Christmas, and he looked like George Custer, had the General survived Little Big Horn and gone on to a sedentary middle age as a convicted child molester. Dwaine introduced himself to my wife. His eyes ate her up; Ellen's eyes ate up Dwaine.

Dwaine and Ellen might have been drunk and stoned on the love drug Ecstasy. Then again, they might only have been overly caffeinated and making general conversation. They talked about the hot tub up where they lived. Dwaine and Ellen shared a lot of private humor between them and touched one another often.

"One thing I don't understand, Al," said Dwaine, "is all that piss that's been showing in the magazine lately. Maybe it's just me, but I want to preserve some of the mystery. In art, there's always the suggestion of the act, and that's a more powerful evocation than just baldly depicting the act itself."

"Kind of like how Chester the Molester was never actually shown fucking a 10-year-old girl, but only smoking a cigarette with her during the afterglow?"

Hardcore sex presented the next great *Hustler* experiment. Larry's initial idea was to shoot actual penetration, but have the sides of the woman's buttocks conceal the point of insertion. "Or the lady can be taking the erect penis in her mouth, and her hand around the shaft can hit up against her lips." Larry hunched his neck and bobbed his head, miming fellatio. He placed his open fist up to his mouth and poked one cheek outward with his tongue. "You cain't really see anything. The readers know it's inside her. There's no other place it can go. But we haven't shown nothing. That's how we get away with it."

It didn't take much thought to grasp Larry's point, and to expand on the original intention. I appeared to have an idea of my own. "We can apply the same principle to anal sex."

Is it possible for a boss to be disappointed and impressed at the same time? That's the look Larry gave me. He trotted out his standard endearment, the one he directed at me almost every time we reviewed photos together: "Does your wife know what kind of a freak you are?"

Hustler's forays into oblique penetration suffered no serious repercussions from magazine distributors or state or secular censors. The stakes were raised. By the opening months of 1998, hardcore penetration shots were inserted in every couples shoot, whether boy-girl or girl-girl. Larry issued a mandate for the photographers to capture flying cumshots. He wanted the jism to be seen as it spurted from the tip of the penis. This particular shot required patience, timing, teamwork, communication and excellent lighting. Or in Clive's case, an inspired proficiency at rigging up a squirt bulb that simulated an orgasmic spray. His duplicity might never have been discovered if not for the betrayal of photo assistants he had hectored mercilessly, and also because he occasionally misjudged the false perspective needed not to expose the workings behind his deception.

In his own estimation, Clive's counterfeit money shots elevated him to heroic stature. Despite preening upon his self-erected pedestal, the senior photographer's presence was not requested at Larry Flynt's bachelor party. Mine was.

I savored my privilege while driving out to the Mulholland Drive party mansion. Cavernous, underfurnished, facing the Valley rather than L.A., the luxury barn was crowded with gamblers and sundry men of questionable though formidable means. The players from Larry's poker game were footing the bill with co-sponsorship by a selection of Vegas casinos. Larry was receiving compliments in the bar. I wedged in next to the golden chair and blocked out a couple of fawning jokers. I clinked my grapefruit juice and club soda against Larry's cocktail glass.

"I always thought you were smarter than me, Larry. Here you go, down the same path I took. To matrimony and misery."

Larry ignored my gambit and leered like a perverted gym instructor. "This is where we separate the men from the boys." Plenty of sycophants other than me were positioning to toady up to the groom-to-be, so I drifted off beyond range of the boss' eye. His threat to separate the men from the boys had sounded sincere.

Flocks of prostitutes had been rounded up as party favors. Men broke into tight twos and threes to handicap the hookers, who arrived in waves. Most of the women were brittle of humor and fit the pro profile. A bookie I met explained the pricing structure.

"Jesus," I said. "You guys *are* high rollers."

For Larry, no expense was spared. The marrying man rolled his chair up to the table of honor. Most guests assumed dinner was about to be served. I sat at a table occupied by a client-relations executive from a Nevada casino and five Las Vegas women who appeared to be working for him. While Flynt's own poker palace was still in the shuffle, Larry's personal jet flew him in on Vegas junkets almost weekly, losing gangster's ransoms in a single night.

A menu had been placed at each setting. For an appetizer, Larry selected a tall brunette with jolting breasts and plopped her onto the table in front of him. He rolled her dress back over her hips, positioned his shoulders beneath her knees, slid off her thong and lunged forward to snuffle at will. Applause sounded, but Larry's foray far outlasted it.

"Now we'll eat," I predicted, but my hooker tablemates smiled grimly. Waiters, balancing salads up both arms, entered as if to begin the meal. A second course in carnality presented herself to Larry. This one was blonde and slouched, her shoulders apparently pulled downward by the weight of her breasts. She took the seat on Larry's table, and he dived in with alacrity, as if he hadn't had a nibble in a week. The salad-bearers retreated. The men seated on either side of Larry lit their cigars, pulled their ties straight and resumed their discreet conversations.

After more than an hour of wondering when the party would start, I had to conclude that it was in full swing. Sitting hungry and ignored in the company of hookers who had sized me up as a no-go was a second-rate experience. Larry went on chewing professional genitalia at the center table, the successive girls positioned like spread-eagle centerpieces, surrounded by guests in various degrees of excitation or discomfort, fiddling with their tobacco or their place settings, none of them having received so much as a leaf of lettuce. Flynt chewed himself through the warmup dishes and feasted on a porn luminary who went by the name of Shane. Petite, sleek and power-packed, a favorite at the office, the girl we fondly referred to as Li'l Shane had posed reliably and good-naturedly in a series of "Bits & Pieces" photo gags. To say that I had harbored an unrequited affection for Li'l Shane doesn't make me any different from many of my office mates, but they weren't sitting there watching her being gobbled up by the turkey we worked for. I said goodbye to the girls at the table and the Vegas wrangler.

The next day Larry threatened to tell the wife what I had been up to, claiming he had photos. He was still high on pheromones.

The wedding, on a summery Saturday in June, 1998, was a less exclusive affair than the bachelor party. Guests at the Doheny Hills house who had not been present at the Mulholland debacle included movie director Milos Forman, Larry's big screen alter-ego Woody Harrelson, Courtney Love, Ed Norton, and self-proclaimed comedian Bill Maher. The Flynt driveway had been converted into a flowery arbor for the exchange of vows.

The wife and I claimed two seats and watched Liz walk down the aisle and stand next to the golden chair with Larry, shoulder to shoulder. Liz deserved her man, the prize. She'd been bedside at Duke University Hospital. Her will had propelled him into a rehab unit. The drugs would have killed him by now. Liz had earned this wedding, and she stood tall, as tall as she could, secure in her matrimonial rights.

The official conducting the ceremony inclined toward Larry. "Do you, Larry, give your solemn vow to be a faithful partner in sickness and in health, in good times and in bad?"

"I give my solemn vow to be your partner in sickness and in health, in good times and in bad."

The vows concluded to warmer applause than had accompanied Larry's dining at the bachelor's stag. Rather than receive the traditional lineup of congratulations, bride and groom split into different rooms in the house. I beelined to Larry and was among the first to greet him as Mr. Liz. He beamed as if his golden-spoked tires had just run over a Republican's neck.

"Did you notice that I left out the 'faithful' part?"

For dinner, the wife and I drew seats at a table of lawyers and their spouses. The attorneys quoted various "Asshole of the Month" passages they had considered particularly ludicrous or cruel. The food arrived more smoothly than at the stag dinner. Fully nourished, the wife and I walked toward our car with one of *Hustler*'s staff photographers. He moved awkwardly, smiling stiffly. He had secreted three magnums of costly champagne in his shirt and pants. As far as girlie photographers go, he was one of the more honest ones I'd met.

Not to give the impression that life was problem-free. Complaints and troubles trickled to me from my staff. Employees always felt they were being taken advantage of by Larry's fiscal policies, such as being forced to pay Flynt to park in his building. Some grievances were more acute. The entertainment editor, Sherman Stanton, stood in my doorway, looking touched by trauma. An Ivy League graduate in a California shlub package, Sherman was in charge of assigning for review the porn videos that XXX companies heaped upon us. I assumed he had happened across a particularly distressing offering, like a recent atrocity that featured a crippled guy being ridden by a Down syndrome shrew. Sherman closed my door behind him.

"I need to talk to you," he said. "I'll resign and sue for workman's comp if you don't stop this."

"What are we talking about?"

"Come with me."

I followed Sherman's stiff back to his office. He was housed in a niche far from the main hallway, seclusion being essential to nearly constant viewing of XXX materials. The editor stood at his desk and pointed at his television.

"See it?"

He singled out a chalky residue streaked across the screen.

"That could be anything," I said. "Hand lotion, shampoo. A dash of dried Elmer's glue." As I spoke, I knew I was lying. It was impossible to convincingly fake that stuff. Sherman's face caved in on itself.

"Catch the guy. I don't care that you did nothing when the tapes started being stolen. This is just my office. I don't live here. I don't need a secure environment. But when the thieves stop and watch the shit and jerk off with their hands on my remote control, and then leave the spill on my screen … I can't deal with this."

"Maybe if you'd leave some tissues next to the set. We could requisition a bottle of Windex, and the intruder might be shamed into cleaning up after himself."

"Find this freak and punish him, or I'm out of here."

I suspected that more than one thief was pillaging Sherman's office. I kept this theory to myself.

"What do you want me to do, Sherman? Do you want me to camp out in front of your door?"

"You're resourceful."

"Did you call Human Resources and report this?"

"It makes me sick enough to talk to you about it."

I hated going to anyone with a dilemma like this. The Human Resources assistant put me on hold. The director soon came on the line. We'll pretend her name was Betty.

"Allan, I'm actually glad you called. I have something to talk to you about. We'll meet in your office."

Ten minutes later, Human Resources Betty and a young blonde who worked in the office of the building management sat in chairs facing my desk. They shut my door behind them, a closure that never bodes well.

"Allan, we have a problem," said Betty. She was graying, 50-plus and manifestly decent. She had a daughter in the junior league and a husband on the board of directors at an oil company. I let her talk.

"The cleaning crew is very upset. Somebody has been leaving Pepsi bottles filled with human excrement in Martin Green's trash can."

Betty's troublesome shit Pepsis trumped the TV screen semen. The blonde from building management was outraged. She was thin, erect, very clean and drove a pastel-colored European sports car that had never seen a speck of mud.

"You don't think Martin is leaving it in his own trash can?" I said.

"Well, I don't know."

I thought of the guys on my staff. Smart, snide, impulsive, all strangers to the balance beam. In truth, I could not cross a single one off the suspect list. If one of them could have done this, and the evidence indicated that one of them may have, then any one of them was capable. Was the guy who was leaving the poop the same guy who was leaving the semen?

"Will you call Martin Green in?" asked Human Resources Betty.

Martin knocked and entered looking abashed. He was large and benign and moved like a shy trained bear. There was no chair available for him.

"Look, Martin, there's a problem," I said, unnecessarily. The closed door and Betty inside were like a billboard advertising the presence of an issue.

Betty took the lead: "The cleaning crew has discovered Pepsi-Cola bottles filled with human excrement in your wastebasket the past two nights this week."

Martin absorbed this news. He allowed an expression of incredulous disgust to come through.

"Well, I didn't do it," he said.

Mary, the building management blonde, looked unconvinced. In her mind, I had to suppose, I was a suspect myself.

"Have you noticed anybody on the floor who doesn't belong here? Have you seen any strangers? Any outsiders?"

Martin thought hard.

"Is there anyone who has anything against you?" said the building girl.

"He's one of the most popular guys here," I put in.

Popularity carried no water for Betty. "Martin, we need you to keep your eyes open. Try to think of anyone who might have done this. We'll be reviewing security tapes, and we may have someone for you to look at."

Of course, they spotted someone for us to look at. Martin and I met Betty and the building management girl in the guts of the parking structure, at the security nerve center. We were led through a room lined with black and white monitors, catching glimpses of our co-workers' daily progress. That was an eye-opener. Stealing copy paper was suddenly less tempting. The tapes were herky-jerky, single frames shot every three seconds; people moved in stutter-starts. A big guy stepped out of an elevator at the third-floor landing and looked both ways. He pulled a key from the pocket of a bulky coat, opened the double security doors and entered the floor that housed Martin Green's office, and mine too.

Betty directed our attention to the time code. "This is after hours, but before the cleaning crew comes on."

Martin denied recognizing the guy. So did I. Human Resources planned to change the locks and make swipe card entrance with employee identity badges mandatory.

"We will find who is doing this," Betty said.

I would forgive this fecal prank, so long as it had not been done to me. I could not afford to have an underling caught and fired on the spot. On the odd chance that the perpetrator was one of my peons, I had to alert the culprit that the snare was being set.

Over the next few hours, I approached each editor in turn and let them know that a mystery anus had been leaving turds in a colleague's trash can. I accused no one and asked for no alibis. Still, everyone looked at me offended, and after a moment's consideration, each suspect looked at me as though I were the probable cause. Naturally, morale took a dump. No one wants to be accused of such an indiscretion. No one wants to be made aware that one of their coworkers may be capable of such an indiscretion. Entertainment Editor Sherman took the accusation poorly.

"Do you think I'm tossing bottles of shit into Martin's office in retaliation for him shooting his wad all over my television?"

"I hadn't thought that," I said, but the scenario did parse out. Sherman watched my face relax into an acceptance of the possibility. His lips formed an O-ringed pout. *Oh, no*, I thought. *Here it comes.* But the anus did not appear. Sherman's puckered mouth remained a puckered mouth. Perhaps I was cured.

Hustler Special Projects

PUTTING TOGETHER *HUSTLER* magazine wasn't as easy as it looked. Distractions could prove disastrous. But try explaining the need for continuous and exact concentration to Larry Flynt. Mr. Flynt likes to squeeze a buck and a half out of every dollar he spends on an employee, so the LFP salaryman's basic roster is always subject to the addition of "special projects."

Certain special projects, compilation issues for instance, are a staple of the skin magazine. Moonlighting editors comb through back issues, designate a theme and recycle previously printed material into cheap one-shots—*Hustler Beach Girls*, *Hustler Couples*, *Hustler's Brown Sugar*, *Hustler's All-Natural*. The slicing and dicing that creates these segment titles exacts minimums of imagination and patience, unlike the truly special projects that befall the trusted long-term servitor at Larry Flynt Publications.

CHAPTER 15

Saving Clinton's Privates

In the fall of 1998, I answered a summons to approach Larry's golden chair, and walked the vast expanse of his money-green carpet. My inner career coach was braying that I'd overstayed my *Hustler* tenure. Fifteen years at Larry Flynt Publications should have been too much for anybody. Taking my seat under the scrutiny of Flynt's gimlet eye, dwarfed in the heavy chair across from the boss' massive desk, I wondered what I was in trouble for now. Larry was at the peak of his cigar habit, smoking long, rich Cubans. He tended toward overindulgence, and his cigar behavior fit the pattern. A typical enthusiast might blow through two or three stogies a day. Larry kept at least one Havana smoking constantly. He fired up a fresh, fat Cuban, sucked hard and gave me time to speculate. I'd recently resolved difficulties with a "Bits & Pieces" editor and a features editor by firing both. The sacked features editor had left behind a cabinet of unopened mail—article pitches, blind submissions, invoices, payment inquiries. Perhaps wind of this disarray had penetrated all that cigar smoke.

"I got a letter yesterday," he said.

Not another one, I thought.

"This character thinks he has a good idea," said Larry. "Give him a lunch. Let him feel like you're taking him seriously."

So I landed in a booth at the Daily Grill on La Cienega Boulevard, chewing thoughtfully on sourdough and pasta while looking into the animated face of an outraged elfin fellow. To hear this gnome sitting across from me tell it, vast right-wing conspirators in Washington, D.C., had aligned with reprobates from trailer parks all across Arkansas in a concerted attempt to hound our chief executive,

William Jefferson Clinton, into submission with allegations of having lied under oath about on-the-job infidelities. My lunch date's active nostrils sniffed something suppurating in Washington.

"They're planning to impeach him, mark my words."

Who seriously believed that the clamor among a few strident zealots to impeach Clinton would gain enough momentum to actually force a Senate vote on removing the President from office?

My mind wandered, and with it my eyes, which latched upon Internet gossip Matt Drudge as he walked into the restaurant. Drudge gave the impression that he was trying to travel incognito, unmistakably so. In case impressionable passersby failed to identify him, Drudge wore his trademark newshound hat, like something that might have lidded Walter Winchell. Drudge had been instrumental in amplifying the name of a loose-lipped White House intern whose moniker would become synonymous with furtive fellatio. If not for Drudge's scandalmongering, I would not be having lunch with the grinning idealist across from me.

"In summation, you're suggesting that Larry Flynt should put an ad in the *New York Times*, the *Los Angeles Times* and the *Washington Post*, offering to buy and publish the stories of women who have banged or are banging current Republican congressmen?"

"Mark my words," said my animated companion, "offer a million dollars. Who won't sell out a dirty adulterer for a million dollars?"

"Offer *up* to a million dollars."

Drudge looked so smug, ordering his lunch from an obsequious waitress who had routinely dismissed my charm. I calculated the man-hours needed to implement the gnome's scheme. Someone would have to concoct the ad's wording, place it, field whatever responses might come in.

As a publicity stunt, the plan promised to be simple and effective. Internet magazine *Salon* had recently monopolized prime-time news with revelations that Illinois congressman Henry Hyde, a loud claimant for decency and for the head of Bill Clinton, had several years earlier destroyed an innocent marriage with unchecked adulterous urges. I explained the idea to Larry. He immediately recognized an opportunity to attach his name to the raging national debate by simply flashing a million-dollar lure. Flynt took a minute of hard consideration to swallow the bitter pill of paying about 80 grand to place the announcement. "Run the ad in the *Washington Post*. The *New York Times* costs too much for what it's worth. The Washington paper is where the action is."

I suggested we contract my animated lunch date to oversee the process. Larry refused. This was a special project, the special type that was specially designed for someone special, such as me. Flynt wanted everything handled in-house by people on his payroll for best control. I spent an hour with attorney Alan Isaacman to craft the wording of the ad, then I farmed out as much as I could—typesetting, proofreading, contacting the *Post* and arranging payment. Friday afternoon, I visited Larry.

"The ad's set to run in the Sunday *Post*."

"Make sure it says '*up* to a million dollars' and not just a million dollars flat."

"Larry, I wonder if we can bring in some temp workers, at least at the start of next week, to handle the added volume." Flynt squinted up at me through a cloud of cigar smoke. I faltered, but went on. "The solicitation, that million-dollar offer, it's a magic number. The publicity could generate a high volume of response."

"Nobody's gonna call."

On October 4, 1998, Larry's full-page ad appeared in the Sunday edition of the *Washington Post*. "$1 Million," screamed the headline. Scream is what it did. "Have you had an adulterous sexual encounter with a current member of the United States Congress or a high-ranking government official? Larry Flynt and HUSTLER Magazine will pay you up to $1 million if we choose to publish your verified story."

An 800 number rang at the desk of Emily, my assistant. I dragged into the office a little after 9 a.m. the following day. Emily hunched over her desk, scribbling madly, transcribing calls from her voicemail. I tried to reassure her.

"That's a bump, an aberration. We'll be calmed down by lunchtime."

I went to my desk. No one but me was available to answer the ringing phone. Newspaper reporters demanded to know what Larry was up to. Upstairs, at the desk of Larry's secretary, the press inquiries were constant. I needed coffee.

"Fetch it yourself," said Emily. "Bring one for me too."

We gulped caffeine and figured out how to forward Emily's number to a backup account. That one soon filled as well. The *Washington Post* ad was being duplicated by papers and news broadcasts all across the country, with Emily's phone number intact. Our message banks would stay filled for three days solid.

A thousand callers a day simply rang up to express their admiration for Larry's gall. Time-wasters, these people were. Less than one hundred messages informed Emily that all scum who toiled in the service of Larry Flynt would rot in hell. Emily scratched out return phone numbers, code names and condensed summaries of the illicit behavior the caller had offered to betray. The more Emily scrambled, the higher the stack of phone numbers that piled on my desk.

Initially, Flynt was content to view the stunt as a publicity triumph. News screens were overfilled with Larry's big, chatting face. The name *Hustler* was spat out in sound bites all day and all night. Phone slips piled on my blotter; they could not all be frauds. I'd been reading "Hot Letters" for many years, and had developed a nose for sniffing out the bogus sexual confession. Among all who called, we had one hundred people who deserved callbacks. I explained to Larry that we should hire someone, the fellow who'd brought us the idea for instance, to vet these potential informers. Our elfin friend had been slighted at not being invited to appear with Larry at any of the various news conferences.

"It wasn't his idea," said Larry. "Keep the thing in-house."

I pressed half a dozen reluctant staffers into service. The passively truculent six assembled in LFP's penthouse boardroom and received their special duties under a watchful portrait of Althea Flynt. Attorney Alan Isaacman codified the procedures for initial interviews of the informers. First, ask for the name of the compromised politician. Was the sexual relationship current or past; if past, how long had it lasted? How had the physical aspect been initiated? What proof was available—photographs? Notes or letters? Phone tapes? Receipts? We offered blanket anonymity, swearing to keep details secret until financial agreement had been reached.

Maybe all those phone slips will be proven false by this time next week, I thought, *and life will return to normal.* Unfortunately, my reluctant staffers immediately pulled in solid leads. I took a sheaf of notes up to Flynt's office and read off viable prospects: senators, congressmen, high judicial appointees, esteemed pillars of moral rectitude, all allegedly unhinged by raging libido. The skin around Larry's eyes tightened. I was kissing away any and all relaxation for the coming six months.

"I'm not convinced," said Larry. A friend of his from Washington, a well-credited Beltway journalist, was due in L.A. "I see potential in what you're telling me. I'd like my friend to take a look before we invest further."

I eagerly welcomed the vaunted journalist. He walked into my office preoccupied by a dismissive attitude. I presented my list of potential scandals.

"Really, you don't have much here to go on," said Mr. Beltway. I could have gone along with his cynicism, and Larry might have blown off the whole special project. But Beltway's condescension pissed me off.

"This one claims she made audio tapes," I countered. "She'll send photos of her and the target having drinks with his hand up her shirt. Either she has them or she doesn't. And this one. She's willing to arrange for surveillance on herself and her boyfriend."

"Why would she do that? It doesn't make sense."

"Fuck over a chick sometime, and it'll make perfect sense. If she can't come through, we'll know within an hour of visiting her." I laid out almost a dozen choice morsels. "This is real."

He hesitated. He was an insider; he wanted to remain an insider. He did admit to Larry that some prospects were "interesting." This small encouragement convinced Larry to kick in more money. The boss flew in a private security consultant whose murky history may have included freelance chores for the CIA. This consultant, code name Ralph, brought along his own investigative reporter, Dan Moldea. Dan stood tall, broad, high of forehead and rabidly partisan of posture. He had taken on the mafia (*The Hoffa Wars: Teamsters, Rebels, Politicians, and the Mob*, Paddington Press) and the *New York Times* (*Moldea* v. *New York Times*). He would have looked at home in a rugby scrum.

Dan Moldea, security expert Ralph and I sat across the massive desk from smoking Larry. Reluctantly, Ralph and Dan agreed to take copies of our lead sheets and evaluate the information for probability and impact. Why shouldn't they? Larry was shelling out fat dollars for their expertise, and their skepticism assured them nothing would be found to disturb any preexisting relationships back home in D.C. I was glad to see all the files transferred to their hands. If the professionals were correct about the stack being worthless, then no more extra work for me.

More than a month had passed since the ad's initial run. Editorialists and television commentators were continuously reporting the million-dollar offer. Emily fielded a dozen calls a day, so I had more potential finks lined up when Ralph and Dan returned two weeks later. Again, the two professionals and I sat in Larry's cigar haze. The investigators had assembled a bulky notebook that prioritized the leads in the exact sequence I had laid them out in the first place, with one big omission. Security Ralph and Dan Moldea had eliminated mention of Speaker-elect of the House of Representatives, Bob Livingston (R-Louisiana). I thumbed through the binders and admired the slick representation of my initial work, displeased only by the deletion of Livingston. We'd received a tip about Livingston from a Republican official in Louisiana. This official had checked out and he provided the name and phone number of a woman he said was Livingston's current girlfriend. Livingston, married more than 30 years at the time, had just campaigned successfully for Speaker of the House. He struck me as an ideal candidate for exposure.

"You left out Bob Livingston," I said. "Bob Livingston should be first priority."

Security Ralph indulged my naiveté. "That guy's from Louisiana. You'll get burned."

"How will we get burned?"

"They play dirty politics down there," explained Moldea. "You never know what's motivated this person to come forward."

"I don't give a shit what's motivating them. If it's not money, then that's a bargain. Livingston's going to be Speaker of the House. If some scumbag has a picture of him fucking a whore, I want to see it. Who cares a fuck what motivates them?"

One great perk of working for Larry Flynt is that you can cuss all you want. Larry took the cigar out of his mouth and squinted through the smoke. "Call the Livingston woman first," he said.

So, Bob Livingston, if you're out there, know that some people did their best to cover up for you. When Moldea finally called in to report his progress, I was sure Livingston had slipped away. At my insistence, Dan contacted the alleged other woman. She told him to fuck himself and clicked the phone down, refusing to answer again.

"That's that," I concluded, prematurely. Twenty minutes later, while dirtying up girl copy for *Chic*, I cut off editor Martin Green mid-sentence and fielded a phone call. The caller identified himself as a reporter from *Roll Call*, the newspaper of record on Capitol Hill.

"I hear that you're working on a story about extramarital affairs and Speaker-elect Bob Livingston," said the *Roll Call* reporter.

What would Larry do? I thought fast, faster than normal: "We are working on a few various things. The financial issues here are not quite finalized, so we cannot let any details out at this time because of confidentiality agreements with our sources."

"I'm going with the story."

"All right," I conceded, resigned to having been outfoxed.

I turned to Martin Green and dared to dream.

"Wouldn't it be great if Livingston folded like Dan Burton and coughed out a preemptive confession?" A caustic Republican representative and Clinton-baiter from Indiana, Dan Burton had attempted to lessen the impact of a *Vanity Fair* article detailing his extramarital calisthenics by addressing the press corps with a self-righteous mea culpa before the magazine was mailed out to subscribers. I imagined Speaker-elect Livingston opting to do the same.

"That will never happen," said Martin.

Less than two hours later, I picked up the phone. It was Larry's secretary.

"Who's this Bob Livingston? He's on TV giving a press conference that he's been unfaithful to his wife. He claims he's been 'Larry Flynted,' whatever that means."

I called Larry at his house and caught him watching CNN and cackling. I gave him the details of how I had used a reporter from *Roll Call* to fake Bob Livingston's dick out of his pants. I wanted Flynt to know from the start where credit was due. Larry was chortling and perhaps missed my point.

Initially, Livingston contended that his adulterous indiscretions did not compromise his ability to govern. Unlike Clinton, he had not lied while under oath. He met with a closed-door Republican caucus and emerged riding a swell of solidarity. Livingston vowed to take the Speaker's chair as planned and preside over the effort to oust the philanderer in chief.

The next day, interview requests overwhelmed Flynt, and he tossed a few my way. A network news crew was disappointed to be wiring me for sound, rather than Larry. It was a Friday. In the evening, my co-workers and I would celebrate at LFP's company holiday party. The news team's producer leaned Democrat. His teeth glistened.

"What precisely is the nature of the material you've found on Livingston?"

"I can't say right now. Confidentiality agreements are still in place, until these last financial details are worked out."

The sound guy had me completely wired up. The producer leaned in, hoping to verify a hunch.

"What we hear from our Washington bureau is that Livingston has been engaging in sexual relationships with lobbyists who are concurrently pushing legislation on the floor of the Congress."

I gave him a sly look.

Finally the camera came on, and the on-air questions began.

"And what precisely is the nature of the material you've found?"

"Right now, a few confidentiality agreements are still in place until the last financial details are worked out. What I can tell you is that we are aggressively pursuing indications that Representative Livingston has engaged in sexual relations with lobbyists who were concurrently attempting to influence legislation on the floor of the Congress."

"Do you think Livingston should resign?"

"Livingston is doing the right thing, sticking in to show that sexual activity has no bearing on the ability to fairly govern. Unless this lobbyist thing pans out."

"So you don't believe the impeachment effort in the House is motivated by ethics?"

"Oh, no. They're trying to steal the government. Go outside and talk to anybody. The brothers on the street all know it's a coup."

I cursed myself on the elevator down from Larry's floor. *The brothers on the street?* Did I have an emotional investment in sounding like a douchebag? I clutched the producer's business card, with his contact numbers. Flustered, ashamed, I summoned my stalwart assistant Emily. The volume of calls had picked up now that Livingston had refocused the limelight on Flynt's million bucks. The callers could hold. I informed Emily of my verbal gaffe, and she howled: "The brothers on the street all know it's a coup?"

I waited while she gained control of herself. "I don't mind that you laugh," I said. Emily had a wonderful laugh. "In fact, I enjoy it. Now I feel less imposing about what I'm asking you to do."

She sobered straight up. "What?"

"I need you to call these people and make sure they don't use that 'brothers in the street' quote. If that runs, I'll never hear the end of it."

"Why not call them yourself?"

"I'm ashamed."

She splurged on me for another 10 or 15 dollars' worth of laughs. "Okay, Allan. I'll do it for you." She pulled herself together to go.

"Here. Use this phone."

"You want to listen in while I call?"

Emily couldn't persuade any of the three associate producers she harried to promise they would not use the "brothers on the street" reference. Her tenacity and the oblique approaches she used in attempting to extract a pledge of no "brothers on the street" impressed me. Still, her best efforts received only an assurance that I would be happy with the way the segment turned out. The network planned to run my comments that night, around 7 p.m., coast to coast.

I retreated to the Hollywood Hills bluffside home. Having showered and shaved, I watched the wife dress for the Christmas party, and also kept an eye on the clock and on several cable news channels. Livingston was holding fast. He, according to him, had done nothing that required stepping down.

"My mom is very excited to see you on TV," said the wife.

I was not excited. First, the LFP party was at 6:30, so I would miss the broadcast. Second, that "brothers on the street" lameness.

"Why'd you say it?" asked the wife. "Did you want the whole country to know you're 'with it'? How do I look?"

"Smug."

The party buzz was happy and momentous. Larry picked up the bar tab for once.

The morning after, I rolled over in bed and turned on the TV. The first thing I heard was that Livingston had resigned. The next thing was that the House of Representatives had voted to go forward with the Senate trial of the President. Clinton was impeached. On the front pages of the *New York Times* and the *Washington Post*, Livingston's resignation was given equal space to Clinton's predicament. It was a dark morning for the President, and his day would have been much bleaker without the Speaker at his side, conjoined in infamy.

"Why the sudden Livingston turnaround?" asked the wife.

"Maybe the stuff I said about pursuing sex with lobbyists." I felt as though I had reached out with one lazy swipe and knocked off the man who was third in line to be President of the United States. His career, perhaps his marriage and certainly his Christmas were all ruined.

On Sunday Larry called; he was lunching at the Four Seasons in Beverly Hills. Flynt needed to see me. I dropped everything and sped over to Beverly Hills. The maitre d' directed me to Larry, presiding over a cluttered table in a back area.

"You want to order a coffee?" said Larry. My stomach growled, but Flynt didn't pick up the hint. Coffee was better than nothing. Dan Moldea arrived while I was stirring in my sugar.

"Did I dream this," said Larry, "or do we really have something on..."

He mentioned a charismatic Southwest Republican destined for the national stage. Moldea had spoken to a career woman who claimed a law degree and photographs, phone messages and gifts that she swore exposed a licentious profile to this new face of the GOP. She'd played Dan the tapes.

"It's not a slam-dunk," said Moldea, "but it's the closest we've got."

Larry had a timetable in mind. The media would tire of him soon and stop calling. He wanted nuggets to feed their interest.

"I want us on the same page for my next press conference."

He pressed his mouth into a tight-lipped smile, signifying that Moldea and I were encouraged to go. Moldea sat tight.

"Larry, I want to talk to you about a bonus for undoing Livingston."

Bonus? All he'd done was call the pissed-off girlfriend.

Unblinking, Larry asked him, "How much?"

Dan named a number that exceeded twenty percent of my ideal salary. Flynt shuddered, but agreed. I fumed on the way home. Where was my bonus?

On the morning of Larry's press conference, news vans were deployed around the neighborhood. I locked my car in the structure where I paid Larry $75 a month for the privilege of parking. Brooding on economic injustices, I arrived at my desk and responded to a panicked message left by Larry's secretary.

"Bonnie Livingston is on the phone," she said. "Bob Livingston's wife."

"She must be pissed."

"Allan, it's awful, what's happening to her family. Larry's got to stop. He can't let that information out. It will ruin them."

"That's Larry's choice," I said.

"Bonnie wants to talk to Larry personally. She wants to appeal to his good conscience. Oh, wait, that's Larry now. I have to patch her through."

"Best of luck to her and Larry's good conscience," I said.

Larry's secretary called me back in about a quarter-hour, sounding less urgent, but still unsteady.

"Larry promised Bonnie that he wouldn't reveal anything further. He agreed the damage had been done and that causing unnecessary pain would be pointless."

"So that's good?" I said.

"But you know Larry. He could go back on his word at any time. Like with the Hugh Hefner photos. He made a big deal about returning those pictures to Hugh Hefner. Of course he made copies."

Larry had ordered the long-hoarded shots of Hefner despoiling a Playmate ("Hugh's Your Daddy?") run in the March 1998 *Hustler*.

"It's so horrible," said Flynt's secretary. "That poor woman begged him. He's going to humiliate her after she begged him."

I put in a call to security expert Ralph, who was in charge of Moldea. Ralph informed me that he had removed himself from the case. Moldea would stay on, but as his own agent. Ralph offered to be on tap if I wanted to call him for advice or contacts, but officially, he was off the project.

"But things are just heating up," I said.

He laughed wryly and disconnected. I kept my own counsel for about an hour, then I called back Larry's secretary.

"I can put your mind at ease about Bonnie Livingston, but first you must swear to secrecy."

She solemnly swore.

"Don't worry about Larry ratting out Bonnie. The truth is that we have nothing on Livingston. We bluffed; he folded."

It took me four or five minutes to convince Larry's secretary that precise details of Livingston's stained honor were unlikely to come from the Flynt camp. She was able to relax, and the ominous circus took on a carnival atmosphere. The only thing missing that afternoon as Larry met with the assembled press were jugglers and sword swallowers. Correspondents fought for vantage in the publisher's office. Plush chairs, settees and tables were pushed aside. I'd never seen the room's vastness remotely crowded, but I was slithering elbow-to-elbow with guardians of the free press. The crooked nose of Matt Drudge wedged forward through the crush. That muck-stirrer would be dealt with soon enough ("Matt Drudge, Asshole of the Month," Holiday Issue, 1998).

A broad protector wheeled in Larry and positioned him behind the desk. One thing about Larry, he knew how to soak up attention. A skeptic up front asked if the White House had been feeding Larry information.

"I can assure you I've had no contact with the White House. I don't get my marching orders from them."

Blind to the absurdity of a man in a wheelchair discussing his marching orders, moralists in the mob insisted that Larry, who had built an empire based on the premise that people should be let alone to indulge in any manner of sexuality that suited them, could not justify his publicity stunt's attack on bedroom freedoms.

"I just wanted to expose hypocrisy. If these guys are going after the President, they shouldn't have any skeletons in their closet. Desperate times deserve desperate actions. Look at what they were doing to the President."

What further squalid revelations could the American public look forward to?

"Several more are going to bite the dust before this is over. I assure you, there are many others to come. We intend to take this to the mat, all the way." Larry rattled off alleged indiscretions, claiming that among a dozen compromised Republicans we had at least one who was "a really, really big fish." This was Larry's Christmas wish list. Eyes sparkling, he addressed concerns about his own credibility.

"I felt I had to employ a very high standard of journalistic proof," croaked the cigar-chomping publisher. "I didn't want to be dismissed by someone saying, 'Consider the source.'"

Livingston caving had made Larry Flynt credible. He could pretend anything he wanted to pretend. None of his questioners had the confidence to protest that he was filled with shit. I had given him this platform of plausibility, and I was bitter. I had my own wish list. Christmas was coming up fast. After the press mob had left, I paid Larry a visit. He sat smoking and smiling behind his desk, reading newspaper headlines about himself.

"I never thought I'd say it," he said, "but I'm in love with Bonnie Livingston. Her phone call gives me a reason why I don't release any details. And I look like the good guy."

"Imagine her face 10 years down the road when you let her know it was all based on nothing."

He paused to imagine Bonnie's stunned look and to admire it.

"Larry, did you go crazy out there or something? What were you thinking, telling those reporters we had all that shit?"

Flynt's public persona doesn't admit to looking sheepish, but that's the look I saw. "Sometimes I cain't help myself."

"Larry, the reason I'm here is that I once heard you say that a person can't get anything unless he asks for it. I'm asking for a bonus for bringing in Livingston."

Money always made Larry serious. He dropped the newspaper and fixed me with a look of respect and compassion.

"You know, Allan, every day I'm more and more impressed by your abilities. When the raise time comes around in July, I plan on giving special consideration to what you've helped accomplish here."

"Larry, July is seven months away." I could be fired twice by then.

I'd written out a memo detailing numerous reasons why Larry should give me money. I walked around his desk and set my argument in front of him. As he read, I narrated along, elaborating my strong points.

"This is the best thing ever done by anyone who worked for you, with the possible exception of Alan Isaacman winning your case at the Supreme Court."

"Okay, okay. You can stop. You win."

"And I want bonuses for seven people who were instrumental in making this possible."

Larry broke down and called payroll. By the end of the day, I was handing out checks. With my cut, I bought the wife a Rolex for Christmas. She pretended to be impressed and wore it for a week.

In the quiet days following Christmas, an anonymous caller tipped Emily that Representative Bob Barr (R-Georgia) had berated his second ex-wife while driving her home from an abortion clinic, furious that her blood had spotted the white-leather upholstery of his Cadillac. "I would do absolutely everything in my power to stop" a family member from having an abortion, swore Barr in 1992, even if that family member's pregnancy was the result of rape. In late 1998, Barr was posing as a Clinton-bludgeoning moralist.

Moldea contacted Gail Barr, the family-values congressman's second ex-wife, and she begged off. Dan reached out again. Under cover of confidentiality, Gail asserted that Barr had cheated on her with his current wife, that he had consented to the abortion of his child, that he had driven Gail to and from the clinic, and that he had paid for the procedure. Gail refused to corroborate the story that Barr had censured her for bleeding on his Cadillac's upholstery, demurring that her ex-husband had in fact been driving a Lincoln Continental. Gail and Barr shared two sons, and she was ambivalent about going on the record. She did, however, confide that she had retained the receipt for the abortion.

Another potential landmine was a middle-aged divorcée whom we can call Penny. Penny proffered evidence of having taken a married lover, a man in the right-wing elite who had been adamant in his condemnation of Clinton. Penny had secretly recorded four bouts of phone sex with this joker. It was tough listening. Penny's demands changed by the hour. Moldea flew out to her home and talked her through. She supplied photographs and hotel receipts that corroborated her stories of trysts with this vocational scold. Supposedly fearing for life, career and reputation, Penny retreated to a bed and breakfast in Newfoundland. She filled my voicemail with rambling 4 a.m. messages. I could not imagine being so hard up for erotic succor as to have an affair with this Penny.

The sexiest prospect was a career minx bumping into her 30s who claimed she was sleeping with one of the vociferous partisans from the House of Representatives. This particular married prosecutor to the Senate's jury had moved himself to tears while describing children who were devastated by the President's moral laxity. His girlfriend negotiated a price tag of a quarter-million dollars. She gave us flight numbers and arrival times for the faultfinder's weekend visit. With Larry's money, I hired a spook from the shadow government who tailed the congressman as he flew out of D.C. and into his lover's embrace. The pair's grabby, slobbering rendezvous was preserved on videotape, the picture as clear and sharp as any on *Cops*. I presume Larry's copy is in safekeeping. Moldea had an opportunity to make a duplicate as well.

The mainstream press so desperately wanted to milk Larry that I became news. A photo of me adorned the front page of the January 11, 1999 *Washington Post*'s "Style" section, above the fold. A larger picture was situated nine pages inside. The reader sees a man whose fists are clenched at the end of a long-sleeved dress shirt. Thick-rimmed black eyeglasses laterally bisect a drawn, dour face. The inside picture includes my desk and conveys a sense of clutter. That jittery man is shown in profile, tense on the edge of a reclining chair, balancing sheaves of paper upon his bony, nervous legs. I studied this overhead view and wondered, *where did my hair go?*

The week of the *Washington Post* article, Gail Barr finally succumbed to Moldea's charm and Larry's cash. I spent an afternoon interviewing her over the phone and fashioning the transcript into an affidavit with one of our lawyers. This draft was faxed back and forth with Gail's attorney, and by the end of the business day we had a complete legal document.

That night I flew coach to Atlanta, safeguarding a massive cashier's check, the payout for Gail Barr. Gail and her attorney had agreed to provide transcripts of divorce depositions from Jerilyn A. Dobbin and Bob Barr, along with the actual receipt for the abortion

Bob had paid for. Every time my eyes closed in the cramped airplane seat, there was a tug on my briefcase. In Atlanta, the predawn city unfurled around the windows of the taxi. I moved through hotel check-in like a self-obsessed zombie. Up in my suite, I ordered room service and passed out in my clothes before the meal had cooled.

A wake-up call stirred me and I dozed in a taxi that deposited me on a stoop outside a suburban lawyer's office. I stood with my overnight bag, straining to recall where I was and what I was doing there.

Inside, I met Gail Barr, second ex-wife of Bob Barr, champion of the 1996 Defense of Marriage Act. Brunette, solid, serene, Gail Barr impressed me as an honest and decent person. What had possessed her to marry Bob Barr? Gail read through and signed the affidavit while I scanned the divorce depositions. Like Clinton, Barr had refused to tell the truth about extramarital sex while under oath. The woman who would become Barr wife-number-three also refused to tell the truth under oath about adulterous acts, on the advice of Bob Barr's attorney. One of the charges against Clinton was that an attorney, on his behalf, had advised Monica Lewinsky to zip her trap.

Of all the people I'd been exposed to in this sleazy undertaking, Gail Barr was the one who deserved a large payday. Handing over the cashier's check, I felt almost as though I had done a good deed. It was an odd feeling, one that threw me off.

Gail's attorney taxied me to the local Kinko's where I faxed documents back to California. The machine jammed, and a Kinko's worker politely asked if I needed assistance. My body shielded the sensitive material from his prying eyes. I sent him away and wondered with some alarm: *Am I a marked man down here in Georgia?* Barr, I seemed to remember, had some relation with the intelligence community. Could he be aware that Larry Flynt's scourge had been booked onto an incoming flight from Los Angeles?

Safe in a taxi, heading back home with the depositions, I fell asleep. I bolted awake as the taxi was circling the airport. The signed copy of Gail's affidavit! I'd forgotten to pick it up before leaving for Kinko's. The taxi driver accepted a ransom of the last of my cash, and we raced back toward the lawyer's office.

"You all must be on some important business," said the cabbie, folding portraits of Ben Franklin.

"My employer intends to expose Georgian congressman Bob Barr's true colors to the world."

"Folks been saying Bob Barr's colored for many years now," said the driver. "Won't be news to nobody 'round here."

The hundreds of cigars Larry had smoked over the past months beat the golden chairman down. Flynt checked into a hospital, and the doctors diagnosed him with walking pneumonia. I hardly finished making my first joke about the "walking" portion of that diagnosis when I was drafted to perform on debate TV, pitted against big-haired commentator John Gibson. A Gibson broadcast crew arrived at LFP headquarters to beam me out. Luckily, I'd worn a suit to work that day, a gray soft-plaid Gucci.

The crew as a whole seemed friendly, so I pumped them for information.

"Which one is this Gibson guy? Is he pretty right-wing?"

"He started out more to the left, now he's leaning to the right."

"Is he the guy with the yellow helmet hair and the sour mouth like an old woman?"

"That might be him."

"He's going to eat me up. I'll look like a schmuck."

"You'll do fine. You look good."

But I had been right. Gibson only booked me on his show to discredit Flynt's revelations. On my attempts to equate Bill Clinton's slippery behavior with Bob Barr's sliding scale of accountability, Gibson preened: "You're comparing apples to oranges."

"No, I'm not," I said. Gibson cut me off.

The broadcast crew silently broke down their equipment and snatched the microphone off my lapel, avoiding my eyes. I tanked. I should have easily swatted that apples-to-oranges nonsense: "No, big-hair, sour-mouth John Gibson. In equating Barr to Clinton, I'm comparing apples to apples—a wormy Red Delicious to a rotten Granny Smith."

The wife and I made the pilgrimage to Larry and Liz Flynt on the celebrity floor at Cedars Sinai Hospital.

"We saw you on TV!" exclaimed Liz.

"I failed."

"No you didn't," she insisted. "Larry said, 'Look at Allan give it back! They cain't shut him up!'"

I appreciated Liz's attempt to console me, but I knew the truth.

"How come you cain't wear some nice clothes?" said Larry. He was hooked up to feeders and monitors and could hardly spare a breath. "You come off looking like some South Central white pimp."

"Those were nice clothes," said the wife. "That's just what happens to nice clothes when he puts them on."

Mid-January 1999: "Penny" accepts our dollar offer and the criteria behind it to rat out her secretly recorded Republican dirty-talker. Penny enlisted a venerable legal team in her hometown to handle the paperwork. It looked like Larry Flynt would be sending out GOP phone sex to coincide with the impeachment's high-minded arguments.

Further research revealed that taping without two-party consent in Penny's home state is a felony. The law provided strict punishment both to whoever made the recording and to whoever spread it. If Larry Flynt were to take these clandestine tapes public, a headline-hungry states attorney would likely strike a deal with Penny to stick the meddling pornographer behind bars.

One last prize was still on the hook: the House Manager videotaped in flagrant embrace with his mercenary mistress. That crafty woman was driving a hard bargain. Prior to the surveillance tape being shot, she had been satisfied to be paid a quarter-million to shaft her married boyfriend. Down at the wire, she wanted the whole million.

Moldea had the best rapport with the girl, but perhaps an adversarial approach might jar her loose. I took a shot. The girl's voice was unnaturally sexy; forceful, confident, throaty and young. Plus, I'd seen her in full make-out action. In her mocking, throaty tone she asked me: "Do you have any idea how much 250 thousand is after taxes?"

"Sure I do," I said. "It's a pile of goddamn money."

"I also intend to remain totally anonymous."

"Running this tape on TV is where we get our money's worth."

"Dan Moldea said I could remain anonymous."

"Dan is in no position to make that promise."

"Talk to him about it."

I chased down Dan who explained that all we needed to do was let the targeted House Manager know that we had the tape, and the target would change his tack. Exasperated, I reiterated our editorial position.

"What does *Hustler* magazine care a fuck if the guy changes his tack? Larry has no interest in a quiet behind-the-scenes life. We'll run the footage, and let the fallout fly, with Larry's face all over the TV with it."

I had one more exchange with the hard-bargaining chick. I liked her a lot. If we were to meet under different circumstances, she might rip my heart right out. I spoke to her as I would speak to a recalcitrant lover: "If you remain anonymous, you could open yourself up to charges of blackmail or extortion. Consider the possibility."

"You'll spend at least a million for me to show my face."

I relayed this information to the house up Doheny Drive, and Larry balked, bitterly. He'd invested thousands in the surveillance taping of this girl and of her sanctimonious married boyfriend. To let that money go for nothing galled him, but not so savagely as the girl jacking up her price at the back end after having agreed to a reasonable sum up front. Such behavior is despicable in a hooker, and it was not attractive in this businesswoman either. She was ambitious, but shortsighted. That Congressional moll could have been reality-TV royalty by now. As it was, her short-term greed and Larry's grip on financial realities left her with a married boyfriend and no pension. She and I could have worked her story into a TV movie, at least. She was so cute, but such a chump.

The *Hustler* Cartoons

IT DOESN'T TAKE a miracle to give the typical guy a basic hard-on. A man of average health can be on his way to church, to the penitentiary, to his mother's funeral, and the sexual impulse will spring upon him like a trap. Approach a man in similar hard-pressed circumstances—on the verge of death, destitution, worship—and wrench a laugh out of him. That hard-won flash of humor is a singular event that might be interpreted as disclosing the invisible workings of divine intervention.

Notorious for explicit sex, *Hustler* achieves a more sublime infamy through its cartoons. To peruse Larry Flynt's flagship is to encounter laughable facets of necrophilia, dildo-strapped nuns, ambulatory turds, walking anuses, the perceived discrepancy in penis size between black and white males, vaginas large enough to envelop an entire man, physical intimacies with anthropomorphic pets, lesbian love rituals, the ills and quirks of male homosexuality, the corrosive effect of vaginal discharge upon automobile upholstery, the danger that freshly licked African-American lips will accidentally adhere to some glasslike surface, bar sluts, gang-bangs, wastebasket fetuses, flatulence anal and vaginal, the handicapped, Ku Klux Klansmen, lynching, anal sex, prison romance, naked females whose faces are covered by paper bags, sex crimes of the rich and famous, sex in full-body traction, retards as playthings, practical jokes committed by Saint Peter, suicide, consanguinity, animal husbandry in the connubial sense, erectile dysfunction, voyeurs, panty-sniffers, menstruation, STDs and philosopher houseflies delivering piquant sophistries while nibbling on corn-studded nuggets of shit. Any publication governed by a reasoned editorial policy bars such topics as joking matters. These precise lapses in decorum are the staples of *Hustler*'s cartoon arsenal, worked month after month into the line-drawn gospel of visual humor according to Flynt.

A perplexed minority of "readers" are horrified by the brash (some say brutal) humor of the cartoons and stop buying the magazine in protest of a particular aberration. A letter to the editors in the December 1999 issue ("Militant Lesbo Attacks") announced the writer's intention to boycott *Hustler* due to a September 1999 cartoon labeled "Six Fags Over Texas." The offending art piece showed oilfields and tumbleweeds as background to a shit-kicker in an open-top Cadillac barreling past a hanging post from which dangle the fly-swarmed corpses of six stereotyped gays, nooses tight about their necks.

One puzzled critic used the September 1996 "Feedback" column to seek clarification for the motives behind the January 1996 selection of drawings ("No Kidding"): "Seeing two African American males lynched from a tree and tied together to make a hammock for a Klansman does not make me see the so-called humor in any way. Where is the humor? Help me understand it."

Hustler's boilerplate reply was typical of the facile rationalizations that were trotted out any time Mr. Flynt's apologists (that would be me and the nimble minds at my command) were called upon to justify the apparently indefensible: "Cartoons are not always meant to be funny. They also offer social commentary, which can touch sensitive chords, as these clearly did with you. Deep feelings are brought to the surface, and they're not always pleasant. Many Americans would prefer to ignore ugly truths and bad feelings. We don't. As long as painful issues exist in society, it will be our duty to address them."

Larry Flynt's rationale for printing what might qualify as visual hate crimes was far blunter than the mealymouthed puff of the "Feedback" rebuttals. Larry pulled me close at a Beverly Hills dinner and cited a cartoon that depicted black men dragged like tin cans behind the car of two Ku Klux Klan newlyweds (February, 1996). "I love that shit," he muttered.

CHAPTER 16

A Wild Bush Chase

ONE LAST TIME, I was in the French Riviera, having my worst trip ever at the *Hot Video* porno awards. I stood on an elevated stage, microphone in hand, surveying a vast auditorium filled with X-rated workers and moguls. Banquet tables receded back toward a far horizon; every seat between me and eternity sold out. An illicitly glamorous congregation of thousands looked toward me with disinterest. It was as if I had waked into a recurring, disturbing dream. I had been summoned to the spotlight and introduced to the assembled throng in a tongue I did not understand. As a whole, this audience of European pornographers and prostitutes had no idea who I was. To them, I was defined only as the nobody who was standing in for the absent Larry Flynt.

A month earlier, I had approached Larry and proposed hitching a ride on his personal jet and flying over to the Cannes Film Festival with him. The French porn magazine *Hot Video* was planning to present the boss with an award for the achievements of his lifetime. My scheme was to cover the award-giving firsthand, fly home in spacious luxury, rest up a few days, then jot down a blurb to accompany the photo of award-winning Larry to appear in *Hustler*. To my delight, Larry agreed that I should tag along.

Days before we were to depart, the chairman called me into his office.

"Bad news. I cain't make the *Hot Video* dinner. Scheduling conflicts. You're gonna have to fly commercial.

"Oh, and Allan," said Larry. "I need you to pick up the award for me. They'll want you to say a few words."

This was truly bad news. I stopped for a mope with Larry's secretary. I found her in the 10th-floor kitchenette, her hands in thick, yellow rubber gloves. She was loading up the dishwasher with dildos she'd pulled out from Larry's desk drawers.

"Did they tell you about dildo duty during the job interview?"

"Larry sucks you in, then you find yourself doing anything for him." The dishwasher door jammed. She repositioned the prongs and slammed it shut. "Actually, I do this for the poor girls. I can't have Larry using Mr. Stiffy on one skank without cleaning off the slut that came before her."

Flynt's secretary poured coffee, and I bemoaned the boss' scheduling conflict.

"Schedule conflict?" She spat coffee back into Larry's mug. "He's having an operation to supercharge his penis pump. The doctor says he should stay close to home on antibiotics for a few weeks."

Crammed into coach, I cursed my boss and I cursed myself for having approached him with hopes of a free trip to France. Later, microphone in hand onstage at the Mandelieu Royal Hotel Casino, I cursed the thousands before me. How dare they congregate, these absurd egotists? Was the world taken in by this ceremony to honor people who made their livelihood by wallowing in dishonor? There I stood, quaking in front of them. A more practical person might have taken a drink in my position. I made do with a cigarette, the first I'd smoked since the day of my wedding, uncountable years ago.

Cigarette and microphone in hand, the statuette commemorating Larry Flynt's exploits clutched in the other, I phrased my opening comments, "I stand before you, who are the esteemed international community of the erotic cinema. In the face of your gathered creative presence, I am humbled. Where else in the world will so much artistic vitality be contained in one room?"

I paused as a shaven-skull European demi-celebrity translated my address into the local patois. The French think they know existential drama. What about me? I spoke into a void, my empty message echoed in words that meant nothing to me, falling upon the deaf ears of a crowd to whom I meant nothing. The portion of the audience that did know me—scummy pricks from back in the States and the tarts they'd dragged across the sea to pimp out indiscriminately—resented my presence. I raised Flynt's statuette forward so that it glinted in the concentrated light.

"My employer, Mr. Larry Flynt, is a man of undiluted vision. Mr. Flynt has sent me here tonight to accept this award and to communicate his feelings that the real heroes of the adult cinema movement are you, one and all, striving forever against all odds to express yourselves in the most honest art form ever invented by man—the adult movie. Larry Flynt salutes you; I salute you; the entire world at large has converged here in the electronic assembly hall to salute each and every one of us! Long live sex."

Prior to my appearance on stage, I'd been seated at a table up front. As the award recipients had wrapped up their acceptance blurbs, I noticed pairs of undulant women in slit-thigh ball gowns leading the honored guests backstage. As I finished speaking, a beefy fellow in a white jacket took me by the upper arm. He wore his hair in a mullet, a fashion I was surprised to see had crossed the Atlantic. He escorted me past a coven of twinkling, precious, spike-heeled femmes waiting in the wings, just beyond reach of the footlights. Their wide-eyed wonder, their juicy-lipped bated breath, their sparkling smiles of sensuality were as one directed forward toward recipients more worthy than me. I was marched through a maze of hallways and finally unhanded backstage, deposited in line for an on-video interview. An officious woman in a tuxedo laid her paws on me and spoke into a headset in a language that might as well have been French.

"How do you find the French people?"

"I am forever amazed and charmed by the urbane hospitality of these gracious hosts."

"What is the future for adult films?"

"The future will be in the past. I predict romance, explosive romance, a return to the epic love story, realism, and production qualities forever improving."

"What is your message for the pornographic public?"

"Use plenty of lubricant, and try to leave your home at least once a day, and be outside while the sun is up."

"You are an associate of Mr. Larry Flynt. Why has he entrusted you on this mission?"

"I am here because my boss cannot stop from playing with his cock. He is so obsessed with playing with his cock that he hires doctors to play with it in ways that he cannot play himself. That is why I am here. Because Larry Flynt has paid doctors to slice open his prick."

I assumed that no one who could hear me could understand what the hell I was saying. "Well, what I just said will be edited for broadcast, right?"

"*Non, mon cheri.* You have been on live television. We did not tell you so you would not be nervous."

A photographer and two earnest assistants were rounding up the actual *Hot Video* winners for a backstage group portrait. Honorees for best threesome anal, best director of an orgy prolonged, best climax multiple and other true bests gathered in camaraderie and fraternity, draping arms about one another.

Clutching Larry's statuette as if it were my consolation prize, I wandered the backstage area, through the service bay and into the kitchen. Eventually, I happened upon the auditorium at large and wended my way forward to the table where I had been seated originally. My neighbors looked away as I claimed my seat. I placed Larry's statuette in the middle of the table, and my dinner mates took turns lifting the gilded award and gauging its heft. A pie-faced American porn woman, whom Christian Shapiro's reviews had repeatedly urged to quit her onscreen copulations now that she had crossed into middle age, moved into one of the empty seats adjacent to me. She was accompanied by a ponytailed man in a tuxedo-front T-shirt who behaved as though he were her husband.

"What do you do for Larry Flynt?" she asked.

"You're not the guy who writes the reviews?" asked the husband.

Why had I come back to the banquet? I could have taken an elevator up to my room and sulked. I left the table, forgetting the statuette, and stumbled toward the exit. Reality had become disjointed, and I felt as though my name were being called from a great distance, from across an insuperable divide. A hand reached out from the other side and tugged at me. I stopped and turned. It was the middle-aged porno queen. She smiled, helpful, sweet, motherly, like an aging waitress. She held out the statuette.

"Honey, you forgot this."

I thanked her for her kindness. Larry would be disappointed if I'd left it behind. I packed the sharp figurine and its jagged edges into my checked baggage. Larry accepted the memento back in Beverly Hills, along with a condensed version of my acceptance speech. He shrugged as though the award meant little to him. The statuette would come to stand on a credenza behind Larry's desk, appearing in the background of any photos taken of him while he worked, hovering over his shoulder as though bestowing legitimate acclaim.

Larry's spirits sagged in the publicity-parched months following *Hustler*'s impeachment meddling, but an idea came to him for reestablishing his status as a current-events sidebar. I'm not sure if he cooked up the notion himself.

"Allan, you know George W. Bush was a crazy kid. Drugs, hookers, the whole bit."

"Weren't we all?"

"He had a lot of money, and he cut a wide path. He must have left traces down in Texas. If we hire a hungry reporter to go down there and turn over some rocks, we can pull up something that might interest the papers. My money says we'll find somebody who'll talk. All they need is to be asked. Bush is too much of a moron to ever win President, but it cain't hurt to give Gore some help. Who do you recommend that we send down to Texas? Someone zealous."

I pressed the features editor to locate a writer and marshal the finances. If anything were to come of these Texas explorations, I would make myself available to take the credit. The features editor had been on the periphery of the Livingston triumph, and had witnessed the notoriety stirred up by that so-called investigation. In this Texas reconnaissance, Features saw an opportunity to make his name. He solicited a pair of young muckrakers whose bylines occasionally appeared in the *L.A. Weekly* and other local venues. This twosome was willing to do wet work for Larry's dirty dollars, but were shy about having their identities revealed.

Features ushered the team into my office for a preliminary interview. One was dark, oily and quick-eyed; the other was blown-dry blond with hooded lids. Their synchronized delivery spoke of long hours cadging drinks through barroom brilliance.

"Our idea is that we work in tandem," said dark and oily, "and *Hustler* gets a skill set that no single journalist can provide."

Light and airy picked up the theme: "We'll share responsibilities and salary; that means increased efficiency and heightened response time."

These two had a cinematic sense of themselves. Even while seated, they posed as though blocking out scenes for a buddy movie. From our first meeting with them, Features and I took to calling our investigative writers Woodward and Bernstein, in smirking homage to the *Washington Post* calendar boys. Would-be Woodward and Bernstein's appeal to Flynt was largely the idea of buying two writers for less than the price he'd been willing to pay for one.

To their credit, "Woodward" and "Bernstein" put in hundreds of hours in Texas tracking down past acquaintances of Bush and ferreting out the slightest indications of electorally significant misbehavior. Woodward and Bernstein's plan was solid: to contact all past residents of Houston's Chateaux Dijon apartments from the early '70s span during which this complex had been home to the presumably profligate George W. Bush.

Flynt buzzed me early one morning toward the end of May 2000.

"Allan. Larry here. Dwaine's dead."

"What?" Had his daughter gone berserk at the nullification of Dwaine's incestuous rape verdict and tossed a running blowdryer into the cartoonist's Cambria hot tub?

"He died in bed last night," said Larry. "He just woke up and died. I guess it's just me and you now."

Could I have heard him right? "Life won't be the same without Dwaine," I said.

Improvements in the work environment should have been immediate, but I knew that Larry would retread some fuckwit from *Hustler* past to fill in for Tinsley, some sallow loser along the lines of Narcisco Smelt. Larry couldn't leave well enough alone, whether with his prick or his magazine. He would fail to see the wisdom in a publishing team made up of just him and me. As I moped over this dumb injustice, Kathleen from the production department approached, misreading my mourning look.

"Are you sad that Dwaine's dead?"

"Why should I be? He's in a better place. He's happy in heaven with JonBenet Ramsey."

Dwaine's funeral service was held in a Presbyterian church at the head of Beverly Hills' famed Rodeo Drive. Young art director Bill rode with me in the black-on-black Chevy Impala. We parked the suitably gangsterish and appropriately funereal car in an underground lot a block from the church. Would this house of worship withstand the ungodly presence of Larry Flynt paying tribute to a man whose life had been devoted to blasphemy of the crassest order?

Young Bill and I took seats toward the rear. Flynt had given all employees the option of taking a half day off work in honor of Dwaine, stipulating that funeral attendance was mandatory. Familiar office faces were mixed in with hardscrabble blood relations of Dwaine and widow Ellen, and with a smattering of longtime associates of *Hustler* magazine, tottering at the opportunity to pay respects to adamant atheist Larry Flynt. Flynt compromised his no-God values to park his gleaming chair next to a front-row pew. The pastor seemed out of place. His generic encomium wafted out like a manufactured breeze in a failing indoor mall.

Larry rolled to the pulpit to eulogize his cartoon mentor. Tears streamed down the golden chairman's face. His throat caught.

"This is going to be tough," said Larry. He wiped his eyes. "I never cried at my mother's funeral. I loved my mother very much. It's just thinking of Dwaine being gone is really tough to deal with. Maybe it's just reminding myself of my own mortality."

The funeral cards distracted me. Somehow, along with *Hustler*'s three contract cartoonists (all of whom had been subservient to Dwaine, and most of whom regularly complained about his shortages of integrity and charity), my name was listed on the program as an honorary pallbearer. Luckily, the earthly remains were not present. I think the corpse had been burned immediately upon the stake being removed from the heart, so I bear no trauma from having lain hands on the Tinsley casket.

After the service, I grabbed young Bill and tried to sneak out through the church courtyard. Cookies and coffee were being served, and Bill stopped for a snack. I came face to face with Dwaine's grieving wife, Ellen. Duty-bound, I racked my brains for something less than cruel to say.

"He really loved his life," I said.

Lit cigarette in her maw, Ellen reached out and clawed my forearm. "Gawd, did he ever."

"It seems cruel," I said, "when someone passes so young."

"Oh, at heart, Allan, he really was young, so young."

"He was so generous," I said. I'm afraid my eyes might have rolled up into my head at this point. I hope Ellen didn't notice. "He put so much of himself into his work."

"But, Allan, he had so much more to give."

I tracked young Bill in the distance, his hands loaded with pastries. What was keeping him? I didn't escape before forcing Ellen to engage in a long hug. My jacket would smell of cigarettes for a week.

"That looked rough," said young Bill as we climbed into the car. As I turned the key, the ignition halfway caught and abruptly went dead. The Impala had never misfired before. I tried again. No luck. I cursed Dwaine with all my heart, but that noble sentiment did no good.

Had the spirit of Dwaine decided to hover over my Impala, thwarting my attempt to move on? Was I doomed? If so, no one noticed any difference. Larry Flynt and our Texas dirt-diggers were hope-filled on suppositions of a George W. Bush abortion, allegedly performed on a pressured girlfriend in early '70s Houston, a time and a place wherein such procedures were illegal. The lead came from a reporter for a local weekly, *New Times*, who passed along contact numbers for an attorney in Texas. On the phone, the lawyer was fully cognizant that Larry Flynt had two years earlier offered a reward of up to $1 million for politically volatile scandal. The Texan presented himself as a temperate, idealistic son of the '60s and claimed to have an ex-girlfriend, one of whose previous boyfriends had facilitated an illegal abortion in 1971 at the behest of young George W. Bush.

The prospect of taunting Bush with a dead fetus enchanted Flynt, so faux Woodward and fake Bernstein signed on to extend their stays in Texas. Between scouring public records in the effort of locating Bush's past neighbors, the intrepid reporters met with a woman whom Larry will refer to as "Susan" in his second autobiography, *Sex, Lies and Politics: The Naked Truth*. Susan's story was that, in 1971, she had overheard an incoming phone call at the apartment of her then-boyfriend. That boyfriend, "Clyde," as Larry will call him, was a self-made millionaire and associate of the Bush family. According to Susan, the phone call was an urgent request for Clyde to arrange an abortion for George W. Bush's then-current girlfriend, a character Larry will name "Rayette." Susan further stated that she had visited the putatively pregnant girlfriend in the hospital on the night before the abortion. Various other friends were also in the hospital room chatting with Rayette. It's hard to find a knowledgeable woman who considers abortion an overnight procedure. It's equally difficult to imagine inviting a roomful of friends to come visit hours before you are set to undergo an illegal operation.

Despite these early warning signs, LFP threw every resource into validating Susan's claims. Our opposition researchers tracked down the doctor purported to have performed the procedure. The surgeon denied the abortion, but admitted he had visited the Chateaux Dijon and claimed to remember Rayette. Woodward and Bernstein interpreted this recollection as a sign of complicity.

"What else could it mean?" said Woodward, seriously. I left it for Features to enumerate the myriad and plausible meanings to the fact that a middle-aged man was able to recall the name and physical characteristics of a vibrant, engaging woman of his youth.

Woodward and Bernstein supplied weekly updates so Larry would feel his money was working, even if it was not buying results. The sleaze sleuths suspected that the target woman, Rayette, had enjoyed a sudden elevation in lifestyle, moving to an exclusive neighborhood, even though her employment situation, in their estimation, was solidly lower-middle-class. This ungainly uptick in abundance would turn out to be an anticipatory misperception shared by Woodward and Bernstein, perhaps marijuana-induced, but the false report looked good on the weekly update and kept Larry's hopes up. Though Woodward and Bernstein discovered that indications of Rayette's sudden prosperity were untrue, these false claims would persist in the mind of Flynt well into the next decade, although with some confusion. One week, Flynt might cite a supposed lifestyle upgrade as evidence to his belief that the supposed abortion patient, Rayette, had been paid off by patrons loyal to Bush (*L.A. Weekly*, "The Texas Abortion Tango,"

June 18, 2004). A few weeks later, he might claim it was the informer Susan who had gone silent after receiving cash from Bush loyalists (*Salon*, "Citizen Flynt," July 8, 2004).

In retrospect, I might have given Bernstein and Woodward more credit for their efforts, but I was flush with a discovery of my own, made in the LFP men's room. One of the great things about working for Larry Flynt is that you never had to worry about him ambling up and standing at your elbow while you were pissing. Still, there was no immunity from the odd LFP urinal shock. Sometime around when Bernstein and Woodward were digging through Texan garbage pails, I'd turned from the sink and caught sight of Earl, a 50-something black man whose military posture and salutatory grin distinguished him from the ordinary computer technician. Earl, I saw in the few seconds between when he'd shaken off his last drops and flipped shut his fly, had been concealing a secret, a gigantic secret.

"Earl," I said, "if I'm being too personal, tell me to fuck off. I think, if you ever had any inclination to go this way, we could find a place for you in the magazine."

Earl did, in fact, have the inclination. Within a matter of weeks after uncovering the initial Earl lead, we'd signed him on for a photo shoot, found the ideal girl (a petite chestnut blonde) to complement Earl's particular strengths, paid our money, and already the set was in the can.

"What was so hard about that?" I wanted to ask our abortion sleuths.

Perhaps chastened, perhaps hoping to illustrate that they had lost neither their focus nor their edge, Woodward and Bernstein located and staked out the modest home of Rayette, the former Bush girlfriend and overnight hospital patient. The dauntless journalists confronted the woman's current husband as he walked down his sidewalk to embark upon his workday. They presented him with the abortion allegation. That night, after conferring with his wife, Rayette's husband denied to the LFP team that there had ever been any abortion, pregnancy or Bush sex. He also informed Woodward and Bernstein that they would be well advised to not be seen again in the vicinity of his wife or of his home.

The story might have ended with Rayette's denial of any George Bush abortion, since the narrative lacked the all-important accuser/victim component, but Larry transported Susan and the attorney whom we initially contacted out to Los Angeles. I sat with Features, Susan, her attorney and our attorney in the plush gaudiness of Larry Flynt's vast, money-colored office. We plotted to devise some way of exploiting Susan's contentions.

"I have an idea," said Susan. "I could approach Rayette and say that I am being goaded by journalists, and that I need to talk to her for her own protection. We could meet in some public place, and our conversation could be recorded."

I wondered how Susan had come up with this idea. It had all the twists and blind turns of a scheme concocted by the zealous brainwaves of Bernstein and Woodward. The merits of this ploy were entertained and debated. Direct questioning from would-be Woodward and bogus Bernstein had alerted Rayette and her husband to our machinations, but even that slip could be used to Susan's advantage. She too would claim harassment by *Hustler*'s attack ferrets, establishing sympathetic bonds with Rayette, making the target feel safe in opening her guts and spilling the facts directly onto tape, preferably video. The plan, stunningly, seemed to be shaping up as a go, but there was a snag. Susan wanted to be paid for her part in the charade. She'd been working with Flynt for months now, and not seen one penny. Woodward and Bernstein were making a living, all on Susan's information. Without an assured cut, she balked at stepping into action.

Almost two years earlier, shortly after the fall of Speaker-elect Bob Livingston, a reporter had caught me off guard at my desk and asked how all this mining for scum made me feel as a journalist. Did it embarrass me? I laughed in his ear.

"Journalist? Embarrassed? What are you talking about? I work at *Hustler*."

I wasn't laughing anymore. It was one thing to be chasing down hypocrite politicians, armed with verifiable dirt. It was a sleazier thing to be hounding Mr. and Mrs. Rayette who, in every instance of being approached by Larry's minions, behaved totally in character with two innocents responding to unjust accusations. Suddenly I was privy to a plot to catch nonpartisan bystanders in an abortion trap. This is what Linda Tripp had done, going to Independent Counsel Starr and the attorneys representing Paula Jones and playing for them Monica Lewinsky's surreptitiously taped admission of an affair with President Bill Clinton. I had sunk to a low to which even real journalists seldom descend, unless they were named Lucianne Goldberg.

While Susan and the Texas attorney were in Los Angeles, I arranged for a lunch at the Daily Grill, across from the Beverly Center. The lunch was attended by me, Features, the Texas attorney and Susan. Woodward and Bernstein were not present. In their place was a Larry Flynt contact from Washington, D.C., whom I am comfortable calling "Skippy."

Skippy was a member of the Clinton inner circle, dating back to the Oxford days. His face was never so familiar as James Carville's, but his real name should be recognizable to anyone who paid attention during the impeachment and attendant sexual smearing of Clinton. Skippy came off as one of these guys you meet and, if you're moderately smart, you realize instantly that he's three steps ahead of you and of everybody else you know. At his behest, I introduced Skippy to the people at lunch by a name other than his own. He quickly got down to questioning Susan.

"Did Clyde specifically say that George Bush was the person on the other end of the phone during that call?"

"He didn't have to. His whole manner changed when he talked to the Bushes."

"When did Clyde reveal to you he'd been asked to arrange for Rayette's abortion?"

"He never specifically had to tell me. I picked it up as much from what he didn't say as what he did say."

"At the hospital, when you mentioned the abortion to Rayette, how did she react?"

"In those days, in that social group, you didn't throw around that word. But you didn't have to. The truth was in her face."

"In the passing years, since 1971, when you and Rayette refer to the incident, has she expressed bitterness? Resignation?"

"I don't remember Rayette and I as actually speaking together, except briefly in a general way, since 1971."

Under the subtle cross-examination of Skippy, it became clear that Susan had never heard the word *abortion* used by anyone involved in the 1971 hospitalization incident. Clyde had never told Susan that George W. had impregnated a girl. Clyde never told her that an abortion was requested or on the way. Susan furthermore admitted that the hospitalized woman had never said to her, or to anyone she knew, at any time in 1971 or since, that she was pregnant or having an abortion. The notion of abortion apparently came to Susan pretty much on her own.

If Woodward and Bernstein had done as objective a vetting of Susan during their initial Texas interviews as Skippy did at lunch, Flynt might have saved a hundred grand. Skippy was polite and respectful to Susan, but he wanted nothing to do with her story. If publicly aired, her contentions would be easily disassembled, and we in the Flynt camp would be exposed as fools. To present Susan would do more harm than good for the chances of electing a Democratic president.

"Incidentally," said Skippy, riding back toward Flynt Towers in my black-on-black Impala, "this story so far. Sloppy. Do you agree?"

I was in no position to argue.

In a last-ditch attempt to toss fetus in Bush's face, Flynt dropped hints to various news producers about a possible Bush abortion, but refrained from naming Susan. By shrewdly keeping his source anonymous, not only did Larry Flynt forgo paying Susan her formidable sum, he also bypassed the risk of having his sole informer revealed as a purveyor of secondhand guesswork.

Bernstein and Woodward were reluctant to let the scent of scandal waft away. Secondhand reports had Susan traveling to New York to meet with editors and lawyers from well-known rags that specialize in gossip and innuendo. If newsstand absence is any indication, none of them would touch her goods. This dearth of coverage was a galling disappointment to our investigators. They consoled themselves by proclaiming Bush's inability to win the election, mere weeks away. I was less sure Bush would fail.

"I'll bet Bush does win," I said. "I'll bet each of you. Twenty bucks a head. I have the worst gambling luck of anyone I know. Me putting money on Bush should make Gore a lock. Forty bucks, if you two win, that's a small price to keep George W. Bush out of the White House."

We shook hands all around to validate the wager. I knew that their evolved and elastic concept of ethical behavior would allow for them welshing on the bet. I would never see that 40 bucks and, if Bush were to prevail, I might truly need it.

Once Bernstein and Woodward had shambled from the office, I went to the restroom to wash up. I had, after all, shaken their hands, and they struck me as favoring expediency over time-consuming, tedious hygiene. Earl, tall, black, rigid and composed like an officer and a gentleman, stepped into the adjacent stall. Earl coughed.

"I wanted to talk to you about my photo set," he said. Earl's pictures had recently been slated ("Earl and Heather: Twin-Tone Tight-Fit," Spring, 2001). Earl and fluffy-tail Heather had been depicted taking a shoe store customer-clerk relationship to an extremely photogenic physical level.

"You looked great," I said to Earl.

"It's not the pictures that bothered me," said Earl. "It's the words."

Had some demeaning terminology slipped into the copy? A sinking sensation accompanied the shut-off of my urine flow, so I put the thing away and asked Earl: "What do you mean?"

"Why is it that my character had to be a shoe store employee? If I were a white man, wouldn't you have made me the shoe store owner?"

I considered this point while Earl buckled in his baby.

"Actually, Earl, we would have made the white guy an employee too. In the *Hustler* universe, we never let the bosses or the rich guys have any good sex. Our philosophy is to give the underdog a bone. Read the magazine; you'll see what I'm saying is true."

"I'll check on that," Earl said.

We parted on pleasant terms, but I wondered how Earl might react if, during his research of *Hustler*'s editorial stance, he were to flip open the December 1997 issue to a series of pictures titled "Mandingo: Damned if He Do..." Shot to Larry Flynt's exact specifications, the "Mandingo" set followed the demise of a massively endowed black slave who, being caught servicing the plantation owner's blonde daughter, is bullwhipped and boiled alive in a cast-iron cauldron while his fellow subjugated Africans kneel powerlessly and pray at the fireside. Earl's shoe-selling clerk had come a long way from being lynched in a soup pot. This kind of progress takes time.

Bush's win paid out in a wealth of raw material for cruel and crude humor. The first "Bits & Pieces" target from the new Presidential Administration was George's daughter Jenna. The girl had done nothing to deserve *Hustler*'s scorn. She'd simply been born into a reigning political patriarchy. Somehow, probably through the embrace of laziness and malice, the "Bits & Pieces" no-brainers were inspired to mockingly offer Jenna Bush money to expose her genitals in *Hustler*, which gave the excuse to run a composite photo of Jenna's grinning face superimposed upon a picture of a nude model splaying her labes ("The Unprecedented $10-Million Beaver Offer: Jenna Bush, This Could Be You," April, 2001). We knew better, but we couldn't help ourselves.

If I'd been less elastic of conscience, I might not have been fielding a call from Dan Savage, author of the "Savage Love" syndicated sex-advice column. Dan asked if we'd heard from Jenna yet to schedule her posing. How about from former Secretary of State and Bush campaign manager James Baker?

"No, he hasn't called either. Actually, we're worried we're going to hear from her father. I'm terrified of that guy, to tell you the truth. Larry isn't, but I am."

"Why offer the money to Jenna and not to her twin sister, Barbara?"

"Jenna's the cute one, and we're interested in the cute ones around here."

"Harsh. What about Barb's self-esteem?"

"The Bushes have way too much self-esteem. It seems to outpace their abilities; so if this decreases the self-esteem of just one of the Bush clan, then we've done a good thing."

I thought I was kidding about being scared of the new President, until the "Savage Love" mention (*Village Voice*, April 26, 2001) was picked up by papers across the country, and news of the Jenna offer jumped to international datelines. Reporters from remote democracies started phoning me for comment.

"From now on," I informed my assistant, abdicating the answering of my phone, "I'm minding my own business, and my own business only. My job is to look at photo slides of naked girls, and that's all I'm doing."

It might have been that afternoon, maybe two weeks later. I checked the photocopies of a young model's ID to ensure she'd been 18 years old at the time of her photo shoot. According to her driver's license, she'd been born in June 1983, almost a month after my Larry Flynt Publications hiring date. When I'd collected my first paycheck for looking at naked women, this particular woman whose womb I was peering into had been herself still in a womb. Staring at her gave me a funny feeling that I couldn't quite define, but I felt sure it was bad.

Hustler's Coming Next

TRANSFORMING RANDOM MASTURBATORS into repeat customers is a trick beyond science. Every day, millions of American consumers are overcome by the need to shoot their rocks, and every one of them has myriad options to effect that launch. Look at all those magazines mobbing the newsrack, flexing cleavage and wiping wet, pink tongues across plump, parted lips. This crowd of sultry-eyed competition is only one face of *Hustler*'s problem. Most of Larry Flynt's target audience is loath to be branded as readers anyway, opting for sexier technology. DVDs offer full-motion, full-sound penetration. Linking up the Internet opens a portal to a sexual universe to be explored wad infinitum, often at no cost. Don't count out the allure of human contact. A man seeking a distant cousin of physical intimacy might slip into an old raincoat and slink into a live-action peepshow. Paper and ink are hard-pressed in the fantasy-flesh marketplace.

The typical copy of *Hustler* is used and discarded like a shameful piece of evidence. The magazine's creative staff accepts that surreptitious disposal as a given. The challenge in assembling the ideal *Hustler* is to implant a response in the male brain so that next time the reproductive impulse strikes, the man again buys from the LFP brand line.

Any massage-shack sex worker knows what must be done: Give the randy bastards the happy ending they desire and then, as the relieved client pauses on his way out through the beaded doorway, promise to provide extra and better at the next encounter. "Coming Next," *Hustler*'s closing page of editorial, was reserved for the kiss-off come-on, touting the subsequent edition's half-imagined delights in teasing photos and pun-rich paragraphs. This closing spiel drooled over the girls to come and played up the timeless importance of the near future's articles. Eventually, erecting the false front of yet another *Hustler* sales pitch raised the same qualms that a weary sex worker faces as she sizes up yet another trick: We've always pulled it off so far, but how much longer can we scrape by?

CHAPTER 17

Tough Times for the
Dept. of Morale

SOMETIMES THE BEST way to appreciate your growth as a human being is to witness the stunted emotionalism of people enduring predicaments similar to your own, and then compare yourself favorably. For example, contrast my relative comfort in the interrogative presence of Larry Flynt as opposed to the damp terror seeping from *Hustler*'s resident porno expert, Mike Albo, in the same situation. Short, rotund, clad in suspendered gray gabardine and bow-tied dress shirt, Albo's dark, harried eyes hoisted matching sets of luggage behind golden, wire-rimmed spectacles. Overall, he achieved the troubled look of a 19th-century pharmacist who has just been accused of dipping into his own stock.

Comfortably within my 40s now, I sat alert but relaxed across from Larry's big desk. Flynt had never looked fitter. Well, never since becoming a sit-down, roll-along man. The influence of Liz brought his face every day to look less the waxen, pale whale and more the emerald-eyed, red-haired shark.

Albo perched on the edge of his chair, slanting forward as if he might pitch his head between his legs and hurl. Unaccustomed to being in the Larry Flynt hot seat, sweat beaded along the ridges of Albo's shaven skull. As editor of *Hustler Erotic Video Guide,* Albo was LFP's ambassador to the XXX industry, a conduit to the smut publicists, to the onscreen carnalists and to the executives of sleaze. Due to his magazine's abrasive and combative stance, Albo was usually not on speaking terms with most of the personages who fell within his beat. At this moment, he would have preferred to be apologizing to any one of his porn-racket enemies rather than be trapped across from Larry Flynt.

"Did you bring the list I asked for?" said Larry.

Albo's eyes popped. He stared at Larry as though at a huge, talking egg. I intervened.

"The list of video companies, Mike. Hand it over."

Twitching into action, Mike stood and leaned over Larry's massive desk. Albo wriggled forward like an English schoolboy squirming into position to take his stripes.

"This is all the major companies?" asked Larry.

Only a slight delay resulted from Albo processing the boss' diction. "Yes. These are the bestsellers. The most popular manufacturers."

"Here's what I want you to do, Mike."

Albo shot me a look of terrified entreaty. Don't worry, my emanations said, relax and listen the best you can. I will fill in any lapses in your comprehension.

"As you know," said Larry, "our Cincinnati Hustler store was raided. We're anticipating an obscenity trial which, when we win it, will set the precedent for how adult materials are distributed in this country from now on out."

Back in the '70s, when *Hustler* had been a moral fungus spreading across the body of America from the unlikely epicenter of Columbus, Ohio, Larry had been convicted of obscenity by the local decency squad and sentenced to slightly less than 6,000 years in prison. Released on appeal, the mad pornographer eventually prevailed in having the conviction tossed, but in all the hundreds of intervening months, every single issue of his beloved *Hustler* had been effectively banned from all store shelves in Hamilton County, home district to Cincinnati. In Larry's mind, the time had come to rectify Hamilton County's *Hustler* deficiency.

In late 1997, Larry had opened Hustler News and Gifts, a store selling periodicals and novelties to the curious citizens of Cincinnati. Initially, the venue's sole purpose was to provide *Hustler* to Hamilton County, provoke a confrontation with local prosecutors (some of whom had spearheaded the obscenity persecution back in the 1970s) and make fools of them in open court.

The problems started when Hustler News and Gifts became profitable. No one had taken into account that the prank store might rake in trash bags full of real cash. Larry abandoned caution and stocked his shelves with hardcore incitements—dildos, edible lingerie, gang-bang flicks. In the face of such scandalous offerings, *Hustler* magazine's profile sank beneath the prosecutors' sights. Cops sent in an underage ringer to shop at Hustler News and Gifts, and a clerk sold the kid copies of splatter videos *Rocco More Than Ever, Part 2* and *Jeff Stryker's Underground*. The store, Larry and his brother Jimmy were all charged with felonies of pandering obscenity, and doing so to a minor.

Being indicted agreed with Larry. The chairman predicted that his trial would be a daily feature on Court TV. Cable-niche notoriety would shoot his star into the firmament of celebrity freedom fighters. Plus, Flynt's role as a prominent defendant offered unique business opportunities. He spelled these out for the editor of *Hustler Erotic Video Guide*.

"Albo, I want you to compose a letter to the heads of all these video companies. Let them know that I'm taking the hit for their benefit. It's only fair that each company should send the store 150 to 200 of their premium tapes to be sold, with proceeds to help finance the legal battle. I'm bearing the brunt of this free-speech fight; it's only right that they should contribute to the cause. They'll all be profiting in the long run."

Albo was doubtful. His cruel reviews and pitiless characterizations of XXX stars in *Hustler Erotic Video Guide* had alienated more potential contributors than they had endeared. "Some of these companies won't even send us screeners," he said.

Larry showed no patience for negativity. "It cain't hurt to ask. You never get anything if you don't ask."

Thus encouraged, Albo painstakingly drafted a solicitation, but Porn Valley was limited in its enthusiasm and declined to expand Flynt's inventory free of charge. Perhaps the smutmongers were shortsighted, or maybe they saw exactly what was on the way.

Freedom, porn's statesmen are often fond of saying, is never free. Neither is anything of dollar value. Despite Larry's schemes to mooch salable product, *Hustler* occasionally agreed to pay for special materials, such as decades-old scandal photos of a young, free-loving Laura Schlessinger. Schlessinger had aged into a stern talk-radio "doctor," marketing harsh Old Testament behavioral guidelines through such books as *Ten Stupid Things Women Do to Mess Up Their Lives*. Crotch shots of this professional prude had defiled the World Wide Web. The pictures documented a time in Dr. Laura Schlessinger's life when her morals and her limbs were both sufficiently limber to spread.

I placed a call to Internet huckster Seth Warshavsky. Seth had poached two of my most productive editors to work at his Club Love website. He'd also attempted to snatch art directing Bill and other key creative cogs from the Flynt machine. Warshavsky owned all rights to the pictures of Laura Schlessinger's embarrassing hindsight. He was quick on the phone.

"Allan?" He pretended not to know who I was, then quoted a price for the Dr. Laura photos that was within the range I'd been allotted to spend. "Do we have a deal?"

"We need online rights too," I said.

"After you run it in the magazine? Sure. Smear them all over the *Hustler* website. These shots won't be worth anything to me by then."

"Dr. Laura's Furburger Furor" filled a half page in *Hustler*'s March 1999 issue. The impact of these photos on the magazine's circulation was impossible to measure, not because Larry didn't have the means of tracking sales figures, but because the increment, if any, was so slight as to be indistinguishable. When Seth had plastered these photos on the internet, news outlets high and low had blushed at the outrage. When *Hustler* finally put them into print? No mention anywhere. The new millennium was half a year away. We were paying premium dollars to print the future in our pages as it was leaving us behind.

Three days after jury selection began on the Cincinnati trial, Larry pleaded out. Hustler News and Gifts agreed to pay a $5,000 fine for each of two counts of pandering obscenity. In exchange, all charges were dropped against Larry and brother Jimmy. Furthermore, Hustler News and Gifts promised to remove all video porn from the downtown Cincinnati store, and to keep the hard stuff out forever. Our wheeled leader had failed to set the precedent for how adult materials were to be distributed in this country from now on out.

Larry claimed victory. After 20 years, *Hustler* was once again on sale in Cincinnati. A few smut manufacturers scoffed that they had been betrayed by a sellout, but Flynt had logic on his side: "Why should I spend millions of dollars in attorneys' fees fighting someone else's battle?" ("One Small Step for Porn: Flynt Cuts a Deal in Cincinnati," *Hustler*, October, 1999.)

As the '90s slipped away, I couldn't stave off a sense of encroaching closure. The months wasted digging for George Bush sleaze in Texas distracted me from the pointlessness of my day-to-day endeavors. Afterward, following the 2000 presidential election, I buddied up to lassitude. Rivals on the LFP payroll were campaigning to discredit me in Larry's estimation and to claim portions of my authority as their own. I retaliated by ruminating upon my latent apathy.

I've always taken my career worries home with me. Skin mag sales were crumbling. In some states, the only way to purchase a *Hustler* was to enter a porn store, where the magazine was eclipsed by full-on hardcore books. The nagging certainty that my LFP tenure was doomed pulled up a place at dinner, at breakfast, hung out on the weekends. The wife soon tired of entertaining my inevitable redundancy.

"Larry will never get rid of you," she said. "Stop dreaming. He likes to have someone around who looks halfway smart."

"But he dumped Alan Isaacman." Alan had been Larry's best man at the wedding to Liz, and his Supreme Court defender. Speculation said Larry had cut out Isaacman after some squabble over the spoils of the Hustler Casino.

"There's a difference between you and Alan Isaacman," said the wife. "Alan Isaacman truly is fully smart."

"Weedy Hood got fired," I said.

"Weedy Hood? That's the kind of drip who gets canned from *Hustler*."

Perpetually mellow Weedy Hood sported the continual loose grin and ocular disorientation of the recreational herbalist. Pushing through middle age, hard of paunch, thinned hair flowed in a vestigial pompadour, always a number of stray bristles protruding from his nostrils, Hood had started at *Hustler* around the same time I had. He was five years older than me, and had been laid off after a few years. Twelve years later, I'd recruited him back. Weedy was put in charge of two niche magazines. For the sake of discretion, pretend that one of Hood's magazines was called *Short Chicks*, devoted to the same, and that the other was fixated upon six-footers, and called *Long Ones*. The two titles came out alternately, each every other month. If sales went well, both would switch to a monthly schedule, bringing more money for me.

That dream soon faded. Weedy's desultory efforts barely covered the call of duty. He wrote unfocused and tired pieces full of familiar phrases and shelfworn scenarios, did little to cultivate fresh photographers, and was lax on his documentation. The rest of the editorial staff—younger, focused, less prone to cannabis excesses—questioned why I had dug him up.

Hood's firing came while I was covering bare-knuckle cage fighting in the Brazilian port city of Recife. Both of Weedy's magazines contained photo sets of men and women engaged in active coitus. Such fluid entertainment, company policy dictated, required accompaniment by appropriate AIDS paperwork. Weedy had mass copied one AIDS test and inserted it into the packets for five different performers, using Wite-Out and creative photocopying to doctor pertinent details. He'd forgotten to alter one defining bit of information: the birth date on all five tests was identical. Oddly, it matched the actual birth date of Weedy.

Hood's incompetent dishonesty reflected poorly upon my judgment of ability and character. The executive who had fired Weedy marveled at Weedy's misguided initiative.

"Imagine that. Rather than simply assembling the correct paperwork, this guy goes through the trouble of taking an AIDS test himself just so he could use the paperwork as raw material for his forgeries. If he could think straight, with that extra effort, he might be a real asset."

Ransacking Hood's office for components to the next issue of *Short Chicks*, I found a suspect invoice demanding payment for two dozen photo sets. These sets, none of which had been slated for use, were all from one company, a well-known crap provider. The invoiced prices were double what the genre's few true artists were normally paid. The photo sets themselves were tricky to locate. Dockets and all, they had been shoved in the space between Weedy's bookshelves and the wall. An editorial assistant fished them out with a ruler and an extension cord and stacked them next to my light table. I put the magnifying lens to my eye, hunched over the material and squinted. The photos were substandard: grainy, ill-lit, stolid. The third packet defied all expectation.

Weedy Hood's tar-yellow teeth grinned back at me. He hadn't taken his shoes off, and he'd left his shirt on in an attempt to veil his hard gut. His erect penis, curved and gnarly like a miniature rhino horn, was glistening in the slobber of a thin-lipped short chick. Hood was modeling in about half of the contested sets, wearing thick glasses to disguise himself, shoving his bent prick into the slack orifices of pallid females, all geared toward *Short Chicks*.

The providers were kicking for full payment. My feeling was that they should not be paid a dime. Hood had never been authorized to commission sets. The providers knew the rules. I sent messages out for Hood to phone me. Weedy finally checked in from a motel room. His wife and the brats had booted him. Hood seemed to appreciate that I did not yell at him. We established that the prices on the suspect invoices were in fact merely suggestions.

"The payment was only to be made on condition of acceptance," said Weedy. "It's not like I'm an idiot."

"No, you're not an idiot," I agreed with sincere and deep sympathy. "But you did lose your motherfucking mind."

Hood had spun crazy in less than a year of LFP culture. How much longer could I hold out? Bored to distraction, I was unable to summon the urgency I had previously accorded to the glorification of all things *Hustler*. I failed to push the young men and women at my command as much as I should have. They were intelligent and current, sensitive to the humored ironies of making a living as we did. Sooner or later, I knew, they would watch me swept from office.

A pair of jetliners was flown into New York's World Trade Center, another plane was crashed into the Pentagon, and a fourth smashed down in rural Pennsylvania. My worries seemed rather petty. Soon after the attacks, right around when traffic manners had reverted to their ghastly pre-tragedy norm, Liz Flynt's secretary insisted that I drop whatever I was doing and join the chairman's wife in her office.

Liz held a corner expanse with an eastward view on the top floor of Larry's building. She drove a 12-cylinder Mercedes sports coupe. She'd taken to wearing suits that might have been Chanel, but were definitely not within the budget of the Nurse Berrios I had met a decade earlier. Like Liz, I had come along. From an adolescent-looking early 30s, I'd moved into my youthful 40s. A navy Prada suit bespoke maturity and stability; I intended the garment to signify dependability with a pinch of panache.

Liz sat alone behind her desk of French lacquer, like a miniature woman. She had the bulk and the presence of an inordinately privileged eight-year-old. A large portrait of Larry leered behind her, bestowing the authority of the king. Liz was on the phone. She raised a hand to me, like a traffic cop ordering a motorist to stop. Gems coruscated upon her fingers, draped around her neck, dangled from her ears. If only Larry would let me pick her up by her ankles, wave her around and keep any jewelry that popped off. Liz finished her phone conversation and turned her preoccupied charm to me. She asked how the wife was doing.

"Well, she just launched her own business, like I was telling you about, and this terrorism thing might kill it before it even starts, not that she can halfway worry about that, seeing that she has so many close friends back in Manhattan."

"That's so great," said Liz. "We're printing up some American flag stickers to send to clients and friends. There's a space on the back for writing, and Larry thought it would be a good idea if we put a message there. You know, people all over the country are ready to hear something hopeful."

The Flynts had come to me for something hopeful. I was touched. Liz turned up the wattage on her smile.

"This goes out in half an hour," she said.

I scraped down for a unifying and uplifting paragraph (respect for the dead prohibits reproducing it here) and delivered it by hand. Liz accepted the paper without comment. She must have been distracted, and not just by the glare of her ice. These trying weeks were stressing all of us in many ways. Maybe two days later, a bouquet of flowers was delivered to my desk. The card had been lost. I racked my Rolodex. Who would send me flowers? I remembered penning the sentiments for Liz. Jeez, my mastery of language and emotion must have totally moved her. Immediately, I called to thank her.

"I didn't send you any flowers. Why would I send you flowers?"

That was awkward. "I thought you and Larry might have sent them for my wedding anniversary."

"Wouldn't you think they were from your wife?"

Liz obviously did not know the wife as I knew the wife. "That must be it," I said.

The card that should have accompanied the mystery flowers was forwarded a day late. The arrangement had been sent by a seldom-used English photographer, a tactful expression of sympathy after the September 11 attacks, proving that classy people do exist in the skin trade.

Soon after 9/11 lost its news monopoly, the *Star* tabloid published a "Beaver Hunt" photo of actor Robert Blake's murdered wife, Bonny Bakley. The snapshot had originally run in the June 1977 *Hustler*, listing the future victim's name as Lee Bonny Bakley. Lee Bonny had expressed her ultimate sex fantasy as "to get it on with either Frankie Valli or Elvis Presley."

A local news anchor requested an onscreen explanation of the Bonnie Bakley photo from someone at the magazine. I didn't want my lofty Hollywood Hills neighbors to see me commenting on a slain woman's open vagina; I delegated the on-camera representation to Sean Berrios. A younger brother of Larry's wife, Sean had been awarded a sinecure in the photo department and seemed eager to spout off on camera. Problem solved, until the anchor asked Sean what would possess a person to send a nude photo of herself to be published by a national magazine. Berrios replied, "Well, you know, when you're young, you do things that are dumb."

A correct answer would have been: "Everybody has a fantasy. Anyone can be a part of the glamour. 'Beaver Hunt' democratizes the cachet of celebrity exposure."

The day after Sean's flub, I was called to the money-colored carpet. Larry warned me not to dodge any future media requests.

"If you say something, at least you won't say something a complete fucking idiot would say."

Could he be sure? Every half-hour, I felt the impulse to say something a complete fucking idiot would say.

U.S. bombs were pockmarking Afghanistan. Reporters were being fed from a single pool of official information. Larry pondered taking a stand.

"Vietnam was stopped because the press was there in the fox-holes with the soldiers. This government has got to realize that the First Amendment extends to America's battlefields."

Larry intended to sue the Pentagon for the right to accompany military forces as they pursued and engaged the enemy. The gesture, he realized, would be empty without placing a reporter in the fray. He had put forth my name in the preliminary court documents as his foreign correspondent. Dodging bullets and land mines, sweltering in desert heat, a prey to sandstorms and scorpions, crapping in the sand—my mind romanticized none of this.

"Larry, I'll be honored to represent *Hustler* overseas. From the comfort of a quaint Parisian hotel."

Larry was being rolled away. He pulled his chair to a stop and said over his shoulder: "If you won't go, find a replacement."

My subordinate on the Bush abortion, Features, had left the company in the wake of that futility, so I couldn't push the reporter search onto him. I solicited a former editor who had traveled under-cover to do *Hustler* service pieces on local prostitution customs in Havana ("¡Viva las Putas! Whore Stories From Fidel Castro's Fantasy Island," March, 1998) and in Rio de Janeiro ("Brazil Is for Fuckers," October, 1998). Close contact with so many professionals had rubbed off on this adventurer. He demanded too much money. Out of nowhere, Features rang up.

"I hear you're looking for someone to embed in Afghanistan. Why haven't you asked me?"

"I've never met your mother, and I don't want our first encounter to be at your funeral."

Features was a Jew, and sending Jews into this hotbed of reli-gious fanaticism—fundamentalist Christians in the U.S. military; Islamic extremists at the opposite end of the big guns—seemed irre-sponsible. Features insisted. "I'd be good for this story."

"We're not after a story. We're looking for a pest who will badger the commanding officers on the ground so that Larry's lawsuit will have the patina of legitimacy. I would prefer to send someone who has done me wrong."

Features would not be dissuaded, and Larry welcomed him as *Hustler*'s man in Afghanistan. Features bought a helmet and a satellite phone, and subjected himself to a dozen inoculations. Larry's free-speech lawyers established contact with press officers at Bagram Airbase, 27 miles north of the Afghan capital of Kabul. No direct flights to Bagram were available, so Features shuttled in through Pakistan.

Chairman Larry looked forward to pressing hard against the Pentagon. "We plan to call Donald Rumsfeld for a discovery deposition. As the plaintiff, I'm entitled to be present for the questioning. Imagine that."

That potential scene, videotaped and played on Court TV, struck me as absurdly entertaining, but Larry's enthusiasm outmatched my own. Dispatches from Features arrived with disturbing irregularity. He had close scrapes in Pakistan while hiring a "fixer" to apply the bribes necessary for travel to Afghanistan. None of this sounded safe or secure. In Kabul, Features rendezvoused with international news vagrants and established residence in a hotel favored by them. His credentials as a *Hustler* writer won over the Bagram Airbase grunts, and his core decency surprised and pleased the higher-ranking communications officers, many of whom were born-again to Jesus.

At the end of January 2002, *Wall Street Journal* reporter Daniel Pearl was kidnapped in Pakistan, from the same streets that Features had wandered blind, and slaughtered on videotape. I flooded Features' message box and bombarded his e-mail account, giving him the Pearl news and ordering him to increase security precautions. He had moved out of Kabul's sole hotel and was lodging with private citizens, an arrangement that saved money and greatly increased amenities. He returned my frantic entreaties at his leisure.

"Don't go back to Kabul," I told him.

"The story takes me to Kabul."

"Stay on the premises at Bagram. You're a soft target. Stay in the compound."

He laughed. A taxi he had been riding in had skidded off the road, flipped on its side and slid 200 yards into a mined pasture. "We followed the tracks of the skid, hopping toward the road, trying to stay on one foot so we wouldn't lose both legs if we hit anything live. About a hundred villagers gathered at the roadside and cheered us in, me and the driver. You should have seen it."

Because of time differences and vagaries of the satellite phone, Features often caught me at home on weekends. I urged him to call every day. He plagued my mind as much as any other aspect of the job. His diary was being posted on Larry's free website. One full-length article, with photographs, had been prepared for the newsstand edition of *Hustler*, with more stories pledged. None of this would make up for Features' head being sawn off.

In a gloomy state, at Larry's personal invitation, I attended a lingerie-wearing contest at the Hustler Casino's sports bar as a judge, sharing that official capacity with Los Angeles Lakers owner Jerry Buss and presidential half-brother Roger Clinton. The winning panty-strutter would be awarded a check and an opportunity to model in *Hustler*. The prize was half a joke: Any girl off the street could take a Polaroid and be considered to model in *Hustler*. The other half of the joke was that most of the contestants would have refused to pose for *Hustler* had they won. My practiced eye had cast its cold evaluation on only seven or eight contestants when a solid Asian man of middle age, tastefully accoutered in gold watch and chains, approached me. His disarming smile inspired confidence.

"You're Allan from *Hustler*."

"Yes, I am."

He introduced himself as the manager of the casino.

"Of course you know about next month's roast of Larry Flynt."

This was news to me. "You bet. I've been looking forward to it."

"Good. Larry says you'll be one of the roasters."

"I hadn't realized that."

"It's what I'm told. Gabe Kaplan is putting on the show. Do you know Gabe?"

"Among the pop-culture ironists of my acquaintance, Gabe Kaplan is warmly remembered as the gruff, nurturing pedagogue of TV's *Welcome Back, Kotter*."

The casino manager's ingratiating manner had, I couldn't tell precisely when, given way to imperturbable authority. "Come with me."

The manager led me away from the women in lingerie and down onto the gaming floor. We wended through the low-stakes tables, our steps muffled by the shuffling of cards and the clicking of poker chips, and arrived at the high rollers. Larry sat in his accustomed place of prominence and granted me a kingly leer.

"Good to see you doing your duty."

Kaplan and I made one another's acquaintance and exchanged business cards.

"If you need any help," said Gabe, "let me know."

In the time taken by this transaction, Larry lost about a grand and a half.

I would have a month to prepare my roast material. The assignment added one more work-related bummer. Features was lingering in Afghanistan, flying in attack helicopters on Special Forces missions and pushing the plunger to blow up terrorist caves, and delusions of indispensability had seized young Bill. The callow art director cornered me in my office late in June and demanded a sizable raise. I hadn't seen a raise in two years. Young Bill had received the top hikes granted under Larry's guidelines. Bill readily dismissed these facts.

"I could go to DreamWorks tomorrow and start at 85 grand, coloring animation."

"What stops you from doing that?"

"You've gotten me money before, and you can do it again."

"So you're saying I should tell Larry that either he pays up, or you'll split?"

"I'm not saying that I will. I'm saying I could. You say whatever you need to say to get the money."

If Bill wanted out so bad, why not walk away like an adult male? Anybody else, I would have told as much, but Bill had stuck close for more than eight years, so I took his case to Larry and pressed it.

"What can we do to make Bill happy?"

"He's put you in a false position," said Larry. "How soon can you replace him?"

Bill seemed surprised that his strong-arm salary negotiation had left him no choice at Larry Flynt Publications. He was booted, and doomed moodiness broke out on the floor.

On the morning of Tuesday, June 25, 2002, an anonymous voice struck back against the prevailing melancholy. Printed out on a sheet of typing paper, a neatly lettered sign had been taped to the art-room door: KEEP YOUR SPIRITS UP.

The inspirational message was attributed, in small type at the bottom of the page, to the Department of Morale.

Was this some expression of bitter irony? God knows, I was not alone among employees who could use a dose of real empathy.

The Department of Morale placed a followup posting on the next morning, Wednesday, June 26: YOU CAN DO IT.

These signs were being placed in a lair of vandals, and nobody defaced them. The Department of Morale directive for Thursday, June 27, read: REACH FOR THE STARS.

I met one-on-one with all employees of intelligence and sensitivity. I applauded the signs, expressed my admiration and gratitude to whoever was behind them. Nobody admitted to putting them up, or to knowing who had put them up.

Friday, June 28: LAUGHTER IS GOOD.

Could the anonymous Department of Morale messenger be the same joker who had placed the poop in the Pepsi bottles?

Monday, July 1: DARE TO DREAM.

I'd returned to LFP's endless treadmill of apprehension after a weekend struggling with the script for Larry Flynt's roast. Had I dreamed anything worth dreaming during the past two days?

Tuesday, July 2: HOLD YOUR HEAD UP HIGH.

All during the day, I found myself looking down. I could not view my work without bowing my head.

Wednesday, July 3: ALL FOR ONE AND ONE FOR ALL.

Young Bill's removal had weakened my defensive lines. I observed three factions on the move to squeeze me out. A hostile pawn was installed as the new *Hustler* art director.

After the Independence Day break, no further Department of Morale posts were taped up at the art-room enclosure. My script for Larry's upcoming roast was shaping up to be foolhardy and fatalistic. I passed through the stations of my job with what I pictured to be the grave dignity of a condemned man.

On the Friday of the roast, I summoned my staff. We met in the ninth-floor conference room, taking seats around a long table situated directly beneath Larry's desk on the 10th. My mind was winding a tragic mythology around my predicament, and I surrendered to an impulse to share it.

"I have something I hope you guys will listen to."

My grumbling about the impending ordeal had been inescapable, and now for these hard-working, dedicated supporters, there was no avoiding a dry run of the roast itself. Their embarrassed, averted faces could not stop me. I stood at the head of the conference table (a position I chronically shunned), nodded once solemnly and read through my Flynt routine from the top.

"...And so I feel that, aside from Larry Flynt, we here tonight are obliged to honor his wife, for he would be nothing without her. Liz, go ahead and stand up. (I'll pause here while Liz stands.) No, really. Go ahead and stand up...."

I slogged on, inadvertently reading the same paragraph twice, accidentally skipping over a punch line, and finally reached the end. "That's it," I said. "I'm finished."

One or two editors clapped wanly. What had I expected? Admiration? Encouragement? The staff stared back at me, reflecting a blank and uniformly dour expression. In the heavy silence, Mike Albo—*Hustler*'s XXX ambassador—raised his hand.

"It's not really my place," he said, haltingly, "but it might be safer to take out the jibe at Liz's height."

A mumble of assent met Albo's suggestion. I considered, and then promised to eliminate that one particular barb.

"It should go over better now," Albo said.

What the fuck do you know? I thought. *You sad, stunted chump.*

Crapping Out

After the roast, on Monday, Human Resources Betty summoned me. Being called up to Human Resources was never good. You cruise up there, thinking all is well, and then an aggravated production artist is filing a complaint accusing you of having taken his cucumber sandwich from the communal refrigerator. I knocked on Betty's door. It eased open. The H.R. director and her assistant sat on either side of her desk, an empty chair between them. Mournfully, they motioned me in.

"Please close the door," said Betty.

I sat down.

"It's about the roast," droned Betty. "Mr. Flynt was very offended by some of the things you said. He's spent a lot of time over the weekend trying to reconcile his feelings. You've been a valuable employee, and he has tried his hardest to put this behind him, but he's been unable to. I'm afraid that Larry has come to the decision that he can no longer work with you, and we're going to have to let you go today."

I felt as if I might float up out of my chair and bump against the ceiling. "I knew this would happen," I said. My elation was from more than just being proven right. Twin anvils had been lifted from my shoulders. I sat up straight and took my first free breath in more than a decade. The world had just blossomed with marvelous, four-color possibilities.

Betty handed me a folder. "There is some paperwork to be filled out."

I opened the file. Two words were printed upon the top sheet of paper: JUST KIDDING.

"So this is what it felt like to be sent back to Vietnam," I said.

Larry and I acted as if the fake firing evened our score; we also pretended to be moving forward in our professional relationship, but there was nowhere to go. I'd been accustomed to Liz Flynt calling me two or three times a week, talking over policy, discussing strategies for problem employees. After I depicted her stripping the pants from her husband, I never heard from her again. I assumed we were quits, then Larry phoned my home over the Labor Day weekend.

"Allan, Bill Clinton called me personally the other day. Bill says it's real important for the Democratic party that this Lindsey Graham in South Carolina don't get elected to the Senate. Bill said they'd be very grateful to us if we can find something on Graham."

Rumors and innuendoes painted Republican Lindsey Graham, at that time in 2002 a North Carolina congressman with a straight anti-homosexual voting record, as in fact flamingly gay. My first and lasting question was: had Clinton really phoned Flynt?

"It might be worthwhile to put a little money into it," said Larry. "For a month."

On Tuesday, I contacted a Washington, D.C., private investigator and negotiated a concerted strike upon Senate candidate Graham.

But Larry and I were not back on the same team. On Thursday, he ordered me up to his office. He coughed, twisted his lips and looked at me sideways, something he'd never done before.

"The reason I called you here is that *Hustler* sales are sliding. I've enjoyed working with you, and I hope to continue to enjoy working with you."

He gave me six months to halt the slide, or he would try with someone else. Sixteen days later, after more than 19 years' servitude, I was offered four weeks' severance, which I laughed off.

From the very beginning of my employment at Larry Flynt Publications, I joked that any day could be the last. I could be fired at any moment. It happened just as I had predicted, although the ax took almost 20 years to fall.

Go back to the moments right after the roast. Roger Clinton had blustered on forever, and then Larry had wrapped up, interminably, but the ordeal had finally finished. The crowd was breaking up. Liz Flynt shot away without looking at me. Through clumps of people, I spied the chairman. Bodyguard Doug stood tall and wide behind the golden spokes, inching Larry toward the door. I moved into place to shake Flynt's hand.

Doug stepped in. "Boss, do you want me to take this joker up to the roof for real?"

"I don't know this person," said Larry. I detected no humor. He looked straight through me and said: "I've never seen this person before in my life."

WHEN SEX WAS DIRTY

By Josh Alan Friedman

When Sex Was Dirty tells of the twilight years of the sexual revolution in New York City. We travel deep inside the hidden sanctums of low-rent model agencies, sexual con men, dubious beauty contests and smut publishers. Friedman documents this Times Square era as America's own Weimar Republic, now a lost world like the Prague or Warsaw ghettos.

"So dirty you'll want to shower afterwards, but so compelling, you'll keep coming back for more."—*Playgirl*

5 1/2 x 8 1/2 • 133 pages • photo section • ISBN: 1-932595-07-4 • $12.95

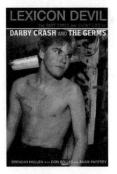

LEXICON DEVIL

The Short Life and Fast Times of Darby Crash and the Germs

By Brendan Mullen with Don Bolles and Adam Parfrey

"The definitive story of L.A. punk's tragic manimal, Darby Crash. Truly obscene, appallingly funny, sad beyond words."
— Jimmy McDonough, author of *Shakey: Neil Young's Biography*

"As oral histories of ANYTHING go, I would put it right up there with *Jack's Book* and *Edie: An American Biography*. Great book!"
— Richard Meltzer

6 x 9 • 294 pages • extensively illustrated • 0-922915-70-9 • $16.95

SIN-A-RAMA

Sleaze Sex Paperbacks of the Sixties

Edited by Brittany A. Daley, Hedi El Kholti, Earl Kemp, Miriam Linna, Adam Parfrey

Sin-A-Rama celebrates in lurid color the bizarre glories of shadowy but revolutionary erotic paperbacks from the 1960s, when sex acts were described with code words, artists and writers used pseudonyms, and publishers hid behind mail drop addresses.

"(An) informative and giddily entertaining book."—*Publishers Weekly*

"... Deeply satisfying... There is much to admire about SIN-A-RAMA."
— Josh Glenn, *Boston Globe*

6 1/2 x 10 • 288 pages • hardcover • illustrated • ISBN: 1-932595-05-8 • $24.95

TO ORDER FROM FERAL HOUSE:
Individuals: Send check or money order to Feral House, P.O. Box 39910, Los Angeles CA 90039, USA. For credit card orders: call (800) 967-7885 or fax your info to (323) 666-3330. CA residents please add 8.25% sales tax. U.S. shipping: add $4.50 for first item, $2 each additional item. Shipping to Canada and Mexico: add $9 for first item, $6 each additional item. Other countries: add $11 for first item, $9 each additional item. Non-U.S. originated orders must include international money order or check for U.S. funds drawn on a U.S. bank. We are sorry, but we cannot process non-U.S. credit cards.

www.feralhouse.com